M000288629

SNAFU
MY VIETNAM VACATION OF 1969

TOM HAINES

SPARK Publications
Charlotte, North Carolina

SNAFU: My Vietnam Vacation of 1969
By Tom Haines

Produced and published by SPARK Publications, SPARKpublications.com
Charlotte, North Carolina

Cover design by Tom Haines and Joel Hassig

Illustrations by Jim Denk of SPARK Publications; Andy Smith, senior illustrator for Marvel and DC Comics; Johnny Hart, creator of *B.C.* and *The Wizard of Id*; Henry Casselli, author of *Master of the American Watercolor*; and Tom Haines, author and artist

Printed in the United States of America
First Edition, August 2019, ISBN: 978-1-943070-55-8
Library of Congress Control Number: 2019936486

Dedication

This book is dedicated to all military personnel who served in Vietnam between 1961 and 1975, with a special tip of the helmet to 76Y20s, 11B10s, dog handlers, and drivers.

Soldier "Victims"

I would also like to make a dedication to all the victims of the defoliant Agent Orange, which contains one of the most dangerous chemical components know to man. This poison is dioxin and is nearly non-degradable. It was supposed to just kill foliage, according to Monsanto, Dow Chemical, and the labs of the US Government. An estimated 300,000 soldiers have died due to their exposure. More are currently dying from the sixteen diseases linked to exposure. I am in the "currently dying" category. The VA has declared me 180 percent totally and permanently disabled. I have eight diseases and conditions related directly to Agent Orange: heart (surgery), prostate (surgery), Hodgkin's symptoms, neuropathy, lung (oops, sorry, that was directly related to second hand smoke at my nightclub, The Attic), diabetes, and skin cancer (which is supposedly not related, but I have had twenty-one skin cancers and other "stuff" removed), and liver and kidney readings are currently being monitored. My brothers and I are thirty-one months apart in age in total, and they have had no skin cancers. Hmmmmmm. And we won't talk about the side effects. I made ninety-four visits to the VA, private clinics, and emergency rooms in 2018. Am I looking for sympathy? No. Am I looking for justice and recognition for those that suffered horribly? Yes.

War Dogs

The US military put to work 3,748 dogs in the Vietnam War. Mostly German Shepherd and Labrador Retrievers, they were used mostly for sentry and scout duty. These dogs saved around 10,000 soldiers' lives. They were thanked by being put in the category of "expendable equipment" to be euthanized or abandoned.

Scout Dog

Sentry Dog

Tracker Dog

Dog

☑ Thumper
❑ Bluper
❑ Chunker
❑ 79

*We've all been told war
is hell; but in war,
hell is not always defined
by the borders of a foreign land.*
– Tom Haines (1998)

Table of Contents

Acknowledgments

I'd like to thank my wife, Nancy, for her patience, valued opinions, and encouragement but mostly for her tireless editing, which, without, this manuscript would be unintellinababble.

I'd also like to thank Robert Fulton, Margaret Van Dyke, Steve Greenway, Brian Kepley, Francis "Shep" Shepard, Mike Ertis, Bill Keller, Barry Friedman, Gay Barger, Paul Seaburn, Darlene Ott, Ellen Hutchenson, Kevin Hughes, Kevin Fitzgerald, Tom and Maryln Ross, Gene Poynter, Daryl Rhoades, Brian Heffron, Mary Asher, Rhonda Stephens Paxton, [Your Name Here], Bryan Entwistle, The Grove Park Inn (Asheville, North Carolina), Wintergreen Resort (Wintergreen, Virginia), the VA Hospital (Salisbury, North Carolina), the VA Outpatient Center (Charlotte, North Carolina), and East Carolina University (Greenville, North Carolina) ... I'm being given the light, so I better stop here.

A special thank you also goes to SPARK Publications and the SPARKlers for making this book a published reality. Fabi Preslar and her team took on this project with genuine enthusiasm and a dedication I have rarely experienced. Their professionalism was over the top. They dotted all their i's and crossed all their t's; I know that is an overused cliche, but damn, it fits. Also a special round of applause to Melisa Graham for her spot-on editing and Jim Denk for his artistic vision in layout and design.

Preface

I took creative license in writing this book in order to present a tale that would flow seamlessly. While some of the details and most of the dialogue are fictional, all of the principle stories are true. Characters were combined and renamed, and anecdotes were chronologically rearranged in order to minimize confusion, heighten interest, and present a smoother flowing narrative, but not to the point of compromising the integrity of the story. In the words of Mark Ethridge, "It's not all factual, but it's all true." In the words of Tom Haines, "I couldn't agree more."

I have included a glossary at the end of the book and highly recommend to all those who are not familiar with military terminology and colloquialisms to look it over before starting to read. Glossaries can be a little boring, so I had some fun writing this one.

Thank you and enjoy the read,
Tom Haines

Steve
4F
Not physically
acceptable for service

Tom
1A
Draft
eligible

John
3A
Married
with child

CONTENT WARNING:

This book includes explicit language and graphic scenarios.

Pleiku, Vietnam

The Beginning of the End

I checked the duty board, scanned the perimeter guard list, and immediately found my name. I was neither surprised nor angry; I just grabbed my ruck (sack) and headed out the door.

Abe Goldberg and I were sharing this hated assignment for the eighth time. A war-weary deuce-and-a-half (two-and-a-half-ton truck) deposited us at bunker number sixty-four without coming to a full stop. Soldiers simultaneously entered and exited from the rear of the sputtering vehicle. There were *supposed* to be three guards in this bunker, not just us two—another example of an Army "SNAFU."

I entered through an opening on the left side of the sturdy, dark monster sporting a tower on its back, slung my ruck down in the corner, and then flipped the flap back. Abe headed to the tower perched on top of the bunker. I pulled out my gas mask and hung it on a nail embedded in a post supporting the bunk beds that were flush up against a wall of black, tar-coated railroad ties.

The gloomy, cramped sleeping quarters provided only turn-around space. The air was thick with the musty smell of dirt. Next out of my ruck was my mildewed poncho, which gave the existing odor some stiff competition. I searched the walls for another nail, found one, and tossed the poncho in its direction. It snagged the liner at a tear in its center. After covering myself with mosquito netting hanging from the ceiling, I emptied the remainder of my ruck onto the worn, filthy, bare mattress, and tossed my sleeping bag to the other end of the bed. A book and a small pile of unanswered letters from "the world" (home) would keep me busy for much of my last twenty-four-hour perimeter guard duty. I loved the sound of that word—*last*.

I figured my tour at that moment to be five months, eighteen days, and twelve hours; minutes and seconds to be determined as time wound down. It felt like a lifetime since May 26th. I couldn't imagine what it would have been like to sign up for two or three tours, and again, thanked God, Sergeant Randall Hart, and East Carolina University for my shortened tour.

Unhooking the blousing cord from the stack of letters, I selected two that I would not beat to their destination, slipped out from under the mosquito netting, grabbed my weapon, and headed outside for my first round of watch. It was 1700 hours and overcast. I climbed the tower ladder and at the top found a large, bright-white "64" freshly painted from a stencil. That meant there were sixty-three more bunkers to the left and God knows how many more of these ominous looking boxes circled to the right, completing a continuous protective chain around Camp Enari, the heart and soul of the Fourth Infantry.

The upper level of the tower was a six-foot square. The sides were open, and the tin roof was supported with 4x4s at each corner. A field phone, wrapped in plastic, hung on one of the 4x4s. An assortment of typed and hand-printed directions, rules, and warnings were tacked up throughout the tower.

I propped my M79 grenade launcher, Thumper, in the corner and opened my letter. Abe, who had brought his own mail, looked over at my weapon and smiled. "So, Tom, expecting a major attack tonight, or are you preparing to cheat in a skeet shooting contest?"

"Nooo, I brought an M79 because I had finished the final cleaning of my M16 before I found out I had guard duty." Picking up the weapon, I held it in the air and mimicked the weapons instructor from basic. "Gentlemen, what I have here is the

Army's answer to the mechanized version of a John Wayne grenade toss. That's right; I'm holding in my grasp, the M79 grenade launcher, capable of launching six 40-millimeter rounds a minute at an effective range of 375 meters. Nicknamed the blooper, the chunker, the thumper, the—"

"Oh, shut up and sit down, Mr. Bad Impression of a DI"—a drill instructor—"The last thing I want to hear is a DI's weapons lecture. I'm having a hard enough time responding to my dad's letter telling me how proud he is of me fighting for such a just and worthy cause," Abe said, not lifting his face from his letter.

A slight breeze tried to interfere with the humidity but was soundly defeated. Abe was thoroughly engrossed in his letter, so I didn't attempt any small talk. He worked at headquarters, and we had known each other since my first day in camp, but not well enough to interrupt correspondence with his dad. I curled up knees to chin on the wooden floor and reread a letter I had written earlier in the day to my cousin Doug.

The tower went silent as Abe wrote at breakneck speed, while I shook my head at my musings. I started most of my letters lightly, but a paragraph later I would be bitchin' about some moronic detail. My rant would then be followed by a paragraph where I droned on philosophically, regarding the inane war we were fighting.

After rereading my letter, I looked up as Abe flipped his pen, end-over-end, ten feet into the concertina wire with one hand while crumbling up his very lengthy letter with the other.

"This war sucks, man," he said, as he stood and tossed the ball of paper into an empty ammunition tin posing as a small trash can. Not a very profound statement from one of the most intelligent people I'd ever met, but very much to the point.

That was, for the moment, the last of his not-so-profound utterances. For the next few minutes, Abe went off on the war with the details of a historian, the emotional vigor of a tent revival preacher, and the convictions of a political zealot. His dad must have really pissed him off. I was astounded by the depth of Abe's knowledge of the war and its very complicated intertwining of politics, economics, philosophy, cultures, religions, traditions, moral beliefs, and human emotions. Then, as abruptly as he started his detailed and eloquent speech—one that could have gotten him elected to a political office or stoned, depending on where he gave it—he stopped.

I stood and joined him at the front of the tower. After rolling down our sleeves, an 0600 daily ritual required by the army, we looked out over the field of wire. Abe broke the silence.

"You know, Haines, we've gotten to that point now where winning this stupid fuckin' war is the main reason that we are still fighting it, *and* we are fighting it in a manner in which we cannot fuckin' win it." He dramatically threw his arms in the air and continued, "Shit, everyone knows America doesn't accept defeat very well, especially in areas where she's always experienced victory. We—"

"Uh oh, did you forget Custer?" I interrupted.

"Hey, I'm fuckin' serious here. Nations all around the world are watching to see how we come out of this *conflict*," he ranted. "We need to minimize our losses because we can't justify being here in the first place. So how do we fight a guerrilla war, take low losses, and win in a short amount of time? The answer—we fuckin' can't!"

Abe paced back and forth in the cramped tower like an angry, caged animal. He breathed deeply, exhaling slowly. "I think I'll go along with those that say we bomb the fuck out of North Vietnam, have the world let out a gasp of disbelief, go on with our lives, and hope we never make this mis—no, I fuckin' don't. Shit, I just know that the way this messed up war is going now, we'll be here at least five more fuckin' years." He sucked in another deep breath and then leaned against the front post.

"You know who I feel sorry for? The poor schmucks who live in this bombed-out shit hole," I said.

"You mean these economically poor, culturally rich, politically screwed schmucks we deal with every day? You mean the poor schmucks that have been told what they want by the Chinese, the Japanese, the French, and now us?" Abe interjected.

"Yeah. What was that again? I need to remember that … economically poor, culturally rich, and what was the third one?"

"Politically screwed," he repeated.

Going over to the edge of the bunker's tower I looked out over the row of concertina wire.

"So what do you think? Do you think maybe, I'm just saying maybe, after more than 400 years of fighting, that these people might be just a tad weary of war?" I created a quarter-inch space between my thumb and index finger. Abe grinned ever so slightly.

We talked and read and wrote for more than two hours. When the sun disappeared, we laid out our guard watch using a tried and true American method; we drew bullets. Straw was in short supply. A complete round got the choice of shifts. For the holder of the empty shell casing, there was no choice. I tossed my empty casing, grabbed Thumper, and headed to bed.

Even though I was exhausted, I lay in the top bunk on my back and stared at the ceiling. My thoughts alternated between Abe's verbal, thought-provoking feast and mental images of going home to hot showers, home-cooked meals, clean soft sheets, and round-eyed women. Then I thought about Suzie and decided they wouldn't have to have round eyes.

Two hours later and still wide awake, I jumped from the upper bunk and landed squarely on both feet. Abe mumbled something about not being able to see diddly, fluffed up his down-filled sleeping bag, and crawled into the lower bunk. Grabbing my gear, I maneuvered my way through the dark and into the void at the front of the bunker.

The area was very small and plain. There was a timber and sod wall behind me and to my left. I faced a wall of similar construction with a large opening that faced "enemy territory." A doorway that sagged comically was on my right.

I sat to tie my boots and smiled as I recalled what I had read earlier in the day on the graffiti-covered wall in front of me. It read, "Ho Chi Minh is a motherfucker," dug in deep and bold. Then on September 3, 1969, old Ho kicked the bucket. Someone had then added a word. It now read, "Ho Chi Minh is a dead motherfucker."

I finished a half-ass job of lacing my boots—lace a hole, skip three, lace a hole, skip three—and got into the "stand and stare" position. Abe was right; you couldn't see shit. You could still smell shit as the last of the feces-filled troughs burned itself out a short distance down the line, but there was no denying you couldn't see shit.

The night was moonless and starless. I'd heard the grunts hated moonless nights more than anything else in Nam, including the monsoons, the leeches, the Asian two-step, and boot lieutenants fresh out of ROTC. With the moon, you could see the well-designed but hodgepodge-looking mess of wire fencing, which ran for uninterrupted miles around the camp, and the tree line a hundred meters directly in front of us. But tonight, without the moon, you saw nothing but a black void. I gazed into the darkness. The world in front of me was very still. The only movement, my eyelids as I blinked.

An hour passed. I continued to gaze into the blackness in front of me. Blink … blink … blink … … blink. I hadn't had any sleep in twenty hours. My eyelids began to feel like lead weights. Slowly, they started to close. I fought; they fluttered, trying to close and stay open simultaneously. A moment later closing won out. My head jerked forward a few inches, and my brain fired the command, "OPEN YOUR EYES!" My head felt light and tingly. I ran in place for a moment and took a deep breath.

The last time I fought sleep that hard was on a road trip from Gannon College in Erie, Pennsylvania, to the University of Maryland in my senior year. There were five of us crammed in my Mustang. I fell asleep just as we hit the outskirts of College Park. The problem was, I was driving. I awoke when I hit the uneven shoulder of the road. It was frightening to realize how close my passengers and I had been to death. Two years later on the other side of the Earth, I had the same feeling.

Midway into my second hour, my eyelids weighed forty pounds—each. My brain occasionally missed sending the signal to raise the flesh that draped my eyes. I went through the standard rituals: blink rapidly over and over, massage eyes with thumb and forefinger every thirty seconds; pour water from canteen over forehead while rubbing face from forehead to chin; shake head until dizzy.

A battle raged between total exhaustion and determined will power. Exhaustion was winning. The darkness began to produce hallucinations, movement of dark objects and contradictory ebony silhouettes stirred against black backgrounds. I picked an imaginary point a hundred meters out and focused on it. I stared until nothingness went out of focus and finally—sleep.

Somewhere in the deep reaches of my brain a nerve twitched to trigger a reminder that this was unacceptable. My brain gathered all its power and sent a message to every living cell under its control. I jerked, my blood rushed, my head snapped back, and my hands reached for an imaginary steering wheel while my foot hit an imaginary brake.

I awoke with a start and shook my head with such vigor my helmet flew off. I ran in place. My heart beat faster. I could feel my blood pounding. In a semiconscious fog, I pulled it together just enough to finish the final minutes of my watch.

At dead-on 3:00 a.m. civilian time—God, the word civilian sounded extraordinary—I poked Abe with my index finger.

"Hey buddy, the wailing wall is all yours," I said, poking him two or three more times.

"Huh … what? Oh, yeah … the Wailing Wall. Yeah, the Wailing Wall awaits." He rubbed his face and shuffled toward the front of the bunker.

Kicking off my loosely tied boots, in one quick motion, I was in the top bunk snuggled inside my warm, soft pile of goose feathers. I took an extra second to let down the mosquito net and then quickly fell into a deep, troubled sleep. …

Abe was poking me in the head with his M16. "Gooks, gooks, hundreds of them!" he screamed. I jumped from the top bunk and hit the ground running. No boots, no M16, no flak jacket, no time to think. My thoughts and actions were disoriented. I grabbed Thumper and headed out the door. Looking out over the strands of wire, I froze as dozens of VC were making their way through two large holes in the concertina, not way off in the distance, but just a few yards in front of us. Abe was in the bunker rockin' 'n' rollin', his weapon on full automatic. "Oh my God! Oh my God!" He screamed loud enough that his voice cracked.

Flares had the area lit up like Christmas in November, and I could see the faces of a half dozen VCs. Without expression, they moved fast and with purpose. The smell of smoke and powder filled the air. I raised Thumper, held tightly in my grasp, and fired. The grenade, which I didn't remember loading, ejected, soared, and exploded, just as it had during all that—what I thought was—useless training.

While my fingers fumbled to select another grenade, I caught a bullet in my left shoulder. Thrown backward and off balance, I looked at my shoulder and saw bone, blood, and pieces of my fatigue shirt. It was a ragged wound that gave the impression that I had taken two rounds. I felt a burning pain. While tightening my grip on my launcher, I started to move back inside the bunker when I caught another round. The bullet struck me in the center of my left leg, just above the knee. I lost my balance and fell hard to the earth, feeling my chest exploding with the third hit. Stretched out on the ground, I spat bright-red blood onto the dull-red dust.

I felt warm, wet, numb, but now—no pain. The flares began to dim. I hugged the earth and rested my blood-soaked cheek flat to the ground, staring at Charlie making his way closer to the edge of the wire. His eyes were riveted on me. I felt alone. I was alone.

My right hand still clutched my empty, useless grenade launcher. Charlie reached the edge of the wire and cocked his arm back to his ear, much like a quarterback preparing to launch a football. The sleeve of his black pajamas caught on the wire. It tore away as he launched a satchel charge, cradled in his small brown hand, toward me. I closed my eyes as he released his projectile. When I opened them, the miniature, homemade bomb sat motionless a few yards away. I could still hear Abe inside repeating, "Oh my God," over and over. The charge exploded at the same moment the flares' dim lights vanished from the black, moonless sky. ...

M79 Granade Launcher

New York State, USA

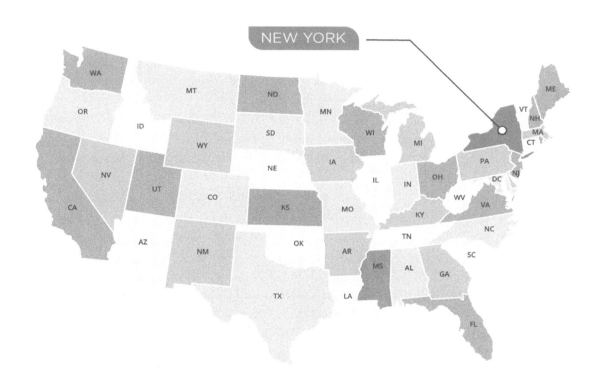

NEW YORK

UNITED STATES OF AMERICA

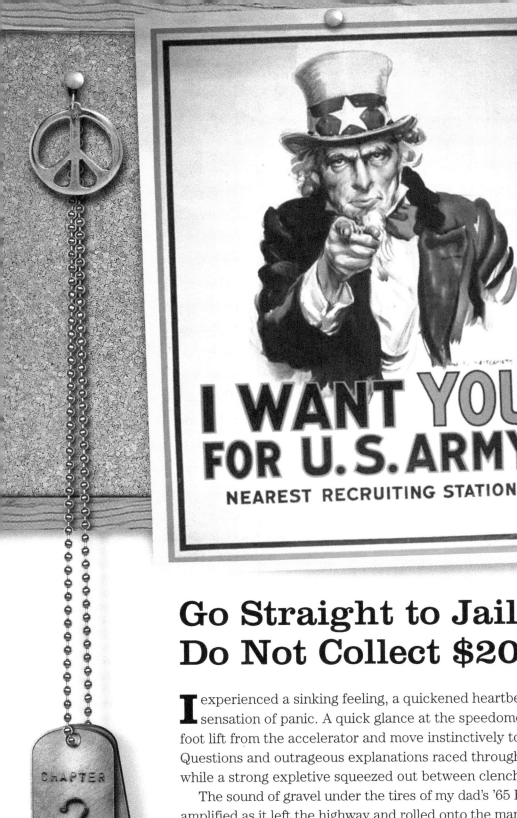

Go Straight to Jail— Do Not Collect $200

I experienced a sinking feeling, a quickened heartbeat, and a sensation of panic. A quick glance at the speedometer made my foot lift from the accelerator and move instinctively to the brake. Questions and outrageous explanations raced through my head while a strong expletive squeezed out between clenched teeth.

The sound of gravel under the tires of my dad's '65 Ford Galaxy amplified as it left the highway and rolled onto the manicured shoulder. Checking the mirror, I was sure whom the officer was following. I rolled down the window while turning off Blood, Sweat, and Tears on the radio. He approached with a ticket pad in one hand, his other hand leaning on the handle of his .38. Adjusting his sunglasses, he bent over and asked, "Where's the fire?"

He, in point of fact, asked me, "Where's the fire?"

"Me! I'm on fire! Can't you tell? Can't you see the smoke coming out of my ears?" My answer was impetuous and without hesitation. I continued to maintain a death grip on the steering wheel.

The silence was numbing. We were both shocked at my response. Releasing my white-knuckled grip, I let out a long, deep breath. I looked at myself in the center of his mirrored sunglasses.

"Look, sir, I just took a full day off work from down in Endicott and drove up here to join the Army," I said. "I got to the induction center at 10:00 a.m., where I spent hours sitting on a stupid wooden chair only to be told to come back next week. I was pissed off to say the least. I stormed out of the center, got in my car, and didn't take my foot off the accelerator until you pulled me over."

The trooper pushed his hat to the back of his head. "Shoot, I drive all over Syracuse looking for long-haired hippie draft dodgers, and I end my shift pulling over someone trying to *join* the Army," he said, talking to himself. "Let me see your license, and then you may slowly take yourself back to Endicott."

"Yes, sir, Sergeant. Here ya go."

Twenty minutes later, at the county jail, I was removing my belt and shoelaces, handing them over to a desk sergeant. The charge: driving with an expired driver's license and speeding in excess of twenty miles per hour over the limit.

The heavy, steel door closed with a loud, echoing clang. My new temporary home, on Friday, June 21,1967, was a single-man cell in the Syracuse City Jail. It was cold, but clean, and sported a fresh coat of paint. It contained a bed slab, a sink, a seatless commode, and not much else. Sitting in the corner of the bed with my back against the wall, I pulled out an envelope that I was allowed to keep when I "registered at the front desk." It contained a statistical synopsis of my life. I dumped the contents on the steel battleship-gray slab and spread them out. My eyes darted from paper to paper: college transcripts, medical history, previous job descriptions, and a letter from my college roommate, Rick "Duke" Davis. Rick had joined the Navy right after graduation and was preparing to become an officer and a gentleman. Another letter from Rick let me know, he's on the USS Corry, a destroyer in the Mekong Delta.

Picking up a DOD form from the top of the pile, I checked it for completeness and inaccuracies. I read line one of section three, "List your last three places of employment, giving dates, and reasons for leaving." With some time to kill, I took the opportunity to reflect on the past summer.

I had graduated from Gannon College in Erie, Pennsylvania, with a BS in marketing in May of 1967. The war in Vietnam was witnessing a daily increase in its intensity. Prospective employers were reluctant to hire someone they might lose to the draft. Being unemployed, single, healthy, and draft eligible, I decided it was time to make some intelligent, logical, mature decisions. Doing what I thought best for my country and me, I packed my bags and headed to Cape Cod for the summer.

My Aunt Alice and Uncle Walter, who lived in Brewster, Massachusetts, extended the hospitality of a guest room. Doug was on break from college, and Wally was on break from high school. We wasted no time. The day after I arrived Doug and I scoured the Cape for jobs. The following afternoon we both hit pay dirt; we became the two newest waiters at a five-star restaurant in Chatham. The eatery's forte was fresh seafood and the Cape's finest and most diverse wine selection.

The first few days were slow and uneventful. When the weekend arrived, however, things got hectic and exciting. Late in the evening on my first Saturday, the proprietor of the famous Pier 4 restaurant in Boston was seated in my section. The owner of this fine five-star establishment that hired me was studying every move I made at a table of six where the proprietor of Pier 4 was seated; he wiped at his brow with a damp handkerchief each time I passed him at the end of the wait station. On one particular pass, I had a towel draped over my left forearm where I was cradling a bottle of the finest wine in the house. My boss' clammy hand latched onto my shoulder and brought me to a quick halt. The wine steward was at a funeral, so each waiter was on his own. My boss was too nervous to let me handle this most important ritual by myself. Without hesitation, I relinquished my towel, my fancy corkscrew, and my way-over-priced bottle of liquid diamonds. I stepped back to the server's station to watch the master at work.

The anxiety cloud that had been moving from table to table brought itself to a screeching halt over VIP celebrity table number one. With small talk out of the way and the corkscrew in place, he gave the fancy handle a quick twist. The neck of the bottle snapped off like a dried twig after a long drought and sent its contents into random flight. He bowed, apologized, and vowed to return with another bottle. I grabbed some towels and went into rescue mode. His bald head glistened with a cover of small beads of sweat as he disappeared into the wine cellar. I concentrated hard to suppress a laugh when he breezed by with a replacement. And, oh yes, he served that bottle with the compliments of the house.

Returning to the table after the ritual of "the wine" had been "properly administered," I made eye contact with a guy, my age, who also did everything he could to keep from laughing. He pushed his glasses up to a large knot directly between his eyes each time our eyes met, and for the next ten minutes struggled with the task of eating and stifling laughter.

Despite doing pretty well that first week, Doug and I were unemployed; victims of over hiring. The real shocker, however, was the restaurant letting Doug go. He was six-feet-four, good looking, and the only one in the restaurant who could pronounce, perfectly, the name of every wine on the menu. He spoke fluent German, French, and Chinese and had an educated understanding of each culture. He was in the process of obtaining his master's degree from Brown University. At a four-star Cape Cod restaurant, Doug was the perfect example of the consummate waiter. We all make good and bad decisions in life. I couldn't help wondering how much thought went into making the decision to let him go.

We spent a month picking up odd jobs, tans, and women, not necessarily in that order, before turning our attention to the serious side of life. Doug returned to school while I headed back to Endicott to develop a plan for my future, one that I hoped to give the proper amount of time, before making a decision. While pondering my future, I got a job on the maintenance crew at the IBM Country Club in Endwell, New York, job number three on the wrinkled DOD form in my hand.

I slid the form back in the envelope and picked up a document my recruiter had filled out. I stared at the cream-colored paper and drifted back to midsummer.

In late July, my dad informed me that he had checked with his connection at the post office and found out that my name was on the next draft list. My D-Day had arrived. In essence, I received my diploma in one hand and my draft notice in the other.

I was sitting at my desk when Dad called. Pulling open the lap drawer and removing the pile of service brochures scattered within, I went to the kitchen and laid them out on the table. In short order, I made my choice: the United States Army.

My decision was made based on the solid laws of logic: my dad was in the Army during World War II; therefore, I should follow in his footsteps. OK, so I got a D in logic, one letter grade higher than I deserved. It was a monumental decision made without any real thorough thought. I wished at that moment that I were in one of my brother's shoes. My older brother by thirteen months, John, was married and had a little girl. The draft did not concern him. My younger brother by eighteen months, Steve, the star athlete in the family, was 4-F and in search of life's dreams.

I got up early the next morning and headed to the Army Recruiting Office. When I arrived, there were two other potential defenders of truth, justice, and "the American way" already asking questions at a rapid-fire pace. I was soon one-on-one with a sergeant decked out in very colorful ribbons, patches, and medals. The display was visually impressive.

Within minutes, this well-rehearsed agent of Uncle Sam had overloaded my very vulnerable mind with more information than it could dissect, digest, and file away for future reference. He had the uncanny ability to make me feel like I needed the

Army more that it wanted me. A few minutes into the interview, I felt I was applying for a regular civilian job. We discussed interests and goals, choices, and benefits. Not much was said, however, about the war in Vietnam.

In less than an hour, he had me convinced that I was a natural born leader just waiting to take charge. A very short time later I signed up for Infantry OCS (Officer Candidate School), at Fort Benning, Georgia, to begin in May of 1968. In a numbed stride, I took it all in. The realities of war weren't realities to me, or, for that matter, to most eighteen to twenty-two-year-olds. In our minds—we were invincible.

The final topic we discussed was a station wish list. I picked three places where I would like to be assigned to permanent duty: Southern California, Germany, or anywhere in the Caribbean. Basic Training, Advanced Infantry Training, Infantry OCS and then on to the sandy beaches of the Bahamas—riiiiight! I had to hand it to that sergeant; he never cracked a smile. I took a second to ponder my decision. Did I give it all the thorough review that it needed, or was I not giving it the thought through that it needed, much like the knee-jerk decision the restaurant owner made when deciding who to keep and who to let go? Life is a string of decisions we make, from adolescence to the grave. Our lives can be dramatically altered by one simple decision. Damn, I forgot the condom: what to do, what to do.

The loud echo of the opening and closing of the cell next to mine brought me back to the present. I figured I had ten minutes left before rejoining my belt and shoelaces. Upon my incarceration, I had used my one phone call to ring the Pi Kappa Alpha fraternity house at Syracuse University to summon a pledge to bail me out. I had just added one more pro to my list of reasons for joining a fraternity while in college. I would never have even thought about committing to the OCS program, if it were not for my previously joining Pi Kappa Alpha. Before becoming a Pike, I was strictly a follower, except for one time in grade school where I was in the front of the line during a fire drill. I found the front door of the school without having to refer to the school blueprint; I was so proud. I never thought that I could acquire the attributes of leadership. But, by the time I graduated from Gannon, I had become the president of three different campus organizations, including founding President of Pi Sigma Epsilon National Business Fraternity and missed being voted president of the student body by just four votes. OCS was pretty much a given.

Those ten minutes came and went. I paced, trying to ignore Mother Nature's call. My attempts were futile. Unable to wait any longer, I dropped my pants to my knees and squatted over the seatless commode. After a second or so of hovering, I heard the main door, ten feet from my cell, open with another one of those loud clang sounds that echoed up and down the concrete and metal corridor. A raspy voice gave instructions. "Step right this way, ladies, and please stay within the yellow lines." Just as I jerked my belt-less trousers back to my crotch, while bent at the waist, I found myself face-to-face with a dozen or so women being given a tour of the facilities. I felt like a monkey in a zoo. One, young lady stared. I stared back. *Thanks for the heads up, jailhouse jerk.* There were two options: turn around and moon the ladies or pull my pants up to my waist and zip. I chose to zip. This day needed no more complications.

After the somewhat flustered tourists had departed, I settled back down to business. Picking up the paper I was handed when I arrived at the Army Induction Center, I read the first two lines. "Welcome to the Armed Forces Examining Station, Syracuse. We hope that your brief stay here will be pleasant." Somehow, I managed to smile at that friendly gesture, but wondered how many others had sneered and flipped the bird at the words "brief" and "pleasant."

Prime Meat

On Thursday, July 27, 1967, I returned to the Department of the Army, Armed Forces Examining and Entrance Station at 805 S. Salina Street in Syracuse, New York, and tried—once again—to join the United States Army.

The day started at warp speed with a battery of mental tests, followed by the security questionnaire to determine an individual's affiliation, if any, with subversive organizations. I wondered if being a card-carrying member of the American Marketing Association would put me on the hot seat. Next came the moral eligibility check, designed to make sure one wasn't of a criminal temperament. After paperwork the day would continue with a very complete, somewhat crude, physical exam starting with height and weight (height minimum of four feet ten inches weighing between 91 and 127 pounds and a height maximum of six feet eight inches weighing between 173 and 227 pounds). The checklist continued with blood, hearing, vision, heart, orthopedic tests, urinalysis, and X-rays, if needed.

The physical was the first experience of the dehumanization process. Herded like cattle, we were poked, prodded, and questioned. Were we, or were we not, healthy enough hunks of meat to become choice property of the US Army?

We discovered there was no standard for the procedure of conducting the physicals. The methodology was strange considering we were all preparing to do everything "the Army way," no questions asked. A dozen of us huddled around a guy wearing a plaid shirt. His selection of clothes wouldn't normally be considered unusual, except that he had on a madras jacket as well. Syracuse was his second time at an induction physical. He was a veritable encyclopedia of information. It seems standardization went out the window, with some of the centers requiring that everyone be completely stripped throughout the process when they finished with the paperwork and staying that way until the process was completed. Other centers had everyone in their underwear, until it was necessary to be naked.

He said that the center in Detroit, the induction city of his first visit, required full nudity throughout the entire exam. Some centers were processing two hundred to three hundred recruits or more daily and had draftees and enlistees wearing nothing but their birthday suits. Charlotte, Milwaukee, Boston, and most of the other induction centers would have America's newest soldiers starting out clothed, most of the time in underwear, and a short stint completely nude. There were seventy-one induction cities and a few "throw-together centers" to handle the overflow.

Our human military encyclopedia, Mr. Madras, said that the structure of the "sans clothes" physicals was, for the most part, designed by the doctors and/or administrators of each induction center. I guess the doctors' vow to protect the privacy and modesty of their patients was placed on hold until the war ended. Immediate subservience was essential. He went on to explain that some thought those in charge of the decision to strip the conscripts of their clothes was motivated by the idea that this would also strip away their individualities. In a serious tone Mr. Madras said they would do this by way of embarrassment, humiliation, and intimidation, aided by the fact that the government employed female nurses for many of the physicals and occasionally had non-medical female clerical staff. The clerks assisted with paperwork throughout the day at the inspection stations, coming and going with forms and reports. This was more rare than normal; however, normal didn't seem to have a definition.

Furthermore, if the doctors or administrators in charge rotated, the policy may switch to the more modest wearables—boxers or briefs. If you weren't wearing underwear, then your birthday suit would suffice as boxers. He went on to say that others, however, believed that mass nudity for the entire physical was for expediency and nothing more. A new voice chimed in with, "Really? Like underwear would hamper expediency. Most guys would be out of their drawers faster than you could say, 'Like underwear would hamper expediency.'"

Mr. Madras was interrupted by the booming voice of what I guessed was a drill sergeant of sorts. As we headed to the next room, I glanced back at Mr. Madras who was talking with one of the new recruits employing his mouth, arms, and hands. I shook my head and thought that the Army was in for a real challenge with their latest entry of a "Rebel with a Cause."

We were shuffled from room to room and table to table in our underwear with small bags around our necks with our valuables: wallets, rings, and keys. Everything was inspected and checked off: eyes, feet, and all points in between. Then it was one-on-one with a very disheveled-looking doctor in his mid-fifties wearing a rumpled white lab coat, a loose-fitting tie, and glasses that hung on the end of his nose. Quick inspections with the usual doctor toys—stethoscope, rubber hammer, plastic gloves—took up about half of the time for this part of the physical. He clutched a leaky pen between two ink-stained fingers on his left hand and a large brown clipboard between nicotine-stained fingers on his right. He placed a sharpened pencil in a shirt pocket already occupied by an almost empty pack of Marlboros and began a quick inspection of my vitals. He then looked me straight in the eye after reviewing my paperwork.

"What kind of shape you in?" he asked. He coughed a raspy-sounding gurgle, leaned over to spit green phlegm into an empty trash can, and waited for my response.

"Except for bursitis in both my shoulders, I think I'm in pretty good shape."

He returned to the clipboard with my paperwork jammed under the clip. "Get into a push-up position," he ordered.

I obliged his request, lowering my six-foot, three-inch, 165-pound frame to the floor. My shoulders gave out three inches into the exercise, and I collapsed to the cold, dirty tile beneath me. "Sorry, but that's the best I can do, Doc," He bent his head to his chest, looked over the top of his glasses, let loose with another raspy cough, and said, "You'll learn. NEXT!"

I felt good about clear sailing from that point forward. I wondered how many stories there were that got people snatched in or thrown out because of some little minor nothing. A friend of mine, Mike Edwards from Durham, North Carolina, took his physical with sixty-four others from the area. This group had an exceptionally high rate of rejection, but he got his stamp of approval after accidentally breaking a doctor's glass desktop protector. The MD was pissed.

I remember Mike telling me, "I could have had one leg, been blind, and in a wheelchair, and those assholes would still have made an exception for me because of my status as a certified glass breaker."

We entered yet another large room and were told to "drop 'em." With shorts in hand, it became pretty clear that next on the agenda were the rituals of head turning, coughing, peeing in a cup, and bending over for the grand finale.

The guy standing next to me, whom I had met two rooms earlier, said, "Hey, check out the chicks."

"What—those nurses by the door?" I said as I pointed to two females wearing scrubs and toting clipboards. They were standing fifteen feet straight in front of us.

"Yeah, except at least one of them ain't a nurse. I don't know about the other one. I saw the cute one on the left at a desk in a room full of office staff while I still had my clothes on. I caught her eye, and she winked at me, or at least it looked like a wink."

"You're shitting me, right?" I asked, as I placed my hands over my genitals.

"Hey, get used to it, dude. We're robots now and soon to become programmed robots," he said as he tried to get her attention again. They disappeared in a flash, and I'm sure they didn't wink at him before they left.

Mr. Wink chimed in again, "Man, this ain't nothin. My cousin had his physical in one of those 'throw together' induction centers that are popping up all over the place. Dudes were lined up naked in the halls. They were heading to the inspection stations in full view of chicks in offices facing the hallways."

He said, "The doors were propped open, and it wasn't even that warm, except for the 98.6 times fifty." He snickered as he added, "Felt sorry for the girls. Evidently, they all had the same urinary problem—lots of trips to the ladies' room at the far end of the hall. Except for the well-hung guys, most everyone held their hands over their crotches."

All of this was easy to believe because of personal stories or antidotes from my family and friends. However, the norm was boxers or briefs. My cousin John took his physical in 1966 in a hotel in Syracuse. He said, "I spent the entire day wearing nothing but socks on my feet, and we all stayed that way all day." He continued, "The most 'what the fuck' moment came when we entered a room with windows that faced an office building across the street. There were some girls I guessed were on break, on a balcony, watching the, ah, activities."

"Yeah, so what; all they could see was the sun's reflection in the windows," I responded.

"Normally that would be true," John said. "But the windows and shades had all been pulled up. I shit you not." John continued, "A shy guy went over to the windows and pulled a couple of the blinds down." A sergeant yelled, "Pull those blinds back up. We need all the light we can get." John finished the tale with, "Yeah, we believed we discovered who was getting paid with dollars or favors for this little service for the ladies. Then again, he may have been nothing more than a perv with a sister who worked across the street."

John added that he had another story more bizarre than the open windows. During his physical, he said that he mentioned he had cysts in his left knee. During his inspection with the Army doctors, they wanted him to be seen by a civilian doc. It was a Monday. They told him that he would get a complimentary room and meals.

"The doctor showed up on—are you ready for this?—Friday and confirmed that I had three cysts on one knee," he said. The civilian doc instructed John to have them repaired and then come back in six months. John said, "I split and never returned, never heard from anyone."

Mr. Wink finished his storytelling with one regarding the urine tests. "At the center in Philadelphia, or was it Dallas … I think, whatever … there were two chicks in lab coats, posted at each end of a urinal trough, handing out cups. I'm not making this up, man. They then observed the flow of pee from the dicks into the cups. When they finished, the cups were retrieved after they were labeled and then placed on a tray. I'm serious man; chicks had to watch to make sure it was indeed the pisser's piss that was filling up the cup. Really! I'm serious as a heart attack. I wonder how many ended up pissing like a fountain." I called an emphatic bullshit on that one and would have bet a week's pay that this guy had a pot pipe in the sack around his neck.[1]

An enormous recruit, right at the height/weight limit, was listening to our conversation; he added his educated two cents. "Your buddy is correct," he said. "My older brother, who's an Army nerd, told me that military regulations stated that it was acceptable to have 'non-medical opposite-gender personnel act as urine collection observers and as chaperones.' I memorized it because I know people would call BS on that little bit of trivia."

"Hey, dude, do you know how they checked chick's pee? Get it … chicks p-e-a, as in the vegetable?" Mr. Wink asked while giggling. We didn't acknowledge his pun. "A female observer—sorry, no males allowed, but that goes without saying— would hand her a cup as she sat on the toilet. The chick observer would turn around and look at the chick recruit in a mirror. Ain't that a pisser? Hey, wow, two puns in two sentences. I don't think anyone gives a shit about male modesty as it's something men don't need to have because … well … we're men," Mr. Wink said, matter-of-factly.

"No, really, man, think about all the YMCAs, today, as well as a shit-load of junior high and high schools all over the good ole' US of A, where the boys *have* to swim naked while girls *have* to wear bathing suits. And if the instructor couldn't make it for one reason or another, they got a substitute who was more than likely a female; probably the chick that teaches the girls.

He then finished with the following scenario. Moms, dads, brothers, and sisters would come to watch the YMCA meet at the end of the season. They called it "family night." The boy's sisters would often invite a friend to come and watch, as well as the female swimmers. At some Y's final swims, there would be crowds of 650 or more. And some of those poor fuckers would get boners. The 650 figure wasn't made up; it was in an article in a newspaper in Sheboygan, Wisconsin. Another article in a New Orleans paper said that over one thousand people watched the final meet. A lot of the YMCAs told the guys to bring swim wear with them. Others gave the boys a choice. He finished with, "Pretty amazing, huh?" "Yeah, I guess I should have cut you off because I've known about that swimming shit since the '50s and was told they have been doing it that way since the '20s. The high school across the street at Gannon, where I went to college, had nude swimming for the boys in 1964. It pisses me off because I'm one of those men with a high degree of modesty, which I apparently must chuck into the same pile as my clothes. I'm just glad my mom didn't like the policy and taught me and my brothers how to swim."

Naturally, our next stop was urine collection, which was where I was able to ditch Mr. Wink. I headed straight to a water fountain where I stood in line with eight or nine other guys to fill the tank. I would need as much as I could hold because I was extremely pee shy. I had no idea how the "peeing in a cup" went because I totally blocked it from my memory along with most of the other stops. August 10, 1967, was not a fun day. It was long, scary, embarrassing, and humiliating. Why else would I have blocked out eighty percent of the experience?[2]

The grand finale took us to a room where we lined up in front of floor-to-ceiling windows along the length of the space. Don't know why, but it appeared there were more people in the room than I thought were necessary. Oh yeah, I forgot, our individualities were being stripped away using embarrassment, humiliation, and intimidation. I guess this was the final ritual of dehumanization for the day. Looking out through that wall of bare windows, I watched a small bird flutter about aimlessly.

I returned to reality when a doctor and his clipboard-toting male aide wearing plastic gloves, the doc holding a flashlight (although I didn't know why, as the light coming through the glass was blindingly bright) appeared between us and the windows. We were soon to experience the infamous, mass rectal inspection. We were ordered to bend over and "spread 'em." In essence, we were mooning the city of Syracuse. At that moment, I wished I were in Washington, DC.

By late afternoon the poking, prodding, and endless questioning were over for the day. We were reunited with our clothes and then gathered together in yet another large, open room. A sergeant entered and banged on the seat of a metal chair. "Listen up, gentlemen. The United States Army would like to thank you for your time. You are free to go—for now."

Vassar, Yale, and the US Army

Endicott was on a straight line south of Syracuse, but a young lady from Connecticut had invited me to alter my direction for a weekend. This invitation came with my personal guarantee to, for the time being, not dwell on my impending future. My new destination—Poughkeepsie, New York.

Lucia Bolton was in her senior year at Vassar. We had met through mutual friends a few weeks earlier. Within hours of that meeting, she asked me to escort her to some fancy graduate get-together at Yale University. I didn't hesitate a millisecond to answer yes.

Almost six feet tall with classic features, long brown hair, large round eyes, and a flawless complexion, she fit my ideal vision of the perfect women. Her speech was a little too perfect, but I tried not to hold that against her.

I spent the night with a few other guys from the "meat market" in Syracuse and headed out on Friday morning to Poughkeepsie, New York. Arriving right on time, midafternoon, seemed to please her a lot. The entire weekend was scheduled to the minute. Dinner, visits with friends (mostly foreign exchange students), a short trip to the beach, and the main event, a cocktail party for graduate students and faculty, were all planned with great care. But even with all the arrangements, everything seemed casual, relaxed, and spontaneous.

My accommodation was an extra room in her dorm suite. At 6:30 on Saturday evening the main event was closing in fast. Looking into an oversized mirror, I pulled the Windsor knot on my tie up to the top of my collar and shifted it from left to right and back again. I removed my hands when it was dead center and stepped back for a self-inspection. I wasn't an Ivy Leaguer, but at the moment, I looked like one.

We arrived at the party on time, actually to the minute—no surprise there. The early evening air was tranquil and cool. We entered the mansion, built at the turn of the century, and surveyed the immediate area. The gathering, distributed throughout the bottom floor, took place in four rooms. Twelve-foot ceilings, intricately decorated cornices, deep-red mahogany woodwork, recorded classical music, and fresh flowers all helped create an elegant atmosphere.

Within minutes, the main room was filled with people engaged in deep conversations. I didn't detect any talk centering on football reported in the morning's sports section of the *Journal*. The collective IQ in the room was somewhere in the hundreds of thousands. The air, filled with chatter, soon shared its space with a mixture of smoke from a variety of cigars, cigarettes, and pipes—lots of pipes.

Meandering around and through the masses, we attached to a group of six, mostly strangers to one another. We exchanged greetings.

"Kit Mitchell, Department of Philosophy," said one. "Darryl Roades, Department of Engineering," announced another. "Jerry Chambliss, Department of Physics," stated a third. "Thomas Haines, Department of Defense," I proclaimed with great pride as I reached around and snagged an unrecognizable something from a passing tray. Lucia tried to stifle a giggle but failed.

We wandered away from the pack of *Homo sapiens* with more synaptic connections than most and headed back out to the foyer. Standing beneath a giant grandfather clock, Lucia began to search the room for a friend she wanted me to meet. She spotted him seated on a sloping spiral staircase and waved enthusiastically.

"There he is. Come on," she said, taking me by the hand while snaking her way through the crowd.

"Tom, this is T.E. T's studying for his MA in history at Yale," she said while still moving. Once stable she continued, "T, this is Tom. He was in Syracuse this morning enlisting in the Army."

T.E. stood out in the crowd because of his exceptionally long hair, wire-rim glasses, and nappy coat with a mismatched tie. Unfolding himself from his almost fetal position, he started the conversation.

"So you just joined the Army. I don't want to seem forward, but would you go to South Vietnam and fight the North Vietnamese if they gave you orders to do so?"

"Yeah, if I receive orders to go to Vietnam, I'll go. I don't plan on doing anything stupid, like volunteering. However, there is a war going on, and I did join the Army, so if they point me in that direction, I'll go."

He seemed genuinely upset. Pulling back his lips and exposing his gums, he went into a lengthy oratory about Ho Chi Minh, the politics of South Vietnam, and our meddling involvement. He cut short his emotional diatribe when he realized that he had gotten the attention of over half of those in the foyer. He continued, in a quieter voice, "Have you spent much time, or for that matter any time at all, thinking about what you're preparing to fight for?"

As seconds ticked away, I tried to gather some schooled thoughts on the subject, but out of respect for myself and those listening, I decided not to sling a line of bullshit.

"Look, as a nation, we voted others to lead us, you know, to make decisions for us in the national interest. I don't care if it's economic, social, military, whatever—it doesn't matter. Evidently, they think this police action in Vietnam is necessary and morally right. To be honest with you, I don't know if it is or isn't. I'm not sure any war can be rightfully proclaimed moral or just. I do think that any war should be a last resort in the grand scheme of resolving differences."

Taking a deep breath, I continued, "As for myself, I've decided that I'll find out firsthand what this is all about. If the evidence indicates that what America is doing in Vietnam is wrong, then I'll deal with it when it happens." Except for calling the war a police action, I believed everything I had just said.

T.E. didn't buy my explanation, but his lips loosened and returned to normal, which I interpreted as a draw in our short but poignant debate. Lucia switched the conversation to a lighter topic, and the volume of the chatter went back to pre-T.E. levels. A short time later he excused himself.

"Tom, I'm so sorry about T.E. Believe it or not, he's a very nice person—very opinionated but a nice person."

"Hey, don't give it a second thought. Being opinionated isn't a bad thing. Everything we believe in has fine lines and gray areas. Our opinions are what makes our lives interesting, and—"

"Tom, I—," she said interrupting.

"—Sorting it all out is a tough task," I continued, interrupting her interruption. "On second thought, make that a monumental task," I said and then changed the subject.

After a short but fun visit to the beach on Sunday, the weekend came to an end. We exchanged addresses and promised to stay in touch.

It was a long trip back to Endicott. I spent some of that time reliving the past weekend. I trusted and hoped that my country and I knew what we were doing.

Welcome to the Army, Ladies

Scores of young men were about to alter the course of their lives forever on Thursday, January 25, 1968, in Syracuse, New York. The induction center, crowded with applicants, enlistees, preinductees, and inductees shared the atmosphere with adrenaline, testosterone, and dozens of emotions: excitement, anger, pride, eagerness, sullenness, nervousness, exhilaration, fearfulness, anxiousness, apprehension, and in truth, a little numbness. I was an applicant; however, at 8:15 a.m., my status changed, and I became an enlistee. I was one of "those men who have been found eligible as applicants and have returned to this station in order to take the oath of enlistment and begin active duty in the service of their choice."

Fifty of us were in a small room that housed a large American flag. It covered most of the front wall. Conversations were interrupted when a short, well-built Marine sergeant entered, followed closely a half step behind by a clipboard-toting private. The sergeant, his hands clasped together behind his back, positioned himself in front of a section of would-be soldiers. His eyes were barely visible under his Smokey the Bear hat. He demanded the attention of everyone in the front section. While scanning the group, his gaze darted from each man to the next. He studied every inductee intently for a fraction of a second. This sergeant seemed to know exactly what it was he wanted or, more aptly, needed.

Visual survey complete, he unclasped his hands, stretched out his right arm, and aimed it at a tall, husky fella with a crew cut. He beckoned the bewildered big boy by repeatedly curling and straightening his finger.

He performed this silent ritual a half dozen times. After separating six men from the rest of us, he made a sharp military turn in their direction and said, "Congratulations, gentlemen. You're now official inductees of the United States Marines."

What the fuck! We were stunned, not unlike a herd of deer caught in the glare of headlights. One of the six appeared to look frantically for an escape route as the group was led from the area. My heart picked up an extra beat, even though I was an enlistee and had no chance of being singled out. I half expected the sergeant to stick his head around the corner and holler, "Just kidding!" That didn't happen. The conversation buzz picked back up.

"Holy shit, can they really do that?" asked a guy wearing a white shirt and solid-black tie.

"Evidently—they just did," answered the guy next to him wearing a torn tank top.

"I wonder why he didn't select me?" chimed in a third voice.

"Hope that son of a bitch doesn't come back for round two," said a booming voice that made a dozen heads turn toward the door.

The noise level continued to grow until an Army sergeant entered and in one long sentence demanded our silence and gave us details about our upcoming schedule.

Those who enlisted took the Oath of Enlistment, while those drafted took the Oath of Allegiance. Everyone received Special Orders 018. We took these orders and our heavy bags of emotions and shuffled to another holding area for shipment to basic training. My new identity was RA 11984846.

As we were preparing to board our bus to Fort Dix, New Jersey, my name was called out. I scanned the area looking for a short Marine sergeant as I hollered, "Here!" An officer approached at time-and-a-half trying to balance a briefcase, a loose pile of papers, and a full cup of coffee.

"Congratulations, private, or should I say, future second lieutenant—oh, shit, that's hot! The Army is giving you your first leadership role. You're in charge of this group. Don't lose anyone."

He directed me to snatch the top DOA form from the loose stack of multicolored papers he was still trying very much to secure. Once the paper was in my possession, he scampered off.

"Damn! I've been in the Army for less than an hour and already have my first detail," I thought. I knew right then and there it was going to be a long three and a half years. With assistance from some real soldiers, I gathered the seven tired and anxious men assigned to my care and headed to a large, silver Trailways motor coach.

The trip to Fort Dix went smoothly. We stepped off the hissing bus into a cold, uncertain, new world. The guy in front of me dropped his bag, raised his arms skyward, and bellowed, "Let the games begin!"

"Games? Games? This is the Army, boy! We're killing people in a war on the other side of this planet, not playing baseball with them! We won't have time for no fucking games! Now get off that bus, ladies. Move, move, move!" screeched the sergeant who "greeted" us.

With heads counted, I gave my paperwork to the sergeant in charge. "Well, son, you did such a good job getting these turkeys to Fort Dix that I'm making you platoon leader of your barracks," he said, hesitated, and continued. "That is, until you screw up."

"Uhhh, thank you, Sergeant," I replied while grabbing my bag and heading into a formation of sorts. *"What good job?"* I thought. *"OK, no one jumped out of any windows while we traveled at sixty miles an hour down the New York State Turnpike in subzero weather; must've been due to my good leadership skills."*

My first duty was to check attendance at formation the following morning. For me, 5:15 a.m. had always been the middle of the night, but in our new world, 0515 hours became the beginning of the day. No matter that it was still pitch-black outside, it was morning and time to be wide-eyed and moving.

At 5:45 a.m., we were dressed and bouncing around like fidgety children, trying to keep warm in a very loose formation, better described as a brisk, broken bunch of soon-to-be battle boys. There were supposed to be forty-seven men, broken down into twelve NGs (National Guard), nineteen USs (draftees), and sixteen RAs (enlistees). Including myself, I counted forty-six people—twice. "Shit, I lost one," I muttered. "Damn, it was so much easier keeping track of everyone on a speeding bus." I tried to control my panic.

"Sergeant, sir, I counted everyone twice, and it appears we're one guy short," I said with sincere regrets as if I were the one who lost him.

"One guy short. Let me tell you something, soldier, I'm one guy who's short"—meaning a small amount of time left in Nam or the service—"and I don't need this shit." He threw his hands into the air and stormed off.

Private Robert Lorenzo, a draftee, was marked down as AWOL (absent without official leave), and we continued our in-service processing.

Non-stop activity and introductions crammed the calendar for the next few days. Introduction to a new language was first on the list. Time was no longer 1:00 p.m.; it was "1300 hours." The bathroom became "the latrine." Picking up trash was "policing the area." If there was not a separate military term for something, then it likely never existed in the first place. Our induction physical wasn't really an exception as we were still citizens at that time.

Probably the most important linguistic distinction made early on was that your rifle is your weapon, and your penis is your gun. If someone called his rifle a gun, he had to hold his weapon in one hand, and his penis in the other. He would then proclaim in a loud voice, *"This is my weapon, and this is my gun. This is for fighting, and this is for fun."* Rarely was the mistake made more than once, except for the occasional pervert who enjoyed grabbing his dick and loudly proclaiming its reason for existence.

We were introduced to a new world of color or, more appropriately, a lack thereof. Our clothes, blankets, canteens, even our shoelaces were all a putrid, dull, ugly shade of green, referred to as OD, olive drab, or Army shade 107. The introduction that affected us most was our new mode of transportation—our feet. My 1965 Mustang Fastback became a fond, old memory.

In a matter of hours, we were stripped of our individualities, forced into an all-male form of communal living, and completely cut off from our former lives. Most did whatever was needed to make the adjustment, while others, like Robert Lorenzo, didn't or couldn't and went AWOL.

The first dreaded ritual of the dehumanization process was the military haircut. There were a dozen men waiting to be buzzed when our group arrived at the small, weatherworn, wooden structure. Every color, style, and texture were represented—blondes and redheads, greasers and hippies, crew cuts and afros were all in abundance as we joined the line of human sheep.

Bush heads entered in the front; bald heads exited out the back. The process took thirty-eight seconds. Instinct had every soldier, without exception, feeling his scalp while he reached for his cap, which suddenly became very necessary.

Each victim exhibited a prominent, notable feature. Some were all ears, while others had giant foreheads or large lips. We looked like a battalion of Mr. Potato Heads. In my case, it was the nose that exploded from the middle of my face and dominated my exterior.

Sporting our fashionable new wardrobes and spiffy new haircuts, we headed to our next adventure—shots. Stripped to the waist, we entered a large, well-lit, clean room. The inoculations were delivered gauntlet style. Sadists, disguised as medics, were lined up in two rows dispensing shots via long-nosed needles and pneumatic guns. The largest guy in the room posing as the noble leader of a pride of lions passed out as it became his turn to prove his dominance at the threshold of the lion's den. And yes, dear movie-going reader, this actually happened with our group.

Gauntlet traversed, we gathered outside to lick our wounds. We rubbed our arms, fingered our scalps, and scratched at the fresh-cut hairs that clung to our bare goose-fleshed necks. We mulled about, dreading what might come next.

A sergeant attempted to gather us with a series of inaudible commands. Frustrated in his attempts to organize us in a swift and orderly manner, he increased his verbal volume and peppered his speech with some insect references.

"All right, you misdirected maggots, form in over here!" he railed, pointing to the ground. We moved at a rate slightly faster than slow motion. The sergeant yelled once again, "This is the last time I'm gonna tell you cockroaches to fall in!"

A large black guy, who appeared to be in a great deal of pain, crossed in front of the sergeant; he was heading in the wrong direction. The sergeant reached out, grabbed his bicep, and pulled him in the right direction.

"Move your ass over here—now" he demanded.

The newly ordained private stood his ground. "No problem, Sarge, as soon as you let go of my arm, which hurts like hell right now."

The sergeant tightened his grip. "I said move it over here now, fly shit!"

The big guy lost it. He jerked away and lifted his fist. The crack against the stunned sergeant's cheekbone could be heard across the compound. The three-striper (buck sergeant) hit the ground like a large bag of Sacrete. I was shocked at the damage caused by just one punch. Out of nowhere, three MPs appeared producing the shrill sounds of hemorrhaging whistles. We were down to forty-six, and the day was far from over.

SNAFU

Processing continued over the next few days. Any free time was spent doing KP (kitchen patrol) and other details. These shifts could last for twelve hours or more. I guessed that the Army figured if we didn't have any free time, we couldn't dwell on our current plight. I lucked out. As platoon leader, my assignment was to guard the barracks for the remaining time in our transition. Most of my time was spent dwelling on our current quandary, writing letters, and getting a jump on memorizing assorted items of military musts: general orders, military hierarchy, and the code of conduct to name a few.

On our last day, January 30th, it all came together. We had our orders and our gear, and most importantly, our individualities had been successfully castrated. Now we were prepped and primed to begin the rigorous training process to become America's finest fighting machine, or second finest behind the Marines, or third finest behind the Navy Seals, or fourth finest behind the Salvation Army. It appears that every fighting military group claims to have the finest fighters in the world. It's impossible to fathom the group that says, "Hey, no problem. We're fine holding down eighth place."

I never had any desire or set any goal to become an expert at killing or maiming another human being, let alone striving to be the best at it. However, I was prepared to push myself to achieve my highest level of performance, physically and mentally, not because of any grand, macho goal of self-achievement, but rather an innate sense of survival and, of course, a temporary overload of testosterone.

With gear in tow, we were herded into a high, one-story, cinder-block building with a cold, cement floor, three stairs down. The room was massive and void of furniture. Each man staked out a piece of floor, dropped an overstuffed duffel bag, and leaned against the hard, green mass. Some wrote letters home; others engaged in small talk, while all created streams of breath that dissipated before reaching the ceiling.

The last soldiers to arrive brought with them news from Vietnam. A major offensive was underway. The noise level of the room picked up and spread quickly throughout the cavernous space. The guy sitting next to me said it was called Tit. He was set straight by the guy sitting next to him. The correct name for the new offensive was Tet. The room fell eerily quiet. A baby-faced black soldier, propped up against the gray and coarse cinder-block wall in the far corner of the room, broke the silence with a spontaneous and haunting rendition of *Alfie*. His magnificent tenor was strong and virile, yet the sound from deep within his soul was bursting with sensitivity. He sang with an emotion you felt you could grasp and hold onto like a security blanket.

When he finished the ballad, silence returned. The soldier next to me broke the quiet. He addressed the person sitting closest to him. "Look around, man. A whole bunch of these guys won't be with us next year to hear great singing like that. Sucks, doesn't it?"

No response. None needed.

Judy – pet monkey of
3/12 4th Inf Div.
Pleiku, Aug. 1969

Fort Dix, New Jersey

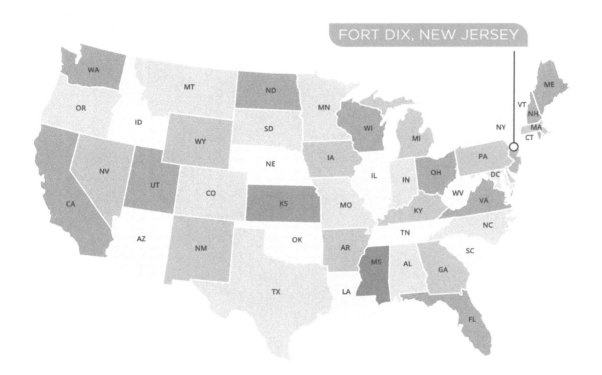

FORT DIX, NEW JERSEY

UNITED STATES OF AMERICA

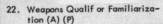

22. Weapons Qualif or Familiarization (A) (P)

WPN	SCORE	QUALIF	DATE
M-14	34	MM	17Apr68
M-16	53	SS	23 Jun 68
M-60	140	IEXP	12Apr68

THE FOURTH LIMERICK

There once was a man from the Fourth

Who blew his pot to the north

didn't take him long

To give his position to the Cong

And now that lad from our Division

Has a deep . . . bloody . . . ugly incision

CHAPTER 6

I Am the Infantry, the Ultimate Weapon, the Queen of Battle

We were loaded into trucks and shipped to different units scattered around Fort Dix for our introduction to war—fighting it and surviving it. I threw my bag and myself into the back of a truck. Sticking out from under a corner of my bag was a copy of our upcoming training schedule. The goals were quite simple: instruct newly acquired Joe Civilian in the basics of effective weapons application, train him to accept orders from superiors without question, teach him proven wilderness survival techniques, show him how to live his life in the proper military teamwork manner, guide him through the inner search for the courage and fortitude that are required to accomplish his tasks, and then watch him evolve into "GI Joe" or as close a replica as possible.

It was still early when we arrived at our new temporary home. The cinder-block structure smelled of fresh paint. The cream-colored interior looked more like a college dorm than a military barracks.

My new address was D-5-3, Second Platoon. I was a member of a squad (ten under a sergeant), a platoon (forty under a lieutenant), a company (200 under a captain), a battalion (1,000 under a lieutenant colonel or a major), a regiment or brigade (4,000 under a colonel), and a division (15,000 under a major general.) All these elements were a part of the whole, the US Army (a million plus, under the president of the United States). Good Lord Almighty—Lyndon Baines Johnson was my boss.

Each room had seven guys assigned alphabetically, so we were surprised that six of us had attended or graduated from college. Education aside, our diversity still proved to be as wide as Mama Cass's ass. Brian Effron, a law graduate, introduced himself to Ken Green, a high school graduate, who joined the Army while working the production line at a toy manufacturing plant. Our geographical diversity became evident as Pat Goodman hailing from, West "By God" Virginia, was introduced to Bill Kessler from Atlantic City, New Jersey, an hour and a half drive from Fort Dix.

Dumping the OD-green mass from my OD-green duffel bag, I introduced myself to the last two to arrive. Walter Hutchison was from New Haven, Connecticut, and Ray Haber was from a small town just outside of Philadelphia.

"I'm sorry, what did you say your name was? Tom, was it? And where are you from?" Walter asked.

"Tom is correct, and I'm from Endicott, New York," I responded, while nodding.

"OK, Tom, from Endicott, New York, I'm going on record … and this is official," he began in a whisper. "I HATE THIS FUCKING PLACE ALREADY!" He screamed his message and then finished his announcement in the same low whisper in which he started. He emptied his duffle bag with a quick snap of the wrist. At six feet eight inches tall, he dominated the room.

I knew right then Hutch and I would become close. "When do we eat?" Hutch asked. His parents owned a bakery, and he drove a truck for them after graduating from Boston College. He mirrored my situation, getting his diploma in one hand and his draft notice in the other. Hutch said that a basketball coach saw him at registration and got so excited he had to put his hands in his pockets. He made a beeline to Hutch and asked him, before coming to a halt, how well he played basketball. Hutch looked at him with a confused look on his face and said, "What's basketball?" The coach walked off shaking his head.

In short order, we were grabbing our gloves, coats, and winter caps and heading out to our first formation. Our sergeant bellowed, "Move it, move it, move it. Let's go, ladies, move-move-move!"

Our surrogate mother was E-6 Michael McNeil. He was six feet tall and had red hair that almost matched his ruddy cheeks. He looked like the stereotypical drill instructor: broad shoulders, flat stomach, bad haircut.

In our ranks, the diversity continued: a solidly built, five-foot-three-inch black guy in front of me, six-foot-eight-inch Walter Hutchison to my left, and to my right, a five-foot-nine-inch Hispanic guy who could stand to lose two or ten pounds. The only obvious ingredients missing from our American melting pot were females, dudes over thirty, and those under four-feet-ten or over six-feet-eight. Walter said he was "dead on" the upper limit. If he hadn't gotten a haircut just before taking his physical, he wouldn't be in the Army.

Introductions continued for the next few days. We learned the proper military way of making beds, folding clothes, telling time, and polishing boots. Military songs, regulations, terminology, customs, and etiquette were also part of the program, as well as a new way to walk, talk, and greet. We learned new, never-before-considered concepts, such as field stripping cigarettes, dry shaving when necessary, and accepting the idea of killing a fellow human being. I believe most of us began using muscles we had never intentionally used before. It wouldn't be long before our main goal was to put as many bullet holes into targets as possible, using a variety of handheld killing machines.

On our third day of basic training, following a grueling morning of more introductions in subzero weather, we were double-timed to a large theater. Brought to an abrupt halt and left standing, puffing clouds of steam, we waited for the order to enter.

After a few minutes, we stepped past the oversized main doors, and our senses delightfully treated to real-world luxuries recently removed. The seats were ass-grabbing comfortable, not a trace of OD green anywhere, and the temperature set at a perfect comfort level. The lights dimmed as we took our seats. An appealing fragrance and nondescript calming music filled the air. The hall fell quiet, without the aid of a DI hollering, "Shut up, you maggots!"

A spotlight illuminated a corner of the room where a lone soldier stood on a giant stage in front of a thick, plush, blue, velvet curtain. In a deep, powerful, yet soothing voice, he welcomed us to the proudest, the most competent fighting force on the planet. Drama was the word of the day.

I leaned towards Walter. "Hey, Hutch, can you believe this shit?" I whispered.
"Wow, where do I sign up?" he responded.

"Easy does it, big fella," I said, "You're already in the Army, and it's too early to re-up—I think."

There was a speech, a film, and an introduction by someone who declared, "I am the infantry, the queen of battle, the ultimate weapon." He was a perfect specimen of what we were supposed to become. This soldier's appearance was so flawless I honestly believed he was the model for those macho military recruiting posters. During the festivities, there wasn't any talk of the politics of the war in Vietnam, just the glory and pride of serving God and country.

Looking around the room, I saw dozens of mouths agape, sucking in all the rhetoric being dished out from the stage. Hutch looked over at me again. "Wow, man, I just gotta re-up. Now."

Even though neither Hutch nor I were buying it, I could understand it. Taking an average, everyday Joe off the street, someone who may have bagged groceries for a living, and turning him into a well-trained killing machine is rarely an easy task. Subtle brainwashing is probably necessary to accomplish this most difficult of missions.

The group that exited the theater was more pumped up, more gung-ho, and more willing than the batch that entered an hour earlier. The percentage of those "won over" seemed to be high. Or, possibly, they were high in the traditional sense.

Back outside in subfreezing reality, Hutch came over and draped his arm over my shoulder. "Well, Private, do you feel like an ultimate weapon yet?"

"Nope," I replied. "If I go to Vietnam and get shot, I'm pretty sure I'll bleed red. But I'll bet a month's pay that some of these guys will bleed an immeasurable amount of OD green."

War Is Hell—
And So Is Basic

Basic training was over. Everyone had packed and headed to well-deserved leaves before reporting to their next duty station. Bill Kessler and Pat Godman were the last to hit the door. Sitting on my stripped-down bunk, I thumbed through my journal. *Why had I even kept a journal?* There was no way I could forget the last eight weeks. I paused at a few memorable passages, including a note from my lawyer telling me the judge had dismissed my speeding ticket and expired license citation when informed that I was in Army basic training. He had no concern of me being convicted after hearing of my fate.

Over those eight long and arduous weeks, the word "normal" had lost its meaning. Reading the entry that began, Thursday, February 8, 1968, I reminisced.

*****

The rock-hard ground was dusted in white. We gathered and fell into formation. The almost weightless snow descended in a frenzy, choreographed by a swirling wind. The temperature was well below zero. Our formation was tight. To keep from freezing, we bounced in place. Sarge wasted no time moving us out to chow. He was as cold as we were and didn't even try to be macho regarding Mother Nature's rage.

The dark of night made way for the gray of morning. Sarge chose a marching song as we double-timed to the mess hall, but it didn't take our minds off the harsh, frigid air. With perfect cadence, his voice boomed, "Hup, two, three, four—I don't know, but I've been told—Eskimo pussy is mighty cold—honey, o babe of mine—go to your left, your right, your left—go to your left, your right, your left." Thanks, Sarge, for the reminder of just how cold it is below numbers of which we didn't want to be reminded.

Moments later we arrived at an imposing block of bricks. The only thing between us and bacon, eggs, and hot biscuits on the warmer side of those bricks was a cold steel monster with eighteen teeth. For most of those bouncing in line, the horizontal ladder was a minor obstacle that put off eating for an extra few seconds. But for the rest of us, it was one of the most dreaded times of every morning. The shiny silver-gray monkey bars were humiliating, frustrating, and helped swell the ranks of the Fat Boys Club. The club was most undesirable. It involved lots of extra running late at night while our buddies were writing letters home or falling into a deep sleep. I looked at those bars and realized one thing: as a kid, no matter how good those Coco Puffs tasted, I should have eaten more Wheaties.

Inching closer to our thrice-daily moment of truth, I considered shedding my coat and gloves but recalled leaving a layer of skin on a frost-covered bar while becoming its first victim earlier in the week. I opened and closed my fists and repeated a quote from a childhood book, "I think I can, I think I can, I think I can!"

Eleven in a row made it. There was some comfort in knowing that Fat Freddie Rigolli was standing between me and the agony of defeat. Freddie, aka, Roly Poly Rigolli, almost always fell from the first rung. He had to have gained a lot of weight between his physical and his induction.

Hutch, who looked like Quasimodo swinging from the bells of Notre Dame, dropped to the ground at the other end of the galvanized structure as Freddie stepped onto the starting rod. He clapped three times and pulled himself up to the first rung. Grabbing the bar firmly with both gloved-covered hands, Freddie pushed off. He swung like a giant pendulum until his body was almost parallel to the ground. Then Freddie lost his grip and fell to the frozen turf. He landed hard, with a dull thud, flat on his back. When the powdery snow settled, Freddie opened his eyes, looked at me, stretched out his arms, and said, "Come to Papa." He rolled over twice and began the mandatory punishment for the unsuccessful: ten push-ups.

Freddie had struggled through two push-ups before I returned 100 percent to my plight. I jumped up to the start position. Without the fanfare of ritual, I grasped the first bar in my right hand and dropped my weight into a swinging motion. My arms, wrist, fingers, and legs fought as a team to reach the next silver bar. I soared forward then fluttered like a wounded bird. Instinctively my left hand sought the second bar. Grasping hard, I pulled my knees upward to help my right hand find bar number three. It was not to be. My left hand slid off the bar as if my body weight had doubled between the second and third steel pipe. Unlike Freddie, some of my dignity remained intact; I landed on both feet. The second my boots touched the ground I ran to the wall where Freddie was still struggling with his push-ups. I dropped down next to him and tried to ignore Sarge's humiliating taunt: "Come on, ladies, bounce those tits in the snow. One, two, three, bounce. One, two, three, bounce."

I unlocked my elbows and lowered myself to the snow-covered turf. When my nose was an inch from the fluffy flakes, I let out my breath and blew the white powder in all directions. Staring at the hard, brown ground, I repeated the mantra over and over, "I thought I could; I thought I could; I thought I could."

Finally, orange juice, eggs, and toast refueled my beaten body. I took my tray to the trash can, scraping the remaining bits of toast into it, then fitted the tray on the stack by the door and felt a movement in my coat pocket. Pulling away, I found myself face to face with Key Hart. This five-foot-five-inch black guy with strong features, a firm grip, and a permanent scowl, was one serious dude. K, as he was called, would reserve fun and games for his next life.

He pumped his fist twice at waist level, and said, "I know you can do it, man." He spun on his heels and left to join the formation that was slowly forming on the frozen dirt field opposite the mess hall. As he hustled off at double time, I reached into my pocket and found a cobalt blue squeeze ball. I pumped it a couple of times and thought to myself, "I think I can; I think I can; I think I can."

When I returned to retrieve my gloves from the table, my bad day had worsened. My gloves had been stolen. Sarge's whistle blasted. Between blasts, I heard, "Fall in, ladies. Let's go, let's go, let's go. We have no time to smell the roses before our march." Sergeant McNeil loved a cliché. His speech was peppered with them, oblivious to proper context. A short phrase, repeated three times in succession, was also a passion. Here, he got a chance to use both.

Double-timing back to the barracks, we grabbed our prepacked backpacks and M14s, then fell into formation. Between commands, I notified Sergeant McNeil of my recent loss of US government-issued clothing.

"Sarge, I have a problem. Some jerk stole my gloves during breakfast."

"Private Haines," reading the name tag on my jacket, "I have all the sympathy in the world for your circumstance. However, our schedule is tight, and I can't think of an immediate solution. So I guess in this situation, a stitch in time doesn't save nine."

"What the hell does that mean?" I wondered. He waved his arm in a circle over his head and bellowed, "OK, men, let's move out!"

We were moving out to our first test of physical endurance, mental stamina, and spiritual fortitude. Marching in standard eighteen-inch steps, we adjusted our cargo and our psyches. Most of us traveled with light packs, but our bodies were well layered in OD green. Most everyone wore two pairs of socks. Boots, underwear, long johns, fatigue pants, fatigue shirt, jacket liner, field jacket, arctic headgear, helmet liner, helmet, glove liners, and gloves finished our ensemble. Minus the gloves, I was wearing everything on that list, including the two pair of socks.

Once our straps, buckles, and zippers were adjusted, fastened, and pulled, our marching pace picked up to time and a half. A mile into our trek we kicked into double time—one hundred twenty, thirty-inch paces per minute.

We double-timed for the better part of an hour. The winds were frigid and relentless. My thin cotton glove liners provided no protection from Mother Nature's stinging breath. I slipped my fingers out of the ten tubular extensions, closed them into a fist, and placed them deep in my jacket pockets. My M14 bounced on my back without mercy.

Sergeant McNeil began a marching song. We left long trails with our breath as we alternated between song and gasping for more icy air. The gung-ho lyrics sapped much of our energy. The shrill cadence sounded hollow in the painful, chilled air.

I wanna be an Airborne Ranger.
I wanna live the life of danger.
I want to go to Vietnam.
I want to kill the Viet Cong.

Some of the guys got off on the singing and belted the words at top volume, while others only mouthed the lyrics to keep the brass happy while conserving our allotted air. I thought the hypnotic chanting might be useful to divert some of our attention from our pain and discomfort, but that was not the case.

An hour into our journey, we acted like children on a long family trip. How much farther is it, Daddy? When are we gonna be there, Daddy? I gotta go to the bathroom, Daddy. We discovered that Sergeant McNeil was an unsympathetic and impatient "daddy" when he answered the first and only inquiry of this nature.

Four or ninety miles into the march, Ray Haber chimed in with, "How much farther, Sarge?"

"It's as far as it is, plus an extra mile for the next pussy that asks that question," he threatened. He ordered us to pick up the pace and, in the next breath, began another inane marching song.

We arrived at a large clearing surrounded by tall pines. We were brought to a quick halt by a booming command from McNeil. "Companyyyy, halt!"

I experienced a feeling that overwhelmed me. A pounding heart and a slight dizziness accompanied weak knees, followed by an all-over tingling sensation. My body, soaked in sweat from the Arctic headgear to my double-wrapped feet, began to shake.

I shivered non-stop. Without the 900 milligrams of sodium from breakfast, my sweat would have frozen on me like a thin shroud; my body jerked out of control. Looking at those near me, I saw that I wasn't the only spastic dancer.

Hutchison removed all three pieces of his headgear in one quick movement. Holding his helmet at chin level, he slurred, "Tomcheckthisshitout." The fog produced by the steam distorted his features. When the wet haze drifted away, I saw his pallid face. The sharp angles of his eyebrows sported tiny white icicles. I wanted to laugh but couldn't.

Hoping to warm up, I continued to bounce in place. Moments later my eyes returned to Hutchison. He was standing on the sides of his boots, next to me—butt ass naked. After removing his steam-filled helmet, he had stripped out of the rest of his wet clothing. In a flash, he dressed his snow-white body in fresh, dry underwear, long johns, socks, and a crisp fatigue shirt. He covered his short, frozen, dirty blond hair with a toboggan and his steam-filled helmet. He had pulled this meticulously folded salvation from his overstuffed backpack.

We had made fun of Walter for lugging all that unnecessary, extra weight. His backpack was twice the size of the others in our squad. He could have said, "Guess whose turn it is to laugh now?" But being the nice guy he was, he didn't. His comfort and relief made the point.

Sergeant McNeil turned his attention to the shivering ice jockeys bouncing in front of him. "I'm not your mother and have no desire to be your mother. You are men. You need to think logically and intelligently for yourselves, without reminders from mommy to do the right thing." He ended his poignant speech with, "And remember, gentlemen, a stitch in time saves nine." Once again I scratched my helmet. *What the hell does that mean?* However, as we picked up the pace of futile movements to keep warm, the main point of his speech was frankly driven home.

Our painful envy was apparent as McNeil picked up his overstuffed backpack, patted Hutch on the shoulder, and headed in silence to a nearby Quonset hut.

The day's temperature rose from way, way below zero to just way below zero. It was going to be a long, frigid day of training. My toes were stiff and my fingers numb, but these discomforts were minor compared to another part of my anatomy that was screaming in pain—my nipples. This useless body part was causing an ache from the cold like none I could recall. They shriveled into tiny white points. Each time my stiff, wet undershirt touched my body, my chest experienced an intense, shooting pain.

The next hour was spent in an outdoor classroom. The instruction centered on the do's and don'ts of handling a loaded weapon on the firing range. I spent my time leaning forward and adjusting my shoulders so that my shirt didn't touch my chest. A soft, dry, fluffy piece of cloth lying on the end of a bench next to the instructor's podium was to become my newest prized possession. After driving home his final point, the captain gave the order to break for chow. I snatched the cloth.

Our meal consisted of a thick, brown and yellow stew, hard-as-sheetrock bread, and syrupy fruit cocktail. It didn't make any difference what food was served in the field because it was all barely edible and tasted metallic. We were instructed to consume our food in a simulated war situation. We were to pretend our company was dining in hostile territory somewhere in Vietnam. I have a great imagination, but this concept was way beyond a real challenge. I cradled my mess kit in the crooks of my sleeves and held my utensils and cup of milk in my cloth covered right hand, all the while blowing into my left hand. My glove liners were so thin I could feel my breath with ease through the loosely woven cotton.

I walked a short distance along a tree line, hearing only the amplified sounds of metal spoons banging against metal pans and the crunch of boots pushing into the fresh, dry snow.

Hutchison was exhausted, scowling, propped against a tree chewing his first bite of the cooling, tasteless, yellow slop. I plopped down next to him. "Come on, Hutch; nothing could taste that bad." Before he got a chance to respond, a very young-looking sergeant approached us in triple time. He came to a halt on top of me. His boots touched the ends of my boots.

"What does this look like to you?" He asked in a deafening and piercing voice, while throwing out his arms in a horizontal fashion.

As I looked around, I noticed that everyone, including Brian, Ken, and Ray, were at least ten meters from the next nearest human for as far as I could see. I guess I forgot I was in the real military. I glanced up at this "kid" that looked more like a school crossing guard than a sergeant in the Army and gave him a smart-ass answer.

"Wow, Sergeant, I don't believe I've ever seen it this bad. These guys must reek like a pound of cigarette butts floating in a gallon of week-old beer."

The young non-com found no humor in my sarcasm. He launched into a long and loud lecture of how I could lose my life in Nam if I joined a buddy for lunch in the jungle. He was talking so fast that I could just make out his face through the large puffs of fog billowing out of his mouth. God, it was cold. The sergeant demanded ten push-ups for my insolence and then directed me to a tree that was so far away, I feared they would call formation before I had a chance to eat.

The wind picked up, my stew congealed, and the snow blustered. Pretending to be in a hot, humid jungle on the other side of the earth while sitting against a pine tree with an inch of ice-snow crawling up its trunk was something even I, with my vivid imagination, couldn't comprehend. The whistle blew as I pushed off the ground, losing the last bit of the pasty yellow mush behind a tree. I pictured some deer discovering it long after we left, taking one sniff and running as fast as Bambi on the opening day of deer season.

Next on the agenda was the ritual of dumping our uneaten remains into oversized trash cans and dipping our mess kits into barrels designed to clean and sanitize. I lingered over a large steel gray barrel full of boiling water, hoping the scalding temperature would thaw some of my body chills. It didn't. The heat from the swirling fog only worsened the situation. Three steps away from the steam, I was colder than I had ever been in my life.

Minutes later, we lined up for our ammunition. I gathered my portion of 7.62 mm rounds and joined a dozen other ice jockeys huddled together in a futile attempt to get warm. The hollow sound of hundreds of bullets entering metal magazines filled the air. Competing with this sound were the low, muffled voices of cursing, except from Pat, whose voice was anything but muffled, mixed with the inexhaustible, shrill tone of the wind. I tried to block it all out.

Some were trying to load their clips with their gloves on, some with glove liners, while still others braved the elements and did it barehanded. I slipped off my liners and picked up a bullet. It fell from my fingers back into the pile. I tried again and again without success.

"Hey, Hutch, my fingers are starting to look like those cranes in the big glass boxes at the county fair trying to pick up a prize," I said, as I made yet another attempt. "Can you help me out?" I added.

Hutch put his hand in his pants pocket and began to fish around, "Yeah, sure, I think I have an extra quarter in here somewhere."

"Thanks, Mr. Funny Guy, remind me to slap you later. If I did it now, I might snap off two or three of these finger-sickles," I said, trying to open and close my fist.

"Bury your hands in your crotch while I take care of this," he said, snapping in one round after another.

"Thanks. I owe you one, or should I say ten."

Whistles filled the air. We lined up, side by side, with our bodies flat on the frozen earth. The cold ground sent a shock through my entire body and soul. I tried to fight back against it by warming the ground with my 98.6 temperature. The earth won. I cradled my M14 in the proper military manner, positioned the sight at the center of the broad-shouldered silhouette boldly displayed at a hundred meters against a hard dirt berm. While waiting for the order to fire, I rested my inflexible finger against the trigger. The cold steel parts of the M14 acted as an additional conduit for the chill and sent my central nervous system into overload.

A dozen second lieutenants and sergeants of various stripes were shouting alternating orders and instructions at the horizontal figures stretched out for fifty yards in both directions. Their drone became an audio blur.

"Ready on the left! Ready on the right! Ready on the firing line! Commence, fire," directed one of the lieutenants.

I closed my left eye, aimed, and strained to bend my right index finger. Nothing. A sergeant I had never seen before squatted down beside me. "The order from the tower said fire, soldier." My brain sent the message to my finger to bend. The message, bouncing around randomly inside my brain, didn't arrive—again, nothing.

The sergeant raised his voice while lowering his body. "I said fire that weapon, boy. This man's army has no room for wimps!"

Grimacing in pain, I pulled my hand away from my weapon and tried to bend my fingers to no avail. The wind continued to cut through the loose knit cotton like a shotgun full of razor blades. Now my entire body was shaking. Brian was to my left and said, "Holy shit, man, are you all right. You look like you could use a dozen blankets."

The sergeant reached down and pinched the end of my liner between his thumb and forefinger. The first round of fire had come to a halt when someone from the command tower announced, "Cease fire." The sergeant snatched the liner from my hand, hit the safety switch on my weapon, and in a voice exhibiting a significant degree of concern, said, "Jesus Christ, man, get up!" I jabbed my elbows into the ground, cradled my weapon, wiping my face against the oily stock, and pushed myself butt first off the frozen earth. Tears squeezed out of the outer corners of my eyes.

McNeil was talking to a lieutenant when the sergeant interrupted. "Hey, Sarge, I've got something you need to see," he said. McNeil took one glance at my blue and white hands, flung open his jacket and shirt and grabbed my wrists. He hollered for a medic as he placed my hands in his armpits and walked backward towards a large Quonset hut while demanding a clear path.

I was a little—OK, hugely—embarrassed by what I thought was a somewhat melodramatic reaction to my dilemma. I also felt a great relief and appreciation for my rescue from frostnip, the early stage of frostbite.

*****

I flipped to another entry in my journal, still aware of the tingling in my fingers. An asterisk in the column caught my attention, another day on the firing range. Unlike February 8, March 6 was warm and breezy. We arrived excited because we were going to be issued M16s, a weapon we weren't supposed to see until AIT, advanced individual training, and in my case, advanced infantry training. No one questioned the change in weapons. Even those who weren't weapons enthusiasts were looking forward to trying their skills with one of the two most respected military handheld weapons on Earth. The other fully automatic, on the list of two, was the Russian AK-47.

The day was partly sunny. The march to the firing range never reached a pace faster than time and a half. Upon arrival, we formed carefully constructed rifle pyramids with our bright new M16s. With the last rifle in place, Sarge yelled out, "Smoke 'em if you got 'em; waste not, want not." Again, *what the hell does that mean?*

After we suffered through an hour of classroom instruction, we were "awarded" a two-minute piss break. Two dozen guys entered an area "in the round." It was enclosed by a six-foot-high corrugated tin fence, and in the center was a pit filled with piss, chemicals, and a rusted steel pole rising eight feet into the air. I assumed it was there to give us a chance to practice on our aim; our next adventure would have us aiming at a different kind of target.

We filled all the available space, standing shoulder-to-shoulder, aiming our "water pistols" at the center pole and trying not to look around too much. Some were righties, others lefties, while a few—without good reason—were two handers.

One by one, streams of pee hit near the rusty brown and silver pole. Those dancing about before entering the pit started first and lasted the longest. Then others kicked in after hearing liquid hitting liquid. Others, like myself, preferred peeing in private behind a locked door. We closed our eyes and concentrated hard to start our anatomical water faucets.

Everyone has their list of tricks, including me—picturing waterfalls, imagining being back home behind a secure bathroom door, or envisioning being hooked up to udder machines sucking out the urine. I really had to go, so I settled on staring at a big dent at the top of the rusted steel pole. Nothing. "Mr. Johnson" began to shrink.

He said, "Forget it, we'll try later." I shot back, "Bullshit, get back out here; we're not giving up yet." "Oh yeah, let's see how successful you are with me in here and you out there." Closing his eye, he slipped my grip. OK, so having a conversation with your penis is bizarre, another distraction that didn't work.

A minute later, all but two of us had finished, shaken off, distributing droplets of urine on their pants, their boots, and on the boots of others. Reholstering their guns, they departed. Soon it was just me and one other reluctant urinator. Showdown.

With his legs spread two feet apart, Mr. Reluctant Urinator mirrored "Mr. Johnson" and me. Holding himself in his left, he pushed his glasses up his nose to a large knot located between his eyes with his right forefinger. My thoughts switched from Gary Cooper in *High Noon* to "Hey, I know this guy." My mind raced, my bladder relaxed, and I remembered: Cape Cod and the busted bottle of bubbly. My piss partner had tried to stifle giggles while attempting to eat a salad. That knot and those glasses were one of a kind, with no chance of being duplicated.

Successfully completing our mission, we made small talk about a small world and hustled back to the formation for our final M16 indoctrination before we qualified as marksman (whew, made it, that's all that counts), sharpshooter (eh, not bad, could have done better), or expert (nailed it).

Forty minutes later, we were in our foxholes eager to learn the fine art of firing the M16 rifle. The pits measured three feet by three feet by five feet deep and had assorted sizes of boxes stacked in a corner for the shorter guys. While waiting, I was entertained by fantasies of adding my name to the legendary ranks of Sergeant York and Audie Murphy while we patiently waited for the DIs to locate their imaginary X marks the spot.

I examined my weapon. With a full magazine of 5.56 mm bullets, she weighed seven pounds six ounces, could effectively fire at targets 460 meters away at a cyclic rate of 700 to 800 rounds per minute, and cost the taxpayers a whopping $127. I named mine Myrtle. She was sleek, solid black, and much lighter and more accurate than my cumbersome M14A1. The M16 was a "she" because once assigned to an infantry unit in Vietnam, we would be eating, sleeping, and becoming one with our new mate. She was a companion that we would love, cherish, and care for till death do us part.

And she was ready for action. I rested her hard, plastic middle in my left hand and turned her over on her back. I pressed a full six-inch clip of ammunition into the open slot on her underside. I pushed hard until the clip clicked into place, fitting firm and snug. Although she was a powerful instrument of destruction, she felt warm and friendly in my grasp. I was secure and in control—and I also thought maybe I'd already been in the Army waaaaaaay too long.

Looking left and right, M16 rifle barrels set on semiautomatic glistened in the warm morning sun. Steel helmets bobbed up and down like the bobble-headed dog in the back of my Aunt Jane's car. Orders echoed up and down the line, rifle barrels aimed across the flat, dirt field in front of us, and safety switches, in chorus, flipped off. I pushed up the rim of my helmet and stared at the cardboard targets thirty yards in front of us. They barely moved in the breeze. Bullets would shred these targets upon impact. Ray, to my left, was rearranging the pile of sandbags for the third time.

After a long silence, the command to fire echoed up and down the line. I took a deep breath, let out half, closed one eye, locked in on my cardboard bad guy and squeezed the trigger firmly five times. All my senses came to a peak. The sight of small clouds of dirt kicked off the ground, the smell of burning gunpowder permeating the air, the deafening sound of bullets whizzing at four times the speed of sound, cracking at decibels well over 150, all contributed to this utterly surreal moment.

While pushing the lip of my helmet up a second time, I noticed a small splattering of blood on my hand. I felt an instant and intense panic. Determining the blood wasn't mine, I began a search for its source. Down the firing line to my left I saw the same chain of glistening rifle barrels and bobbing helmets as before; looking to my right, a link was missing from the chain. The foxhole to my right was helmet-less.

I pushed up and out of my pit. "CEASE FIRE, CEASE FIRE, CEASE FIRE, CEASE FIRE!" I screamed, trying to compete with the cracks of rifle fire. I was moving in slow motion, my body and mind in two different time zones.

The firing line fell silent at the sight of my hysteria, but I continued the command, now in a whisper, while I gazed into the hushed, dark hole. I didn't remember who was to my right. Even if I had, I wouldn't have recognized him. Slumped in a contorted mass of bright red and olive drab at the bottom of the foxhole was a faceless soldier who had fired his weapon on full automatic into the underside of his chin. I closed my eyes and turned away at the same moment a DI and a second lieutenant arrived. My body went hot, then cold. A brisk breeze chilled the gooseflesh rising on my neck. The lieutenant commanded that I return to my position, patting me on the shoulder as I retreated to my foxhole, disoriented, in shock, and moving at a staccato pace. Whatever noises were filling the air up and down the line, I didn't hear them.

"God, oh God." I closed my eyes for a long time and prayed for the bloody mess that lay in a crumpled heap less than ten feet away. I also prayed that I would never again have to witness bone, blood, and flesh opened to the earth.

We've all been told war is hell; but in war, hell is not always defined by the borders of a foreign land.

SNAFU

I started to close my journal, but the reminder of a faceless suicide stole the elation I had been feeling about the recent completion of eight weeks of … of … of … something I couldn't quite find the proper words for. I wanted—I needed— to cover it with another memory, a pleasant one. I flipped forward a few pages. I stopped. March 21st contained, without a doubt, that story. In the margin, blocked off in red, were the words "physical combat proficiency test" (PCPT).

The last PCPT: an examination of our physical proficiency, a trial of our personal fortitude, and a supercharged challenge to our testosterone overload. Most worked hard for eight weeks to prove to themselves and their comrades that they were up to the tasks required of them. Some set personal goals while the Army took care of goal-setting for those not so self-motivated.

For eight weeks, we had been pitted squad against squad, platoon against platoon, company against company, and most importantly, each against himself. Our armed forces were masters of motivation through competition. Like Pavlov's dogs, we were rewarded with praises and prizes for beating the other guy. Competition applied to everything from the best spit-shined brass belt buckle, the most proficient forty-yard low crawl, and the most accurate firing of an M60 machine gun.

March 21, 1968, would be our miniature, one-day Olympics. If company B heard me make that analogy, they would do everything they could to acquire a Russian ringer. Total scores and individual scores were witnessed and logged. Earlier in the week we had finished qualifying as marksman, sharpshooter, or expert with our M14A1s and awarded the appropriate medals to decorate our dress greens. Now our final attempts to attain a combat-ready score—the forty-yard low crawl (thirty-six seconds), the horizontal ladder (thirty-six rungs in one minute), the dodge, run, and jump agility run (26.5 seconds), the grenade throw (fifteen points), and the mile run (eight minutes and thirty seconds in combat boots)—were just moments away. Each event was worth 100 points with a maximum score of 500 points. A minimum of 300 points was considered passing, and a soldier must achieve a minimum of sixty points per event to be considered "combat qualified."

Activity in the quadrangle was at a fevered pitch. Sergeant McNeil had a stack of DA Form 705, the Physical Fitness Testing Record, gripped in one hand and his OD pen in the other. The air was still, the sky clear and blue, and the temperature somewhere in the fifties. I was standing on the bottom step of our barracks.

Hutchison, sitting on the top step, looked at me while polishing his belt buckle with his shirtsleeve. "We're counting on you, Haines," he said. K, passing by with Ken, looking more stern than usual. He stopped a yard later, strutted in reverse, and came to a halt a foot from my shiny boots. He looked up at me with great confidence and said, "I know you can do it. You know you can do it. Company B doesn't have a clue that you can do it." He broke into an uncharacteristic grin, bit his lower lip, winked, pumped his fist once at waist level, and strode off with his signature bouncy gate. Ken followed but turned around and gave me two thumbs up.

It seemed that I had become the Cinderella athlete story of D-5-3 when I graduated out of the Fat Boys Club after being a member for one looong week. I traversed the ladder from end to end at the conclusion of day eight. When my foot hit the bar at the end of the ladder, there was a smattering of applause, followed by a few congratulations. I took a moment to stare at the ground where I had always dropped to do my push-ups and vowed never to return to that spot again.

The ladder became a passion, with higher goals set every time I stepped up to the starting bar. I got tips from a gymnast, strength through training, and speed with practice—lots of practice. Everyone thought I was nuts to spend any more time acting like a monkey than I had to. On this final day, I knew I would score the full 100 points; it was just a matter of how many seconds would tick off the clock in the process.

Formation came together without delays, as everyone was anxious to "let the games begin!" Some were excited about the competition, while others were more excited about having the remainder of the day off.

We arrived at the park, divided into groups, and waited patiently for the start of the first event. I finished the forty-yard low crawl in thirty-four seconds, just under the standard of thirty-six. In the dodge-run-and-jump I finished at twenty-eight seconds, three longer than the twenty-five considered the norm. My "combat ready" score (300 minimum) was 369, which I guess meant that I was a little more qualified to kill another person but not as good as others who were qualified to "collect fingers." If I had only scored a 192, would they have taken away my chance to kill the "enemy"?

My heart began to beat faster when I heard the second platoon being called to advance to the horizontal ladder. Hutch finished the dodge-run-and-jump and joined me at the center of the field for the announcement to line up. Walter and I assisted each other with our stretching exercises and tried to pump each other up with words of encouragement.

"I'm expecting a full 100 points from you, Haines. You got any problem with that?" Hutch said, as serious as anything he'd ever said to me.

"A hundred. Shit, I'll hit that at the thirty-six second mark," I responded, talking more confidently than I felt. I took a deep breath. My mouth went dry, and butterflies began bouncing off the walls of my gut.

I ended up close to the end of the line. The wait wasn't pleasant. My palms began to sweat as I watched some struggle to get in thirty-six rungs in sixty seconds, the standard for this event. For the most part, good scores were logged onto the chart.

Soon there was no one between the first shiny silver pipe and me. A DI with a clipboard in one hand, a stopwatch in the other, a Smokey the Bear hat on his head, and a whistle in his mouth stood at the base of the ladder. I took another deep breath, grabbed the first bar firmly in my right hand, stretched out to the second with my left, leaned forward, and waited. I was utterly focused on the third bar, unaware of the crowd that had gathered to watch.

A short burst of an ear-piercing sound emitted from his whistle. I pushed off with a vengeance. Three, four, five, six, seven, eight came fast and easy. I was in a flow. My timing was perfect. Twenty came and went within seconds. My heart pounded faster; adrenaline shot through my system. I was soon at the standard of thirty-six and not slowing up. When I reached fifty, I heard K holler out, "You can do it, man—fifty-one, fifty-two, fifty-three." Time was running out, and my body began to feel the strain. I felt leaden and started to lose my smooth swing. I experienced pain in a half-dozen places, but I didn't slow down. The sound of the whistle cut through the air at the end of what seemed like a very short minute. Applause and whistling filled the air around me.

I dropped fully to the ground and looked up at the DI. "Seventy-six rungs, one hundred points, and the new leader for the total number of bars. Good job, son," he said as he wrote. I allowed my knees to buckle, landed with a thud on my butt and, for the first time in my life, smiled through pain.

P.T. Test

Start with the Local Bars
Then join the 150 Yd. Self Motivation
Participate in Dab & Dodge & Hop
Witness the 20 Yard March
Finish with The Mile Stroll
Are we sweating yet?

AIT—Déjà Vu All Over Again

I arrived back at the base from my weekend pass an hour early and killed some clock watching new recruits reporting. It had been only nine weeks since I began my military initiation, yet I felt a kind of superiority over these guys. They didn't have the faintest idea what was in store for them. Watching them made me wonder if there would be someone scrutinizing me as I entered AIT and thinking the same thing, and then again when I started OCS, and yet again when I got to Nam, where the cycle would come to an end.

D-5-3 was now a part of my past. My new alphanumerical identification was A-3-1. When I arrived at my new address, I was hit with a visual shock. After spending basic training in a college dorm type of environment, I didn't expect to take a backward step in time regarding accommodations.

My new home was a one-story wooden structure that I guessed was built sometime during World War II, or for that matter, maybe, World War I. It sported a fresh coat of white paint. The grounds were sparse but well kept—very little grass, lots of dirt.

The interior was typical of what we grew up seeing in the movies: two rows of bunk beds on either side of a long, narrow room with a wide center walkway, a large iron furnace perched at the far end, and a small room to the side for the sergeant. A footlocker was at the end of each bunk and a stand-up locker at the other end. To the right of the main room was the infamous latrine: a large open shower, a row of toilets measuring just inches apart, and a line of sinks opposite the toilets. There were no partitions of any kind, anywhere. If you were sitting on a toilet and spread your legs just a few inches you could be touching knees with the guy sitting next to you. A lot of guys peed siting down so as not to splash on the guy sitting next to you, as well as being eyes to genitals only a couple of feet away. Awkward.

The one thing missing from the silver screen scene was the sergeant slapping a horsewhip in his hand, yelling at the maggots who had the misfortune of being assigned to his care for the next eight weeks of hell, all the while sadistically squinting at everyone and everything.

I tossed my duffel bag on the bed and tested the mattress for firmness. Our sergeant appeared out of nowhere. Everyone scrambled to attention. After a long silence, he introduced himself. Staff Sergeant William Logan welcomed us to his home. He made a few announcements: our training schedule, his rules and regulations, and when to be ready for our first formation. He had a friendly demeanor and a strong, commanding voice that didn't rise above fifteen decibels. He wished, with great sincerity, that all of us do well in A-1-3. The room was quiet until the screen door closed behind him. "Hey, didn't this guy see the movie," I said to the private standing next to me. He didn't get it; I didn't explain.

Unlike Sergeant McNeil, who was tall and walked with a slight slouch, in a slow, almost awkward manner, Sergeant Logan stood around five-foot-nine and moved with his shoulders back and chest out, as if he were marching in a parade. His face and body were angular and well defined.

After the door closed, the room became loud with the simultaneous start of dozens of conversations. I introduced myself to my bunkmate.

"Hi. Tom Haines; you want the top or the bottom?" I asked, not caring what his answer would be.

"Vincent Cal Verduchi, but just call me Vinny. I'll take the bottom bunk if you don't mind, and besides—" he said before we were interrupted.

"Haines, you sorry fucker," came a voice from the other end of the room.

I followed the sound and spotted big old goofy-looking Walter Hutchison leaning into the walkway, holding onto a bed frame.

I held up a finger to Vinny in a "hold that thought" manner and hollered back. "No, it's not me, Hutch, you sorry son of a bitch. I'm my mother's invisible sister's two-headed daughter looking for a section eight."

We walked toward each other, not breaking from our conversation. "I can't believe we got assigned to the same AIT unit," he said catching my hand while in full stride.

"Well, if you think about it, we did graduate—is that the right word? Yeah, didn't we graduate with honors from the same basic training unit?" I responded.

Vinny introduced me to a new friend, Chip Flattery. Before I had a chance to introduce Hutch to Vinny and apologize for walking away in mid-sentence, Sergeant Logan returned to jump-start our next eight weeks.

He briefed us on our upcoming two-month mission. In five short minutes, Sergeant Logan filled our heads with lots of names and numbers: the M79 grenade launcher, the M72 LAW rocket launcher, the M16 rifle, and the M60 machine gun. We were also told that we would become proficient enough for survival purposes at map reading, first aid, and bayonet use. The list finished with us learning the uses of the varieties of gas that were at our disposal, as well as the gases employed by the North Vietnamese. Also on the agenda would be extensive training regarding small unit tactics at the fire team and squad levels, radio procedures, land navigation, escape and evasion, and artillery fire adjustment. Last on the list was wilderness survival techniques. Our upcoming eight weeks would also contain many hours of marching and PT squeezed into our already over-bloated schedules.

"Damn, I wonder if they'll allow us the time to take a shit?" whispered Hutch.

"Only on command, son," Sergeant Logan fired back, almost before Hutch had a chance to finish the word "shit." No one ever whispered anything within a hundred meters of Sergeant Logan again.

*****

It had been seventeen weeks since I stepped off the bus at Fort Dix. I sat on my stripped-down bunk in an empty room. I flipped through the yellow program that I hadn't even glanced at during our graduation ceremonies. Whoa, it was like déjà vu—all over again.

There I was—again—the last person to leave at the end of an eight-week training program. I guess there would have been some deeper meaning to that reality if it hadn't been for the fact that my parents called and said they would be somewhat late. It seems there was a problem at my dad's real estate office. Just how long is "somewhat"? Sometimes it's a real pain in the ass to own your own business, but owning my own business was exactly what I hoped to do. Over the previous eight weeks, I had gotten lots of practice in "pain-in-the-ass" training.

I opened to the center of the program. Jack Lewis was voted outstanding trainee—no argument there as he was just what this Army was looking for and more. Except for the fact that Jack was black, there was little difference between him and the "I am the infantry" soldier we met on a fancy stage in basic training. Company A beat Company B in almost every category: PCPT, patrolling, and proficiency park. Company B, however, did edge out Company A on the M14A2 rifle and the M60 machine gun. I tossed the program on top of my duffel bag and picked up my blue book.

My journal was slighter in AIT, consisting of short notes or phrases next to a few scattered dates. My eye stopped at a red asterisk in the column next to April 10, 1968.

*****

Sergeant Logan entered the barracks for an announcement. "Gentlemen, there has been a change in the training schedule. The assignment you are about to hear is not a joke but rather a very grim task that I don't want to see anyone treating flippantly."

We were issued M14 rifles and bayonets and ordered to fall into formation. Two other staff sergeants and a captain joined Sergeant Logan. Curiosity was at a peak. With no time to waste, the captain stepped forward to speak. "AteeeenHUT!" bellowed one of the sergeants. "At ease men," followed the captain. "For the next four hours, you will receive riot-control training, after which time you will attend a briefing for possible deployment to a college campus."

"Hey, Hutch, did he say 'college campus'?"

"If he did, I sure hope they send us to Smith or Vassar."

"I don't fucking believe it; they want us to break up a demonstration or whatever on a college campus." The captain stopped his speech and directed himself to Hutch and me.

"Do you gentlemen have something you'd like to share with the rest of us?"

I flashed back to the eighth grade and Sister Honoreen asking me and a buddy, word for word, the same question.

"No, sir," I said, "I just wanted to make sure—you did say college campus, correct?" Hutch leaned a few inches in my direction and whispered, "Ask him if we're breaking up a panty raid or a science project gone wrong." I unsuccessfully tried to stifle a laugh.

"That's right. America has no problem with free speech, but it does have a problem with students trying to take over their universities," he said with conviction, adding, "You see anything funny in that."

"Oh, no, sir," I said, trying really hard to stifle the giggles "I just, you know, couldn't help thinking that we were going in to"—snicker—"break up a panty raid." I guessed that somewhere between twenty and thirty others joined in on the giggles and laughter.

"OK, enough with the frivolity. Let's move out," said the captain with a smile. I looked over to Hutch and said, "Sorry about stealing your joke, but I couldn't pass on that."

Hutch shot back with, "Are you kidding? I can't believe you had the balls to say that."

The next four hours we practiced three variations of squad and platoon movement for crowd disbursement. The captain's favorite was "the wedge." Things must have quieted down because we heard nothing more about the unrest in our institutions of higher learning. We went back to our normal schedule of learning how to kill "Sir Charles."

*****

At the bottom of the next page, the word "cough" was punctuated with a half-dozen exclamation points and was printed in the margin in big bold letters.

Gas class, we were told, was a very vital part of every soldier's training, as was hand-to-hand combat the day before and bayonet training the day before that.

We started with a couple hours of classroom instruction on the uses, effects, and treatment of nerve, mustard, tear, and CS gas exposure. We then spent a half hour on the proper use of our gas masks and then marched to a small wooden structure at the edge of a tree-filled area in an isolated section of Fort Dix.

Strung out in a long, jumbled line, we practiced our gas training ritual over and over until we could perform it as a reflex action: place mask over face; test air intake; enter building; pull in a lung full of air; report to the officer in the center of the room; place hand at bottom of mask at chin level; pull upward and remove mask from head; give name, rank, and serial number to the officer in charge; place mask back over face; exit building. No problem.

When we were within a dozen yards from the building, we could detect a slight odor, our cue to put on our masks and repeat the ritual one last time. Minutes later,

SNAFU

I was escorted to another line, this one much smaller, inside the old wood and concrete structure. I watched through a thick, gray, swirling fog as each guy took a deep breath, snatched off his mask, and reported to the officer in the center of the room. Chip was the third in front of me and nailed every "rehearsal."

Deep breath, snatch off mask, report. Deep breath, snatch off mask, report. After a little longer than forever, it was my turn. Snatch off mask, deep breath—holy shit! I had just slurred the word "sir" when my entire being went into shock. My eyes stung, throat burned, stomach wrenched, and head pounded, all while both lungs tried to expel the CS gas I so heartily sucked in. I was determined to report because getting in line again was not an option. I reported, "Sir—(cough)—Private Haines—(cough, cough)—Thomas L—(cough, cough)RA1—(cough, cough, cough, cough, cough)—RA 119748—(cough, cough, cough, cough, cough, cough, cough)—" The lieutenant finally interrupted and said, "All right, already, get the hell out of here."

Once outside, I continued to cough until I puked. I sat down against a tree, sweat pouring, throat burning, eyes stinging, tears flowing. I went over it one more time: deep breath *first*, you dumb shit, *then* remove the mask, you dumb shit, then *report*, you dumb shit. Greetings like, "Hi, Tom—(cough)—how's it—(cough, cough)—going?" lasted for days.

*****

Flipping to the next page, I winced. It was dated a Thursday in early May, and I'd noted we were past the halfway point—it was downhill from there. Oh, how wrong I was. On the agenda was a twenty-four-hour bivouac capped off with a march to the range for training on the M60 machine gun. The thought brought back fond memories of camping out on an overnight weekend with the Boy Scouts.

By the time dusk rolled around, new, not-so-fond memories were finding a home. The march out was five miles at time-and-a-half with full field gear. I reached far back into the memory portion of my brain and recalled arriving at our Boy Scout camp in a station wagon, which also carried our gear.

After the five-mile march, we set up camp with the bare necessities of life. Sarge made sure that the twentieth century had little to do with our overnighter. I remembered our scout leader taking out brand new Coleman accessories from their boxes and using those boxes to start our fires.

When it was time for dinner, I reached into the C-ration box and pulled out something labeled hash. Better luck followed with the second can: fruit cocktail. I could still remember the look that covered the scoutmaster's face when he opened up his cooler and pulled out six large ground beef patties.

I was trying to deal with my hunger pains when Vinny came to the entrance of my tent and said, "Tom, you don't want to miss this."

We ran past all the tents spread out over a football-field-sized area and came to a clearing. There were twenty guys in a circle watching this farm boy from northeastern Mississippi stalk a huge chicken with great caution. Within seconds of my arrival, he succeeded in nabbing the once-elusive fowl.

"Hot bird in less than an hour. Who's coming to dinner?" He snapped the bird's neck in one movement.

I didn't hesitate to join in, "Save me one of her legs." Chip chimed in with, "I'll take a tit. May be the last I'll touch for a loooooong time to come. Pun intended." "Classy, Chip, classy," I responded.

I had never given much thought to the process of eating meat before, but that changed when my plate arrived. There, sitting at the bottom of my mess kit, was a well-cooked chicken leg—claw still attached.

*****

My finger traveled down the page looking for one more journal entry to help pass the time, when I ran across one written in green ink.

With two and a half weeks left, I was wearing down fast. The training was a pain in the ass—not unbearable—just a pain in the ass. I was in good physical shape, but real tired.

"Hutch, I need outta here for a day or two. What are my options, besides going AWOL?" I asked while he finished brushing his teeth.

"You look like shit, man."

"Huh? What do you mean?"

"You heard me; you look like shit. You should go on sick call."

"Ooooh. Yeah, not only do I look like shit, I feel like shit."

"Quick, sit on the floor. I'll go get Vinny."

"Hey, Vinny, toss the shoe polish, man, Haines is sick as shit."

"Really, what's wrong with him?"

"I don't know, but he's real white and breathing funny."

"Tom. Yo, Tom, look up at me buddy. How do you feel?"

"OOOH, I feel nauseated and dizzy and … and, like, you know … you know, really shitty."

"Do you think if you vomited, you'd feel better?"

"OOOHH, don't mention vomit."

"Give me a hand, Vinny. Let's take Tom to Logan; he's on duty at

HQ. I mean, I hope so."

"I'll go get his jacket. Keep him company, Hutch."

"If you want to pull this off, Haines, you'd better come up with something better than 'and, and, or and' as a symptom."

"Hey, eat my shorts, will ya? It's not like I had all day to plan."

"Here's his jacket, Hutch. Put his arm around your shoulder. TOM, CAN YOU WALK?"

"He's sick, asshole, not deaf. Come on, let's get him to Logan before he dies on us."

"Careful of the door, Vinny; we don't want to add a concussion to his disease."

"What do you mean disease? What disease? Do you know something I don't? Jesus, man, why didn't you tell me he has a disease?"

"I don't know if he has a disease. I just know he's real sick and should be in a hospital."

"OOOOH."

"OK, buddy, we're in front of the stairs, one step at a time."

"Vinny, help me get 'em inside and in a chair and then go knock on Logan's door."

Knock, knock!

"Who's there?" Logan responded.

"It's Private Hutchison and Private Verducci, Sergeant. We got Private Haines with us, and he's real sick."

"Private who and who? Never mind, come on in."

"Hey, Vinny, only one of us can fit through this door at a time."

"Sorry, Sergeant, but we brought Haines with us because we didn't know what else to do. He's in the front room. He's real white, and shaking, and breathing funny, a—"

CLUNK

"Oh, shit, Hutch, he fell off the chair!"

"OK you two, don't move him. Let me in there."

"I don't like the way he's breathing and shaking. Loosen his belt. It appears that he needs mouth to mouth."

"Hey, Sarge, what's that white stuff coming out of the corner of his mouth?"

"Never mind mouth to mouth. Keep Private Haines warm; I'm going to call the medics."

"Got a sick one for you, Doc," the medic said as he wheeled me into the base hospital. He was a big guy that appeared to have just entered his twenties. "The guys from his company said he was real white and shaking a lot and breathing real funny," he continued.

"Take him up to the ward, and I'll be there in a minute," said a doctor as he rapidly tapped a pen on his clipboard.

In a matter of minutes, I was undressed, in bed, with a thermometer in my mouth. The matronly nurse, Janet Wilhelm, according to her name tag, who had assisted with all this activity, scampered off to retrieve an extra pillow.

"What's your scam, man? Hey, I'm a poet and don't know it," came a voice from the next bed.

"Huh?" I responded.

"Hey, I don't know if you is sick or you ain't, but if you ain't, then you have one minute to get that glass tube in your mouth to read 100 or better. Rub it on your blanket, man, but not too much. Run it up to 106, and they'll put you in a tank of ice."

It read 101 in a matter of a few seconds. Bingo. Just as I put it back in my mouth, the nurse returned, pillow in tow. She held the glass tube up to the light, squinted at it as she twirled it back and forth, and then took my pulse. The doctor arriving in a real hurry, asked me a few questions, and then told the nurse to watch me overnight. She pushed a pencil into the bun of her salt and pepper hair, patted me on the arm, and left. Glorious victory!

When I woke, I felt rested but warm. The same nurse arrived at 0600 to check my temp. The thermometer in place, she took my pulse, never leaving my side. Oh well, a few hours respite is better than none. Lifting her head, she checked the results through the glasses perched at the end of her nose.

"Well, I guess it's time to join my unit, huh?"

"Not today you won't, your temperature is higher than last night—102. Make yourself comfortable, sweetie, I'll be right back," she said while exiting the room.

"Shit, I must have caught something from you," I said to the guy in the next bed.

"Not a chance. I'm here on a scam. I'm allergic to eggs. So if I got a day from hell on the agenda, I eat just enough to get me here for the night."

The next four days were spent trying to get my temperature down. It was a nasty virus. One day later and I would have rotated to the next AIT where I would have been back to scratch. My first and last scam was a bust. Never again.

*****

I wanted to end my recollections with one final "moment." I rushed through my brain to find the moment I could label as "most fun." It didn't take long for me to decide that qualifying on the M60 machine gun was it. When I was growing up watching war movies, my biggest desire, if I ever had a chance, was to fire a machine gun. It was a warm day, with a spattering of clouds. We got the typical instruction on the fine points of firing the M60, the specs about weight, type of ammunition, and a whole bunch of etceteras. After the lecture, we lined up for our moment of "fun." When it was my turn, I could hardly contain my excitement. I did everything I was instructed to do and added a medal to my dress greens by qualifying as an expert. Then the fun escalated. We were all given an M60 and assigned a partner. They told us to walk toward a berm with Charlie cutouts randomly placed in the sand. The assistant carried a belt of ammunition by my side and fed the 60. I never once thought that it could be possible to do this same thing with real VCs standing in the sand shooting back. But, hell, I was having too much fun with *claka claka clacka.*

*****

My mom and dad arrived. Hugs, a handshake, and the standard question, "How was your trip?" ensued. They brought me back to the moment. Semiconscious, I began to gather my stuff. Throwing my duffel bag over my shoulder, I noticed my dad inspecting the room. Studying the pained expression on his face, I knew better than to ask what he was thinking.

He served in the Third Army, Twenty-Sixth Infantry Division, 104th Regiment during World War II under the watchful eye of General Patton. My dad was wounded in France during the Battle of Montcourt Woods on October 22, 1944. In a cross-fire sniper attack, every member of his squad had been shot. A bullet caught the edge of his entrenching tool, misdirecting its path through my dad's body, just missing his heart. My brother, Steve, told me Dad was the only one who lived. Dad was released from the hospital six months later on April 28, 1945, three days after I was born. He was awarded the Purple Heart, the Bronze Star, and five battle stars. He never talked about the war, and every time one of my brothers or I asked him a question about it, his response was really short, and he would then change the subject.

I stared at my dad from behind. Looking like a DI, he stood in the middle of the room—rugged, angular golf-tanned arms locked behind his back. My mom waited in much discomfort at the door, watching him in silence and most likely recalling his nightmares that went on for years. PTSD back then was referred to as shell shock. He stood motionless. Bowing his head, he said, "Let's go home." His eyes were moist.

I took one last look at the red and green wildcat that Vinny, Chip, and I had painted on the front of the building and searched for the hidden FTA. I found it, smiled, and marched off to round three of "how to kill Charlie and survive 'The Conflict.'"

Home cooked meals, cutoff jeans, a Mustang with a full tank of gas, and some real quality time with a member of the opposite sex—no wonder the Army handed out leave passes with a certain amount of reservation. They were breeding grounds for AWOLs. Like many, I dreaded the start of round three. The letters A-W-O-L didn't sound too bad spoken one letter at a time. But I made a commitment and sucked it up and headed to Fort Benning for the start of Officer Candidate School (OCS). Good God almighty, what have I gotten myself into that will change my life in a dramatic fashion for the rest of my time on Earth?

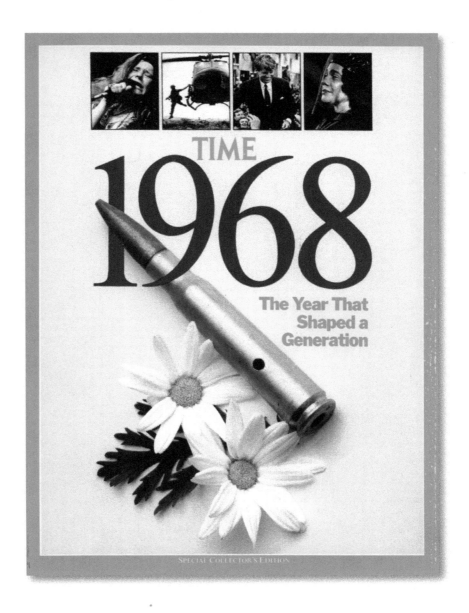

Fort Benning, Georgia, USA

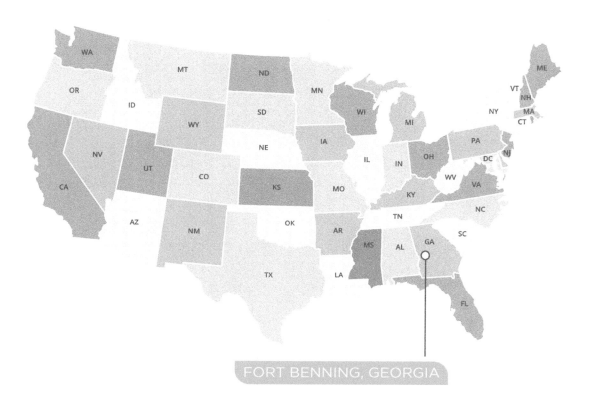

FORT BENNING, GEORGIA

UNITED STATES OF AMERICA

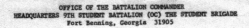

OFFICE OF THE BATTALION COMMANDER
HEADQUARTERS 9TH STUDENT BATTALION (OC) THE STUDENT BRIGADE
Fort Benning, Georgia 31905

Dear Mr. & Mrs. Haines,

This is to inform you that your son has arrived at the Infantry Officer Candidate School, United States Army Infantry School, Fort Benning, Georgia, where he is enrolled as an Officer Candidate.

The mission of the Infantry Officer Candidate School is to produce Infantry combat platoon leaders of the highest caliber. That your son seeks the tremendous responsibility of leading our Nation's youth in battle does him credit, however, the hard work which is necessary to prepare him for this responsibility will be a great challenge.

His typical day during the next six months will start early in the morning and end late at night. During the training day he will undergo a great deal of stress both physically and mentally. The standards are tough and demanding to better prepare him for the task ahead.

I encourage you to write him often. Although his replies may not be as prompt as you desire because of his schedule, a letter from home will encourage him to keep pushing ahead toward his goal--the commission of an officer in the United States Army.

If I can be of assistance to you please feel free to call, or write me at any time.

Sincerely,

R. A. FITE
LTC, Infantry
Commanding

Telephone: Fort Benning, Georgia
545-2141 (Area Code 404)

Sir, Right on Time, Sir

At 2000 (8 p.m.) on Saturday, June 8, 1968, I arrived by bus at a seedy hotel in Columbus, Georgia, to spend my last night of freedom. OCS would last a long six months. I checked into an old hotel in downtown at the same time two other guys were signing the register. We discovered during introductions that Lee Lucas, Derek Richards, and I were all assigned to the same OCS class. After paying our tab in advance, we grabbed our gear and headed to our rooms.

The corridors, wrapped in cardinal red wallpaper and dark green carpet, were lit with low-wattage bare bulbs. A strong, stale smell became more intense as we approached our rooms. While dumping our gear, we decided that the hotel was much too depressing of a place to spend our last night of liberty.

Once we hit the muggy night air outside, Lee lit a cigar. "Go wherever you guys want because my one and only concern tonight, whether it takes my charms or my dollars, is to get laid." We bid him farewell and good hunting.

At checkout the next morning, Lee was twenty-five dollars poorer, and Derek and I were nursing hangovers from the consumption of six—or sixteen—beers. Lee read his orders and discovered there was no time listed. "Well, guys, how does lunch and a movie sound?" He dropped his bag in the corner of the lobby.

"We aren't there yet?" Derek said moving with purpose to the entrance.

After the consumption of three cheeseburgers that had a Goldilocks feel to the order—one well done, the second a perfect medium, and the third had Lee mooing after each bite—we checked the newspaper, then walked two miles in the scorching Georgia heat to watch *The Party* starring Peter Sellers.

After two hours in a theater that had more in common with an ice box than a movie house, we stood on asphalt hot enough to feel the waves of heat enter our pant legs. As much as we could, we followed a path of shade back to the hotel. We picked up our bags, untouched in the corner of the lobby, and caught a taxi to Fort Benning.

We arrived at the OCS compound at 1815, greeted by a first lieutenant who collected our orders and began to check items with a red pen.

"Where the hell have you gentlemen been? Your orders call for you to be in class 0522. You missed that by at least an hour. I'm sorry, gentlemen, but class 0522 is full. You'll have to wait for the start of the next class," he said with a considerable amount of irritation in his voice.

"But, how long will—" Lee asked no one because the lieutenant had vanished in a flash. He returned a few minutes later with our orders still clutched in his hands. "You're in luck; another class starts first thing tomorrow morning."

We were sure he knew that information before leaving the room but apparently wanted to watch us sweat for a while, which we did—profusely.

Then came the papers to fill out. Shoving aside a letter lying in the middle of the counter, I began the process of processing. Paperwork completed, I picked up the form letter I had pushed aside and read:

OFFICE OF THE BATTALION COMMANDER
HEADQUARTERS 9TH STUDENT BATTALION (OC)
THE STUDENT BRIGADE Ft. Benning, Georgia 31905

Dear _____,

    This is to inform you that your son has arrived at the Infantry Officer Candidate School, United States Army Infantry School, Fort Benning, Georgia, where he is enrolled as an Officer Candidate.

    The mission of the Infantry Officer Candidate School is to produce Infantry combat platoon leaders of the highest caliber. That your son seeks the tremendous responsibility of leading our Nation's youth in battle does him credit; however, the hard work that is necessary to prepare him for this responsibility will be a great challenge.

    His typical day during the next six months will start early in the morning and end late at night. During the training day, he will undergo a great deal of stress both physically and mentally. The standards are tough and demanding to better prepare him for the task ahead.

    I encourage you to write him often. Although his replies may not be as prompt as you desire because of his schedule, a letter from home will encourage him to keep pushing ahead toward his goal—the commission of an officer in the United States Army.

    If I can be of assistance to you, please feel free to call, or write me at any time.

Sincerely,
R. A. FITE
LTC, Infantry
Commanding

Oh great, just what my mother needed to read: "… your son seeks the tremendous responsibility of leading our Nation's youth in battle …." Forget the fact that my mother had read this; I just read it, and it hit me like a pneumatic sledgehammer redefining the form of a rock quarry. Damn, am I seeking the tremendous responsibility of leading our youth in battle? Shit, I guess I am. Fuck, we're all in trouble now. Wait a got-damn minute, son-of-a-bitch—I'M our nation's youth.

Adjusting for OCS wasn't a lot of trouble. For the most part, it was an intensified basic training and AIT with an emphasis on leadership stressed to the highest level. Our goal: discipline and commanding respect.

For the first eight weeks, we participated in a variety of tactics training, weapons training, bayonet training, compass training, and plenty of plain old "damn good training" training. Instruction in the classroom and in the field started early in the morning and didn't let up until late in the evening, just like the lieutenant colonel said in his letter to my mom and dad. Any gaps in our tightly filled schedules were plugged with the constant and relentless harassment by the senior students and "newly ordained" officers. A brand-new second lieutenant feels compelled, almost required, to inflict—ah, I mean administer—the same punishment—ah, I mean discipline—onto the scum—ah, I mean officer candidate under his power—ah, I mean care—that he suffered—ah, I mean tolerated. You know what I mean.

No time was allowed to reflect on our feelings, changing philosophical beliefs, or shifting attitudes about the tasks we were so thoroughly trained to undertake. But just before crashing into sleep, I did take the time to think about those things and to anguish over them—long and hard.

Framed

Placing the end of my ruler against the wall, I checked the distance one more time. Four and one-quarter inches—perfect! I took a step backward in my stocking feet (boots would have marred the floor) to marvel at my world of perfection. It was just as the manual called for: bed three feet from the north wall, six inches from the west wall, and six inches from the south wall; dresser four and one-quarter inches from the north wall, four and one-quarter inches from the west wall, and twelve inches from the door frame; desk two inches from … damn, I almost lost control of my metal ruler because of the heat it was getting from one hell of a workout.

Furniture placement was only part of the program. Everything in the drawers, from underwear to pencils, had to be displayed by the book. No deviations accepted. I bounced a quarter on my bed for the tautness test and then snatched the coin on its ascent from the blanket. Last up, I straightened the eight-by-ten-inch frame positioned three inches from the back edge of my dresser, grinned, grabbed my boots, and headed out to formation.

It was still dark and somewhat chilly when I joined the other forty-two "would be" second lieutenants assigned to B company of the 197th Infantry Officer Candidate School at Fort Benning, Georgia. Looming to the north against a flat-gray sky were silhouettes of the airborne jump towers.

"Attennnnnhut ... dress riiiiight, dress!" hollered the candidate assigned to be in charge of the day's formations.

Next on my list was a quick self-inspection. Uniform fresh, crisp, double-starched—check. Brass polished and properly placed—check. Boots shining like a pool of oil in the noonday sun—check. And face scraped smooth as a baby's butt, stoic expression in place—check.

Upon command, I snapped to attention, rigid and unflinching, with that stoic expression frozen until ordered otherwise. Silence fell. The wind and the shrill voice of a young officer whining commands to the company in the formation twenty yards to our right were the only sounds heard.

The mess hall odors began to permeate the air. They were just strong enough to overpower the smell of a chilly, damp, early morning in a jungle of concrete and blacktop.

Rigid as a toy soldier, I rotated my eyes. To my left, lines of men were stiff as stone, cookie-cutter uniformed and expressionless, just as the Department of Defense demanded. The Army must have been very disappointed that some of us were five feet eight inches tall and weighed 145 pounds, while others of us were six feet two inches tall and weighed 205 pounds. I felt sure there was a team of scientists tucked away somewhere in Utah charged with finding a way to standardize all armed service personnel. It would have to be a secret, though, because if the Marines found out, they would demand a separate, larger size.

The short silence had given all forty-three of us time to wonder, reflect, or panic over our upcoming sixteen hours. A lieutenant broke the hush by barking one word, repeated three times, each time many decibels louder.

"HAINES," shattered the morning's stillness. My blood flushed head to toe and back again. A fraction of a second later the boom of "HAINES" reverberated around the walls of the quadrangle. My stoic expression disappeared. A third and final blast of "HAINES" roared through the ranks, making me more than aware that my just-discovered little practical joke wasn't received in the spirit intended. I fell out of formation in the proper military manner and reported to the officer with flecks of white foam coming from his mouth. Of the three officers I faced, my guess was "Ole Foam Face" had dragged my name from the depths of his bowels. Right again.

Foaming and fuming, the lieutenant directed me to my room. He dug his meticulously shined boots into my painstakingly polished floor and stormed across the tile. His index finger was so stiff it shook as he pointed around the room and remarked in a calm, soft, almost eerie manner.

"Your bed is perfect, your floor is perfect, your desk is perfect, and your foot locker is perfect." His voice was strained yet somehow mellow. He got specific, "Your #2 pencils—perfectly sharpened." Then he got personal, "Your underwear—folded perfectly perfect." He was beginning to sound a tad redundant.

As my attention flagged, his arm swept 180 degrees, and that quivering index digit halted one-half inch from the eight-by-ten-inch frame placed just so on my dresser, three inches from the back and four inches from the left side. The lieutenant's soft voice returned to the bellow he had used in an attempt to wake the dead just minutes earlier.

"What the fuck is this?" he screeched. His voice and eyes demanded a quick, logical, acceptable response to his direct but crude and unmilitary question. He snatched the frame from my dresser and brought it to my face. I bit the end of my tongue to keep from snickering.

Inside the frame, the only personal space allowed within the entire Fort Benning complex, except the trunks of private cars, was a collage of photographs. The frame overflowed with the likenesses of communism's elite, punctuated with a fond message from each. There was a solemn Fidel Castro wishing me the best while I was in the Army, Nikita Khrushchev was telling me to look him up after my discharge from the service, and Ho Chi Minh confirming our meeting after my graduation from OCS. My tongue tingled as I relaxed my jaw. I lowered my head and responded in a soft voice, "I'm sorry, sir, it was just a joke, sir. I didn't mean any harm, sir."

He pointed that ever-present index finger at my roommate's frame. It held a picture of his very attractive girlfriend. "Why can't you do the same?" My immediate smart-ass thought was to proclaim, *"Sir, because I don't know her, sir."*

Instead, I leveled him with a quick-thinking lie, "Sir—because my girlfriend died eight months ago, sir." His vulnerability showed, and his soft voice returned. "OK, how about a picture of your family?" he suggested.

I couldn't resist: "Sir, because I am dead to them, sir."

His rough and gruff, mean and tough demeanor vanished. "OK, I don't care what you put in there; just replace this," he said in the mildest tone of our short conversation.

SNAFU

I hoped that my ill-conceived deception wouldn't be uncovered because it was
a little mean-spirited and almost certainly would have gotten me in a shitload
of trouble.

That evening my communist friends were gone, replaced by a photograph of a
field of dead cows ripped from a magazine located in the trunk of my roommate's car.
He never said anything about the replacement, but I often wondered if he thought
those were my cows.

Mickey Mouse Happy Horseshit

Pledging a social fraternity and joining a military training organization are similar: both are structured and filled with tradition, and both attempt to instill a sense of obedience and leadership, making men out of boys, so to speak.

I had made it through the Pi Kappa Alpha pledge period, endured the acceptable levels of humiliation and harassment, enjoyed the camaraderie and sense of belonging, and grew in the areas of leadership, teamwork, community service, and sports. However, four years later, I threw in the olive drab pledge towel of the military fraternity better known as the Commissioned Officers of the United States Army. The harassment didn't do me in. Long hot days in the July Georgia sun didn't slow me down. Extensive, compacted infantry training was tough but not insurmountable. What brought me to a screeching halt was the slap-up-the-side-of-the-head, heel-of-the-palm-to-the-forehead, snap-of-the-finger realization of my eventual goal. Joining a fraternity in college was simple because the goal was simple: paaaarty! OK, it was more than that, but still, very simple. This time, the goals were anything but simple. It took me eight weeks, but I finally discovered my path was damn serious and frightening.

It was during my eighth week that I made the decision to quit—ahhhh, I mean "leave the program." The colonel called me to his office to try his military best to convince me to stay in the program. Without apprehension, I made my way to his office. After all, my reasons for leaving the program were very, well … ah … simple.

I arrived and, without any hesitation, began to pound the doorframe with the heel of my palm, the same one I used on my forehead the day before. I repeated the ritual three times as instructed in chapter 10 of the "How Things Are Done in the Military Way" invisible handbook. I responded respectively and pushed open the door when I heard his firm and official one-word response: "Enter."

Before I was able to remove my hand from the super-polished doorknob, the colonel snapped to a picture-perfect salute. Without blinking, I whipped my head around faster than the barrel of a Gatling gun set on rapid fire to acknowledge the general behind me. I was perplexed; there wasn't one. Because of the intensive training I had just received, teaching me to think fast and weigh all possibilities in a fraction of a second, I reviewed the situation and drew the conclusion that the salute was intended for me. Seeing no reason to embarrass myself any further, I mirrored his salute and put myself at ease.

He didn't waste any time on small talk. While shuffling papers, he went right into his, "Convince the Candidate to Stay in School" routine. He expounded the virtues of my record, exaggerating some of my accomplishments as he read. I wanted to accept the flattery, but I knew the truth.

After a couple of minutes of back-patting, he went for his speech-ending reminder of the awful fate that awaited all OCS dropouts. He delivered the frightful reminder with the slickness of a professional gunslinger standing in the middle of Main Street, the sun glistening off his still-smoking six-shooter pointed firmly at the hole in his victim's heart—his mouth the holster, his tongue the gun, his words the bullets. I never had a chance. His lightning quick draw was, however, unnecessary because everyone in OCS was painfully aware that if you quit, you did not pass go, you did not collect $200. Quitting was a one-way, nonstop ticket to Vietnam as a "bush beater," a "grunt," a "Charlie eliminator." His reminder wasn't necessary, but it did act as an inflated exclamation point at the end of his brief but poignant speech. Arms stretched, his hands on the corners of his smaller than usual desk, he took a deep breath, leaned forward, and put my balls—I mean, the ball in my court.

"Why, for a man with your talent and leadership abilities, do you want to quit? According to your records you were the president of three campus organizations."

Taking the question like a cue in a school play, I began to rattle off my answer like a well-rehearsed speech from act 2, scene 1. "There are three reasons why I'm shortening my stay here," I said, taking care that I didn't use the word "quit."

"First, I've decided not to make a career of the service. If I stay, I spend three years and four months in the Army. If I leave, I spend one year and nine months in the Army," knowing that I would get three extra months shaved off my sentence if I returned to college.

He bristled. I continued.

"Second, and most important, I looked deep in my heart, deep down in my bowels, and deep into my soul, to find the answer to questions I've pondered for the past eight weeks: Can I lead forty-two other human beings into battle? Can I accept responsibility for their lives? Can I take responsibility for their deaths? The answer to all these questions is a resounding, emphatic, no!"

Bristled was replaced by an inner awareness. I continued.

"And third, this program is the biggest bunch of Mickey Mouse, happy horseshit I've ever encountered in my life."

Inner awareness turned into shock. I was on a roll.

"Spit-shined brass belt buckles, eating 'square meals,' and memorizing stupid songs does not prepare men to lead other men into battle. Sure, all those things help build a better sense of discipline and acceptance of orders without question and maybe even create a bond with peers. But since the course is just twenty-four weeks long, it should consist of sixteen-hour days of intensive training and next to no time for bullshit traditions and silliness. It is scary and absurd to watch guys fall asleep during compass training because they were up until three in the morning polishing the tiles of a floor, so one could shave in the reflection. Many of these guys pledged fraternities in college. They don't need to pledge again. They do, however, need to learn how to win battles and save lives with quick, expert decision-making. In college, you had twelve weeks to turn a freshman into a frat man. Here you've got twenty weeks to turn a frat man into a fighting man, one that is knowledgeable, trained to lead, and ready for anything. How many lives has the Army lost because someone fell asleep in compass class? And how many lives have been lost because that same someone couldn't put a perfect shine on a tile floor at two in the morning?"

Shock had turned into a blank, pensive stare.

My little speech probably sounded a little too rehearsed, but that's because it was, and I delivered it without any pauses so that the colonel wouldn't have an opportunity to interrupt my flow. There was a long silence. The colonel took a step forward, shook my hand, and saluted.

"Well, soldier, it appears that you've given this a lot of thought. I appreciate your honesty and your suggestions about our, ah, program. I sincerely wish you all the luck in the world. You're dismissed."

I nodded, said something with the word "sir" in it, and closed the door. "Oh, shit! I'm on my way to Vietnam as the responsibility of a second lieutenant trained in OCS at Fort Benning," I thought. I could only hope for one trained in the proper use of a compass and not one trained in the execution of the finer points of floor polishing.

Two days later at 0700 hours on August 6, 1968, I sat on my duffel bag, which was propped up against a tree at the north end of the barracks. I watched dozens of officer candidates jockeying for proper position in formation. Fidgeting, I waited for the other seven dropouts to join me for the long, hundred-yard walk to the holding area where we would receive our orders for Nam.

Formation complete, the noise level was greater than I had ever heard. One of the other dropouts emerged from the jumbled mass and tossed his bag next to mine.

"What's with all the noise? Did the war end?" I asked the dropout while lighting a cigarette.

"No, but maybe the next best news," he said. "It seems the ol' man has gone soft and eliminated walking tours, hand-polished floors, and daily room inspections. And from what I gather, that's just the beginning."[3]

"So where was that son-of-a-bitch when I walked three two-hour tours last week?" asked drop-out number three.

I smiled, slung the bag over my shoulder and joined the others as we walked the longest hundred yards of our lives.

Gone to the Dogs

We walked in silence, hearing only the sound of leather slapping against cement. Inside my head, I listened to my thoughts become louder and louder with lots of high decibel questions. *Where am I going? Did I make the right decision? Will I come back? If so, in how many pieces?* A thousand questions with no known answers.

The repeated sound of "pssst" broke through the still air. Like puppets on a string, we glanced to our left in unison. After all, we had just been out of OCS for a matter of minutes. Peeking around the corner of a long, white building was a first sergeant, beckoning to us with hand movements similar to those of an Air Force runway director guiding planes to a hanger. All that was missing were the batons. Like a small herd of sheep, we turned in his direction. It must have looked like a scene from a bad B movie.

Our diversion from hell introduced himself as Sergeant Derek Richards, the first sergeant (also known as "Top") of the United States Army Scout Dog Unit, located less than a mile away. Without wasting any time, he got right to the point of his mission.

"Gentleman, I am very aware of your current status and your more-than-probable destination."

Pausing, he stroked his chin with his thumb and index finger while resting his other hand on his hip. He was short, had angular features, and appeared to be in his early forties. His uniform was impeccable, his pant creases stiff and in perfect alignment. The one deviation from military perfection was the cap he wore tipped way back off the top of his forehead. His eyes were wide and seemed to focus on each of us individually.

"I have the authority and permission of higher-ups to offer you a chance to remain in the States another twelve weeks," he said very matter-of-factly.

I experienced a verbal hard-on; my ears turned pink from the rush of blood and felt as if they doubled in size. We sucked in a lung full of air and then held our mutual breath for the next words of ecstasy.

"I need four scout-dog handlers to walk point in search-and-destroy missions in Nam," he continued in his very matter-of-fact style.

Collectively we exhaled; I felt the blood drain from my flaccid ears. He then began to explain that training would keep us in the States for three additional months and fluffed us with, "Who knows, the war might be over by then."

The eight of us exchanged quick glances. This step would alter the shape of our destinies, and there was no time to weigh the pros and cons of such an important decision. Would one of us toss our hand into the air, or all eight of us, or just the four he requested?

"Volunteer" began to ring in my head. I was thinking about my dad's advice the day before my induction. I anticipated a long speech but was surprised when Dad said just three words, shook my hand, and wished me good luck. The words "don't ever volunteer" became emblazoned on my brain.

Daydreaming about my dad's advice caused me to miss some of the first sergeant's words. As I drifted back to reality, I discovered that I had my hand swaying back and forth just above my cap. My hand movements were in unison with those of three others.

Why was my hand waving? Did I think my dad was just kidding, and what he really meant was that I should volunteer every chance I got? Was there a gnat flying around my cap? Did it have anything to do with the fact that dogs had always been an important part of my life? Who knew? The one thing I did know for sure was my arm was vertical, and I was about to meet my new best friend with four legs.

We grabbed our stuff, bid farewells to the incredibly stupid (or incredibly wise) remaining dropouts, and loaded onto a waiting truck.

As we rode that mile from the OCS compound to the Scout Dog Unit, I thought what a strange scenario had just taken place. Where's the red tape, the forms to fill out, the military, by-the-book system? I closed my eyes and pictured the scene: DOD manual 6, chapter 8, section 3, paragraph 4, "Changing Your MOS" (military occupation specialty)—fill out form 368-A in triplicate, take said form to the center of the base, and look for a sergeant peeking around the corner of a long, white, wooden building making a "pssst" sound as he beckons you with waving arms. Strange. Very, very strange.

The more I thought about this bizarre adventure, the more I questioned my decision. Hunting down a bottle of Maalox became my newest priority.

The four of us reported to First Sergeant Hartman at 0800 hours the following morning. Two extra hours in bed was a good thing since it took an extra two hours to get to sleep. A highly polished wood counter split the room in half. The first sergeant sat on the other side behind a single desk that swallowed up most of his space. We watched while he dished out orders to three waiting specialist E-4s (SPC-4s or "spec fours").

My sense of smell was diverted. For almost thirty weeks in the Army, the air had a certain scent to it. It was not an aroma easily described. I thought of it as a military smell issued the first day of basic training and resupplied daily after that. Now that changed. Our new home had a different odor—dog shit. A soft breeze carried the pungent fragrance in waves. The aroma got stronger as the day got warmer.

The dogs were all German shepherds. We had spotted them as we arrived the day before. Strong, regal, friendly, and intelligent—they waited patiently to be fed after a heavy day of training.

The SPC-4s received their assignments and scooted off. Top turned his bulky swivel chair in our direction and gave us his undivided attention. Like the day before, he wasted no time on pleasantries. He stood and approached the counter. "Gentlemen, I lied to you yesterday," he said stone-faced.

"Don't ever volunteer" rang in my head like giant cathedral bells. If someone kicked me dead center in the crotch, I don't think I would have responded. I was numb. His next sentence exploded the bells and left me weak.

"I don't need scout-dog handlers. I'm up to here with scout-dog handlers," he said placing his hand just above his very short cropped flattop.

"What do you … I mean … but I thought …," stammered the guy next to me as he twisted his cap in his hands.

"What I do need," interrupted Top, "is a truck dispatcher, a clerk typist, a veterinary technician, and a supply specialist."

Sergeant Richards seemed to revel in his little deception. With a glance to each of us no longer than a blink of an eye, he continued. "You guys have college degrees. You're already trained to think. Take five seconds to think which of these jobs appeals to you and report to the following duty stations," he said while laying out a pile of papers to be filled out and signed.

"I'll take the trucks," said the guy who had stammered incoherently seconds earlier.

"I can type forty-five words a minute. Can anyone beat that for the clerk typist job?" declared the guy to my left.

"I was a biology major in college, so veterinary technician has my name written all over it," said a voice behind us.

"If a degree in marketing qualifies me for the supply room, I'll take it," I said. We had settled our fates in just over five seconds and with no conflicts. The first sergeant didn't seem at all surprised. He just smiled and excused himself to other chores.

I grabbed his attention just as he turned, "Excuse me, Top. What if I still want to train a dog?"

"Well, I guess you'll just have to re-up," he said while turning half-way back to me." "Right now, I need your ass in the supply room. Any more questions?"

"Ahhh, nope," I added as if I might have another.

With forms filled out, I was ready for supply school. I had traded my M16 and a dog I never even got a chance to meet for a #2 pencil. Dropping to the floor in the hallway I tried to take it all in. I felt a little disappointed in not being assigned a dog. For two hours, the night before, I had wondered what it would be like to walk point in search-and-destroy missions with a dog I had trained. But then again, from time to time, I had also wondered what it would be like to be sightless, or be adopted, or grow up in Vegas.

I had a comforting thought at that moment: *I got a dog waiting for me back home. Keep warm, Mopsey.*

NOTE: For explanation of symbols and abbreviations see AR 320-50

DEPARTMENT OF THE ARMY
Headquarters United States Army Infantry Center
Fort Benning, Georgia 31905

SPECIAL ORDERS   10 April 1969
NUMBER   100   EXTRACT

31. TC 241. Following reassignment directed, Individual will proceed in military uniform to the place
assigned and will report at the hour on the date specified in port call. TDN. CIC 291A03. ASSIGNED TO:
USAOSREPLSTA Ft Lewis WA 98433 for fur asg to USARV VN Trans Det APO SF 96307 for fur asg to WOBR VN Trans
Det APO SF 96384 Port Call data: Report on 25 May 1969 not later than 1200 hrs to USA OVERSEAS REPLACE-
MENT STATION (6A-6021-01) Ft Lewis WA 98433 UNOINDC Request No. 0335 Leave data: 30 DDALVAHP UNOINDC PCS
(MDC): ZZE9 OPO C&L No: VPS UNOINDC Auth: OPO DA Ltr EPADR-E 28 Mar 69 Subj: Sel Enl Pers for OS Svc
(SEPOS)(39-25) UNOINDC AR 614-30 AR 614-215 AR 55-28 PPSC: A UNOINDC EDCSA: 25 May 69 UNOINDC
S P E C I A L   I N S T R U C T I O N S:
ACPATT. Bag alw of 66 lbs and ex bag alw of 135 lbs personal eff is auth indiv while tvl by acft. Sp
orien is rqr IAW Third USA Reg 612-2 prior to dprt on PCS fr prsn unit.
                        Pers needing corr eye lenses WB equipped with mask, protec-
tive, field M17, and nec corr eye lenses prior to dprt fr CONUS. Indiv clo will not be shipped as
unaccompanied bag but will acmp indiv while in a tran status. Indiv WB POR qual IAW AR 612-35. The
introduction, pur and poss of privately owned wpn is prohibited in the Republic of Vietnam. Army Green
uniform is rqr for indiv tvl in uniform in CONUS during winter season; and upon arrival at POE indiv
will have in his poss only those items spec in app IV, AR 700-8400-1, as changed. Mail adrs: Personal
Mail Section APO SF 96381. Cncr tvl of depn and shpmt of POV not auth. TPA. *CC trans auth.

KING, JOE P US53612364 (251-78-9437) PFC 76430 Co C 818th Engr Bn this sta OPO C&L No: VPS 569 BASD: NA
BPED: 29 Feb 68 ETS: 28 Feb 70

ROY, ALBERT C US67062262 (038-28-7181) PFC 76X20 524th Pers Svc Co this sta Line: 5721 PPSC: B BASD: NA
BPED: 7 Mar 68 ETS: 6 Mar 70

*JONES, WILLIAM L RA67019446 (301-46-4533) SP4 76W20 177th Avn Co (Mdm Hel) this sta Leave data: 25
DDALVAHP Line: 5718 BASD/BPED: 29 Jul 68 ETS: 28 Jul 70

HAINES, THOMAS L RA11974846 (060-38-0790) SP4 76Y20 HQ Det 26th Inf Plt (SD) this sta Port Call data:
Report on 20 May 1969 not later than 1200 hrs to USA OVERSEAS REPLACEMENT STATION (6A-6021-01) Ft Lewis
WA 98433 OPO C&L No: VPD L103 Auth: OPO DA Ltr EPADR-E 11 Mar 69 Subj: Sel Enl Pers for OS Svc (SEPOS)
(039-44) BASD: 25 Jan 68 BPED: 8 Nov 67 ETS: 24 Jan 70 EDCSA: 20 May 69

LINEBERGER, JOHN J RA12812340 (239-70-5349) SP4 76Y30 (76Y20) 26th Inf Plt (SD) this sta Port Call data:
Report on 20 May 1969 not later than 1200 hrs to USA OVERSEAS REPLACEMENT STATION (6A-6021-01) Ft Lewis
WA 98433 OPO C&L No: VPD L105 Auth: OPO DA Ltr EPADR-E 11 Mar 69 Subj: Sel Enl Pers for OS Svc (SEPOS)
(039-44) BASD/BPED: 22 Jan 68 ETS: 21 Jan 70 EDCSA: 20 May 1969

FOR

OFFICIAL:

MALCOLM R. BAER
Colonel, AGC
Adjutant General

JIM D. KEIRSEY
Colonel, GS
Chief of Staff

DISTRIBUTION:
40 - Consolidated Orders
 1 - AG Orders
 1 - AG Records
 2 - Svc Sec
 3 - AG-MPB ATTN: S and A
 2 - FAO ATTN: Svc Con Div
30 - 197th Inf Bde
45 - USAIC Trp Comd
25 - 5 ea indiv CO, USAOSREPLSTA, USAPERCEN (6021) Ft Lewis WA 98433
17 - USARV Trans Det APO SF 96307 (For MR and Other Admin purposes)
 5 - WOBR VN Trans Det APO SF 96384
 1 - Postal Off Ft Lewis WA 98433
 1 - POR Board
185 - AG-MPB ATTN: AJIAG-PE (OS)

CHAPTER 13

"Alert Notification for Overseas Movement"
(Militareese for "You're going to Nam")

Time raced around the clock despite the fact that my new temporary station in life was numbingly boring and about as challenging as opening a can of soup. Six of us ran the supply and arms room operations located in the basement of the USAIC HQ Detachment, Twenty-Sixth Infantry Scout Dogs Platoon, 197th Infantry Brigade, our official home until the Army decided otherwise.

SNAFU

By the end of the first day, I knew which of the five others would become a close friend. Physically, except for his receding hairline, John Lawson and I were mirror images. His very distinct accent took the guesswork out of geography placement. It was just a matter of where in the south he hung his hat. Somewhere in the second sentence of our first conversation I learned he was from Tryon, North Carolina, a short drive from Western Carolina University, where he had graduated in 1967 with a bachelor's in management. By the third sentence, I knew he, too, had dropped out of OCS in August of 1968.

Even though we had become part of the Army's Remington Raiders, we still had to take the exam to see where we were on the proficiency totem pole. There were twenty-three in our class. Tests were never on the list of my strong suits. That's why I was shocked that I came in sixth. This could only mean two things: I'm a lot smarter than I thought I was, or there were supply rooms all over Fort Benning that were being run by people in the double digits on the IQ chart.

Months became nothing more than a blur of time. Trips to Atlanta, once every three or four weeks, helped us to maintain a small amount of our sanity. A much-needed trip to Panama City, Florida, for spring break in April gave us a chance to forget that we were even in the Army. Then again, four guys with really short haircuts might have been a giveaway.

John and I had hooked up with Travis Howard and Chris Geller for the trip. Chris was our "bait guy." In 1968 a top ten TV show, *Mission: Impossible*, was created, written, produced, and directed by Bruce Geller. Chris was Bruce's nephew. With those credits, our trip could have been called *Mission: Impossible—The Bruce Geller Show.*

We arrived midafternoon and were at the motel, out of our clothes, in our bathing suits, and on the beach in eleven minutes flat. We put together a plan: whenever we got into a discussion with a group of girls, we would put the "bait guy" to work. We hit pay dirt on the second group. It couldn't have been better. There were four of them: three were hot, and the fourth one was cute as a button. They were students from Auburn. After fifteen minutes of small talk, we asked them if they wanted to join us for dinner. One of them, Joy, a tall blond, said she would have to pass as she told a guy she met earlier in the day that she would join him for dinner.

Chris took this opportunity to put on his "bait guy" hat. "Oh, that's a shame. It was real close that these guys were going to be a group of three, which would have worked out perfectly. I joined them after changing my mind about where I was supposed to go."

"What was your original plan?" Pam, the cute-as-a-button girl, asked.

"My uncle is Bruce Geller, and I was going to be on the set of an episode of *Mission: Impossible.*"

"Are you serious? Your uncle is Bruce Geller?" asked Tammy, the most "endowed" of the four. "I don't believe this. I haven't missed a single episode of MI since it started in 1966. Oh, my God." Tammy turned to Joy and said, "Cancel your date. I'll make up the best excuse, or lie, I've ever come up with. I promise."

While looking at me, Joy said, without any thought, "Sure, why not."

"I know a perfect place, not expensive, and it has a great patio and awesome music," said Gina, the fourth girl. "It's called Captain Dave's on the Gulf, in Destin. Is that OK?"

The girls offered their van, and I volunteered to be the designated driver. We all went back to our motel rooms and got ready for the excursion. We loaded into the van, eight people, two cases of ice-cold Bud, and a radio on full blast.

Tammy hooked up with Chris, no surprise there. Travis and the Button hit it off. Being six-three made five-eleven Joy and me a perfect fit. John and Gina were happy with their match-up. Amazingly, there were no overlaps regarding seat arrangement at Captain Dave's. Top would have been so proud.

Beers on the way to CDs, beers at CDs, and beers on the way back from CDs. Uh oh, bets were about to be placed on who would be hugging porcelain first. We all met back up at Travis and Chris's room to finish off the party.

The Button found a deck of cards and held it in the air and slurred, "Hey, hey, y'all, anyone up for a game of striiiiiip poker?" Four jumped in with an immediate, "Hell, yes." The remaining four hesitated for a few seconds and then collectively said, "Hell, why not." We all voted on standard poker because anything more complicated would be insane to attempt.

After a few hands, there was a pile of flip-flops under the table. Then Travis lost a white dress shirt, Joy a head band, Gina a bracelet, Chris a baseball cap, me a Hawaiian button-up, Tammy a ring, John a belt, and Pam a scarf. A half hour later we saw a pile that included two bras, three pairs of guys' beach shorts, and a sundress. A second pile was in the process of growing as well. The string of people around the table were a blurry, human collage of shades of white, pink, and bright red.

Then it happened; Pam was the first victim. She lost and had one piece of clothing remaining—her panties. She stood up and took a bow and placed her thumbs in the waistband on her hips and hesitated. The girls were actually the loudest in chanting, "Take 'em off! Take 'em off! Take 'em off!"

Pam finally spoke up, "I can't, y'all … becaaause … it's … ahhh … it's that … ahhh … time of the month."

Gina couldn't resist saying, "What are you worrying about? You still have one piece to go." Everyone broke out in a prolonged bout of laughter. With four more down to their final piece of clothing, Tom among them, I called an end to the game to the relief of most. Pam put a hand on my shoulder, slurred a thank you to me, and grabbed one last beer.

"Don't forget it was your idea, Pam," I said.

"Yeah … yeah, but poker's myyyy, my game. I paid over one half, or maybe almost a one half of my tuition—seriously half, with my poker winnings. That's right, winnings, not *looosings*. I was truly, really expecting to beee the only one looking at a room full of nude, naked people." Pam continued. "Who would have thought. Damn, I didn't get to see one naked nude penis dick," Pam slurring her redundant answer.

A big relief to me was that I almost went commando for the evening, I thought to myself.

An hour later everyone staggered out of the room clinging to each other for support. Joy and I, the most sober of the group, decided on a walk on the beach. It was a long trek. When we got back to my room, we showered and crashed into a tight cuddle.

At breakfast the next morning (or was it afternoon?), we all ordered scrambled eggs to keep company with heads that were beyond scrambled. No one ordered a bloody mary.

At one point the table became very quiet for what seemed like minutes. Chris broke the silence, "You know if we got together again here in two years, one of us probably wouldn't be able to make it." Everyone looked at him, like, "I can't believe you just said that." If we had gotten back together in two years, Travis would have been the one not joining us. He didn't return from Vietnam. He was, and still is, missing in action.

*****

My only regret of our trip to Panama City Beach was that I didn't consider the sun for what it was—a blistering trip to hell. I returned to Fort Benning bringing with me the worst sunburn of my life. I arrived at work on Monday morning wearing flip flops. The lieutenant who was not in a good mood, asked me why I was out of uniform. I said that I had sun burned to a pretty shade of scarlet while in Florida.

He said, "Boots on your feet in ten minutes or you'll be court-martialed."

"For what?"

"Destruction of government property," he said in a serious manner. He then changed his mind and said that I would get an Article 15, one step down from a court-martial.

I just stood there in silence, thinking, *"What an asshole."* We stared at each other for a few seconds before I turned around and went back to my room to retrieve my boots. That was, without question, one of the most painful days of my life. Thirteen wasps stinging me at the same time still holds down first place.

Daily humdrum settled back in, and checking a day off the calendar became our most cherished moment of each day. I had no idea what time it was at any given moment. However, I do know where John and I were at 2359 hours on December 31, 1968. That moment will forever be etched in my memory. One problem after another kept us on base for three hours and twenty minutes past our planned departure time on New Year's Eve.

"John, what time is it now?" I asked, for the third time in less than thirty minutes.

"Exactly 3:58 p.m. Eastern Standard Fucking Time, and if Top isn't back in two minutes, I'm calling off our trip to Atlanta, buying a case of Ripple, and throwing the bottles—after I empty them—at road signs between Columbus and Phoenix City until 12:01 a.m. Eastern Standard Fucking Time," John said, just as Top entered the room. In a matter of seconds, we were on our way to Atlanta, 104 miles northeast of Fort Benning.

"Hey, John," I said as we passed through small town number three en route to the big city, "If you threw empty wine bottles at road signs in Columbus, Georgia, at 2359 hours and then drove over the bridge to Phoenix City, Alabama, to finish off a sign at 0001, you'd have to wait an hour."

"What? Huh? Oh yeah, I forgot about the time line. I sure wish Atlanta were in Alabama. I'd like to get back at least one of our three lost hours."

"Uh oh, prepare to lose some more time. You ainnn't gonna like hearing this, but we're outta gas," I said, as the car sputtered to a halt.

"Shit, shit, shit! I don't remember seeing a gas station for miles. But hey, we're in luck. There's a wine store," John said, taking the news much better than I thought he would.

At 1816 we were again back on our mission to self-destruct at midnight. At 1904 hours we hit the city limits of Atlanta and spent the next forty minutes looking for our motel.

A neon sign proclaimed our destination. Bouncing into the parking lot, I found a space between two identical, old, black, Ford Galaxies. I turned the key to the off position, but the engine decided it would continue to run against my wishes. I cussed at her a couple of times, at which point she decided to shut the hell up.

The front desk clerk was decked out in New Year's Eve regalia—a bright orange lei around his neck, a black plastic top hat resting on his ears, and a balloon tied to a belt loop at the back of his high-water pants.

"Are we checking in, or are you checking out?" John asked the clerk.

"I'll check y'all in, but if somebody comes in here at 11:59, I'm a telling 'em to come back next year. Git it? Next year?" He laughed at his imitation of a joke as he gave us a sign-in card.

A few minutes later we were in our rooms timing out the remainder of the year 1968. Showers and eating were next on the list. Dialing 04 on the phone got us room service.

"Yeah, room service, this is room 308. We would like two of your Hotlanta Burger Platters," John said into the phone. "We want one somewhere between rare and raw. If it moos when you take it off the grill, that'll make it just right. As for the other one—set that sucker on fire. And we'd like two ice-cold Cokes to wash down our undoubtedly sumptuous banquet. Thank you. Oh yeah, will we get this before the New Year?"

John often talked out of the center of his mouth, keeping the corners tight and curved. Three dimples framed his mouth, two on his cheeks and one in the center of his chin. The look was very effective when he was being sarcastic or mischievous. In this case he was both. He wasn't mean; he just loved messing with people. For the most part, his victims also loved it.

After a half-hour, we were assured that our food was on its way—and assured again every ten minutes for the next half hour. At 2240 hours our food arrived. Everything was cold except for the Cokes, which were just a few degrees below room temperature.

At 2306 we were in the car, attempting to start the engine. Turn the key, "Damn." Turn the key, "Shit." Turn the key, "Fuck."

By 2319 we had successfully flagged down a taxi. At 2354 we hopped out of the cab, threw more money than we should have on the seat, and waded through the confetti on the street toward the entrance. Once inside, we encountered a small line. When we became customers number three and four, the bouncer checking IDs said, "Sorry, but we're over capacity. We have to cut the door off."

Ten or so others joined in behind us. At this point, pleading "what's a couple more gonna hurt" wasn't an option. At 2359 the couple in front of us said, "I can't believe this shit. You wouldn't believe what we went through just to get here on time." John and I fell out laughing until we heard the sounds of noisemakers and the singing of *Auld Lang Syne* coming from the room twenty feet to our left. We could also see what appeared to be total strangers kissing each other.

I reached out my hand to John. "I guess this will have to do. Happy Fucking New Year, Hoss."

Two days later we were back at Fort Benning, where placing an *X* on the calendar in the supply room at the end of each day was still our number one mind-saving ritual.

At the end of my sixth month in supply hell, I brought my parents up to date.

Dear Mom and Dad,

Sorry I haven't written in a while, but we've been working late a lot— nothing unusual. Most of the inspections are over, and we're trying to get some new personnel downstairs.

You remember me telling you about the four guys we dubbed the "Misfit Four"? Well, here's the update. Howard Franklin is being held on $10,000 bail for armed robbery. Chris Ellison totally screwed up the arms room and is waiting for his trial for marijuana possession. Roy Smith received an undesirable discharge for general misconduct. And Bill Washington was just convicted on his marijuana charge.

Oh yeah, Jamal Jalen volunteered for a tour in Nam. Well, I'm down to 353 days left in the Army, and I'm beginning to think about volunteering for a short visit to the Orient this spring—but I doubt I will. However, this place does make you think about it a lot.

I guess when it's all over, there will be some things relating to the Army that I will have appreciated. But I can tell you right now that making 18 cents an hour won't be one of them.

Thanks for the care package. Could you please send my cream-colored jeans and my burgundy sweater in the next package? Thanks.

All my love, Tom

Early 1969 was nothing more than days turning into weeks and weeks into months. John and I knew, through the grapevine, that our orders for Vietnam would come across Top's desk every two months. He would then pass them along with a compassionate plea to allow us to remain in his unit because we were indispensable. I translated that to mean he didn't like going to the OCS compound on dropout days to snag unsuspecting would-be grunts. Then in late March, First Sergeant Richards went on leave.

I had just less than ten months remaining in the Army when I received Disposition Form 2496-1 on April 5, 1969. John received his orders at the same time. Under "subject" it said, "Alert Notification for Overseas Movement." Translated into regular English: "You're going to Nam." All of a sudden, we were dispensable. And Top would have to practice his *pssst, pssst, pssst* when he returned from leave.

Taking my envelope outside, I tore it open. Inside was a single sheet of paper marked Special Orders number 100. I sat on the warm cement steps outside the main entrance to headquarters and searched, in a helter-skelter fashion, for the important whens and wheres.

There were five names on the extract. My name was second from the bottom. It read:

HAINES, THOMAS L RA11974846 (020-88-0490) SP4 76Y20
HQ Det 26th Inf Plt (SD) this sta Port Call data: Report on
20 May 1969 not later than 1200 hrs to USA OVERSEAS
REPLACEMENT STATION (6A-6021-01) Fort Lewis WA 98433
OPO

C&L zno: VPD L103 Auth: OPO Da Ltr EPADR-E 11 Mar 69
Subj: Sel Enl Pers for OS Svc (SEPOS) (039-44) BASD: 25 Jan
68 67 ETS: 24 Jan 70 EDCSA: 20 May 69

While studying the dates and numbers, I noticed that four of the five people on the list were short timers. Rumor had it that Nixon was escalating the war. Sending over short timers seemed to verify the rumor.

As a taxpayer, I was impressed to see that almost everything contained on the extract was abbreviated to fit on one piece of paper. However, also as a taxpayer, I was irritated that the Army felt it necessary to distribute 358 copies of our orders to various destinations throughout the Department of the Army. "The powers that be" had decided that it was necessary to give forty copies to Consolidated Orders; one copy to AG Orders; one copy to AG Records; two copies to Svc Sec; three copies to AG-MPB ATTN: S and A; two copies to FAO ATTN: Svc Con Div; thirty copies to 197th Inf Bde; forty-five copies to USAIC Trp Comd; twenty-five copies to five each individual CO, USAOSREPLSTA, USAPERCEN (6021) Fort Lewis WA 98433; seventeen copies to USARV Trans Det APO SF 96307 (For MR and Other Admin purposes); five copies to WOBR VN Trans Det APO SF 96384; one copy to Postal Off Ft Lewis WA 98433; one copy to POR Board; and 185 copies to AG-MPB ATTN: AJIAG-PE (OS), whatever the hell that is.

Not printed on the above list were the copies the other four transferees and I received, plus copies that were perhaps mailed to my parents, my recruiter, my Aunt Alice, and maybe even one to my dog, Mopsey.

I spent a few more minutes reading about luggage weight limitations and not being allowed to purchase or possess privately owned weapons in the Republic of

Vietnam. Folding up my orders, I let it all sink in.

"So, super soldier, what do you think?" came a voice from behind me. John's question jolted me back to the real world. He was clutching his orders in his left hand and a fresh cup of coffee in his right.

"Well to be honest, I'm excited, apprehensive, frightened, ecstatic, relieved, curious, and a whole bunch of other things all at the same time," I said while trying to think of all the emotional adjectives I could come up with in a few short seconds.

"So have you made up your mind yet? Are you flying over as a hawk or a dove? No pun intend—OK, pun intended," John said. His tone was as serious as I had ever heard him speak, pun aside. I was surprised by his question. We never had conversations regarding the war and whether we thought it was right or wrong.

"I don't know man. After four years of college and a year in the Army, I'm still straddling the political fence. But I guess I'll fall off that sucker sometime over the next six months," I said. "How about you?"

"I'm a hawk for now, but depending on how I get kissed in Nam, I could easily turn into a dove," John said. He downed the last of his coffee and switched subjects. "So, my man, are you going to go for an early out to go back to school?"

"Hell yeah, but I don't want to get a master's. I've been considering getting a degree in art."

"If you do, check out East Carolina University. Man, it is one great party school. Shit, you already have a degree. I'd go for partying 101, advanced prophylactics 205, and an easy three credits for the advanced study of the social, economic, and physiological effects of getting shit-faced. No, seriously, it's a really good school with an exceptional school of art; you should keep it in the back of your mind."

"And you? Any plans for going back to school?"

"I'll investigate those waters after I've been in Nam for a while; plans are just day to day till then," he said without hesitation.

John tossed his coffee cup in a fifty-five-gallon trash can with a dog's head painted on it and went for cup number two.

I was given forty days to savor life, begin researching shit-faced 310, and pile in enough new memories to get me through my tour. The day that logged the best memories of my young life was April 25, 1969, my twenty-fourth birthday. I would relive those very private twenty-four hours many times over during the following six months.

Taking a bus from Benning to Atlanta jump-started the forty days. I was going to meet my mom and dad at The Regency Hyatt House. They were in Atlanta on business. When they arrived at the hotel, they asked if I had arrived yet. The sign-in crew said no. When I arrived, I asked if my parents had arrived yet. They said no. This went on for about an hour. At one point, we both arrived at the desk at the same time. We asked those working how this could happen. They truly did not have an answer for us. So they gave us the presidential suite. We forgave them.

The next day we went to the Atlanta airport to go to Binghamton, New York, with a stop-over in New York City. The plane looked and smelled like it came straight off the production line at Boeing.

After we had taken off and settled in, I made a beeline to the restroom. There were two ahead of me. A book that the stewardess was reading caught my eye, so I asked about it. She was almost to the end and said she was thoroughly enjoying it. I asked if she had time to talk about it as I had just finished reading it. She answered in the affirmative. We introduced ourselves to each other. Her name was Cindy. I sat in a way that I could keep an eye on the line to the restroom.

She asked about my destination. I said, "Endicott, for a short stay before heading out to another journey, a visit to the other side of the planet for a little vacation in a country called Vietnam." I immediately sensed something wasn't right as I looked into her amazing blue eyes, that at that moment had a very sad appearance.

"Do you want to share the sudden change in your fully smiling face?" I asked. "No, I'd rather not, but thank you for your concern," she said after hesitating for a couple of seconds.

It was my turn for the washroom. Upon my return, we picked up where we left off, minus any discussion about Vietnam. After a few minutes, she had to dispense drinks and snacks. After that chore she stopped by and tapped me on the shoulder and gave me a come-hither by curling her finger three or four times. I wasted no time following her digit request.

When we were both seated at her station, I continued my no-wasting-time approach and asked her if she was available for dinner and a show. She said, "Yes—and if you didn't ask me, I was going to ask you." I thought to myself, "Hmm, I think I just fell in love."

I returned to my seat and explained to my parents that my flight plans had been altered. My mother had no idea what was up. My dad smiled, put his hand in his pocket, pulled two Franklins from his clip, and said, "Have fun, and we'll see you tomorrow."

"Thanks, Dad. Make that a big thanks, and I'm your man to put the shelves up on the three walls of the garage." My dad wasn't going to ask me to do any projects on his list while I was home on leave, but I already planned on three undertakings.

Cindy and I had an evening that was added into the category of "one of the best ten dates in my life so far." At dinner, she explained about her change in her facial expression. Her brother had been killed in Vietnam eight months earlier. She emphatically stressed that had nothing to do with her accepting my invitation to dinner and a show.

I took her back to her hotel, where we exchanged telephone numbers and addresses. A sweet kiss brought our dream night to a close.

From NYC to . . .

South Vietnam

Pleiku, Vietnam

Welcome to
Nam, Gentlemen

Our stop in Fort Lewis, Washington, was both hectic and relaxing. The weather was warm. The sky was full of large, white clouds that surrounded Mount Rainier, just a short distance to the west. The atmosphere seemed subdued and businesslike. Tens of thousands were processed through this base each year. When not wondering or worrying about what was in store for us in Nam, we were kept pretty busy with our processing.

First came the obligatory paperwork, followed by the issuance of our jungle gear, both necessary before we were allowed to become inhabitants of the land of "Sir Charles." We stood in front of a sea of olive drab and were loaded up: OD fatigue pants, OD boots, OD socks, OD underwear, OD jungle shirts, OD caps, and even OD handkerchiefs. I wondered, "If the Army issued condoms, would they also be OD?"

John got the chance to use his closed, curved-lip sarcasm once again when he demanded, "All right, you supply maggots, give me blue, red, yellow, and orange madras. I want purple stripes, rainbow-color plaids, and pastel solids." They gave him a rousing laugh for his demands and OD green wearables to fill up his OD green duffle bag.

As evening arrived, the air began to fill with redundant conversations. They don't need recounting because they were mostly boring and had no intuitive musings regarding our unknown destinies. Although exercising our jaw muscles was the main activity of the evening, some spent their time getting wasted, others wrote letters home, while still others went to bed early and lay awake staring into the unknown. I spent at least an hour of my final evening in the real world sipping on a beer at a small club on base. I listened to "Hey Jude" over and over on an old and faded jukebox.

Around 0500 a bugle sounded over a PA system. Soon after, in the low sun of early morning, we marched single file into a World Airlines Jet. Destination: Cam Ranh Bay, Republic of South Vietnam.

The raspy-voiced pilot welcomed us aboard and gave us the usual weather and other assorted statistics. He then leveled us with the length of our journey. "Your flight to Vietnam, gentlemen, with a refueling in Yokota, Japan, will take almost two trips around your watch. So sit back, relax, and enjoy your flight."

"Jesus," I thought, "I'm still reeling a little from the jet lag I got from my flight from New York to Fort Lewis, Washington."

After sixteen hours of eating, reading, and water watching, I fell into a deep sleep. An unknown amount of time later I woke abruptly. *What? Really? On a plane? Really? A wet dream on a freakin' plane?* Thank God John was sound asleep, or I would never have heard the end of it. I grabbed a pillow and headed to the rest room. Traveling commando didn't help the situation. Naturally, the restroom was occupied.

A stewardess asked me if I was OK. I'm not sure which expression I sported on my face, but it wasn't a happy valley grin. I told her I was fine, just a little nervous. "A little? If I was exiting this plane to face what you guys are about to face, I would be in that john for the whole twenty-three-hour trip," she said.

We chatted for a few minutes. I pegged her to be a hippie when not flying the friendly skies wearing her stewardess costume.

While looking at her name tag, which read Felicia, I said, "So, Felicia, when you are not on the plane, I see a headband, bellbottoms, and lots of beads around your neck."

"Wow, you're good," she said, as the guy in the john finally came out. We danced a couple of steps of "pick a direction" before he knocked the pillow out of my hand.

I looked at the cute hippie while retrieving the pillow. I felt a very vulnerable embarrassment, but Felicia put me right at ease, or at least close to it, when she said, "You're not the first and won't be the last. Hang tight, I'll be right back." She returned with a hair dryer and said, "This might help. And seriously, ditch the embarrassment. I've even had one on the plane."

She did take the edge off of my embarrassment. When I was as back to normal as I could get, I exited and handed Felicia the dryer and thanked her. She said, with a wink, "You're welcome; sweet dreams." This time I had the happy valley grin, as did she. I seriously thought about asking her to dinner and a show. I guess that would be taking her to the mess hall and watching a movie projected on a sheet hanging by six nails on a wall. Yeah, twenty-three hours on a plane can really mess with your head. I returned to my seat and fell right back to slumberland.

After I woke up for the second time, I entertained myself with more hours of monotonous water watching, thinking so many different thoughts that they slammed into each other in my skull. Finally the peaceful, uncluttered coastline of Vietnam was an oddly welcome sight. We landed with the usual skipping and skidding of tires on hot concrete. While we taxied, I began to have the same thoughts I had after quitting OCS, and yes, these were some of the same questions we discussed the night before. Where will I be stationed? Will it be in a "safe" area? Will I see any action? Oh, God, will I kill anyone? Will my officers know their butts from first base? My brain went into a quick overload.

The red lights went off simultaneously with the ding sound that signals the all clear for movement. The scene that usually follows on most flights—passengers scrambling for their carry-ons, jockeying for a quick exit and wishing the best to their seatmates—didn't take place this time. There were no loved ones waiting in the concourse, no shuttles to take one to luxury hotels, and no pretty women with leis welcoming passengers to paradise. We all took our time making our way to the exit. When I arrived at the red sign with the cutout letters, EXIT, I looked at my new best friend and winked at her. She winked back.

A tall, good-looking guy with sideburns that looked longer than regulations allowed was walking in front of me. He held an old, beat-up gym bag in one hand and a small, off-white canvas bag in the other. When he arrived at the door of the plane, he dropped both bags, placed his arm around the waist of the stewardess, who was in the process of dispensing farewells, and kissed her in the grand style of the great lovers of silent films. He then picked up his bags, looked over his shoulder, and declared over the high volume of cheers, "What are they gonna do? Send me to Vietnam?"

I looked into the last pair of round, although somewhat flustered, female eyes I would see for months, ducked my head, and walked smack dab into 112 degrees of breath-snatching heat. Comments were quick and plentiful.

"Holy shit, it's hotter than a branding iron on a calf's ass."

"Hey, did I miss out on being issued my allotment of breathable air?"

"Good Lord, there's no AC over here, is there?"

Within minutes, we were all soaking wet. Priorities switched from surviving the war to not drowning in my sweat. Within a couple of hours, I was walking bow-legged from chaffing. I had a classic screaming case of crotch rot. I wondered if not having any underwear on made it worse. I didn't feel too silly, however, because half of those I was with were walking in the same manner. "Make way, make way, c'mon, c'mon, make way for an activated cowboy reserve unit from Lubbock, Texas," announced a guy near the front of the pack as we waddled across a plank walkway. The cowboy reference seemed fitting because we were herded around camp like cattle on a round-up for the next two days.

During one of those round-ups, a few hundred FNGs (Fucking New Guys) filled a sterile, cavernous auditorium for a speech force fed by a general. Dozens of overlapping conversations created a loud buzzing noise. This gathering brought about a lot of instant short-term friendships. The guy next to you became, however briefly, your new best buddy. Almost everyone was edgy and anxious. We were looking for and filing away any information that seemed to have any value. I looked around for Mr. Madras while cringing at "fond" memories of the infamous induction physical. But with a sea of OD bouncing around in front of me, there was less than no chance of spotting anyone sporting madras.

The order to attention echoed around the tin walls as we all obeyed the command without hesitation. An officer of unknown rank tapped the microphone a couple of times and, without a lot of fanfare, introduced a general with a single star on each of his shoulders.

The starched and shined general welcomed all of us to the Republic of South Vietnam. After verbally waving the flag for a minute or two, he promised to keep his remarks short and to the point so that we could get on with the mission at hand. He said that his comments would cover just two subjects: malaria and marijuana. John removed a pen from his pocket, ceremoniously clicked the point into view, and pretended to take notes in the palm of his hand.

"You will only be here for a year, gentlemen, so make it as safe a year as possible, and take your orange and white pills as directed. Taking these pills as directed will help prevent you from acquiring marijuana," he said, oblivious to his faux pas. A minute later he switched to his second topic and opened with the statement,

"Malaria—it's cheap, it's available, and it's potent. But remember this: you're not just buying malaria; you're buying a whole lot of trouble."

Jesus, Mary, and Joseph, the son-of-a-bitch did it again. I was thinking, "Hey, if this is the general speaking, I shudder at the thought of a second louie speaking. Oh, my god, we're as good as dead. John and I exchanged glances, removed our caps, held them over our hearts, and shook our heads.

Then I thought, "Well, maybe he's dyslexic, or dumb, or both." I didn't care. My only concern was finding out where I was going and what I would be doing. An hour later I found out: I was going on my first detail.

A sergeant entered our barracks with a clipboard and a leaky pen. He pointed his Bic randomly around the room at a half dozen ill-positioned soldiers. He barked, "You, you, you, you, you, and you, prepare to burn shit at 1300 hours."

"What do you mean burn it? I thought they just recycled it through the mess hall," John said. He got our names, added John's to the list, and exited.

Even though I knew he could tell time militarily, I felt he didn't explain our detail in the proper military jargon. I soon found out the activity we were about to engage in was the "eradication of human feces through the process of incineration" assignment, or like the sergeant said, we were going to burn shit.

At 1300 hours, we loaded onto a deuce-and-a-half and headed for the latrines. On the way, everyone, except for myself, put on his gas mask. I thought, what a bunch of wussies. I had just spent a year inside the largest kennel in the military world and envisioned this to being put on a rose-cutting detail for the general's wife. Wrong!

We pulled up to a long, thin, wooden building. It had a screen door in the center of its eight-foot-wide front. We went to the right side of the building, kicking up small clouds of dust as we approached the three-foot-high doors lining both sides of the unpainted structure. I reached down and pulled open the doors housing the first row of fifty-five-gallon drum thirds and gagged like I've never gagged in this or any previous life. My eyes watered, my head pounded, and my breakfast rose. The air was already heavy, hot, and lifeless. The addition to the atmosphere of this putrid stench was nothing short of a curse from beyond.

We grabbed each drum by the lip with our gloved hands and pulled them out of their dark confines into the bright sunlight. Dragging a drum to its new temporary position, we quickly released our grips, jumped back a few feet, and gasped for fresh air.

At first, we were only assaulted by our sense of smell, but then our sense of sight was attacked as well.

"Man, oh man, oh man, check this shit out—literally," said John. "Let's see what we've got here. It looks like a coagulated mass of shit, puke, piss, undigested food particles, wads of military-issued coarse toilet paper with wood chunks, and in that first drum, check it out, check it out—a live rat."

"What should we do with him?" asked a short, skinny guy who looked a whole lot like the rat we were discussing.

The SPC-4 in charge chimed in, "Well, here's what we should do. First, we let him enjoy his meal, and then we floss his little teeth, and then we send him on R&R to Hawaii. That's what we should do, but what we're gonna do is leave his ass alone and get this shit on the truck!"

The use of gas masks proved to be a futile idea. The heat and odor were inescapable. John and I had practiced deep breaths and skyward looks for a while before we approached the problem of lifting the drums onto the truck. I discovered that hot, humid afternoon what the meaning of the phrase "heavy as shit" really meant.

Two skinny guys with minimal muscle power may not have been the most intelligent pairing, but we managed to execute our system to perfection. Tilting the drum to the side, bending at the knees, placing one hand on the lip and the other underneath its rusty bottom, seemed to work rather well.

One, two, three—lift, stand, lock knees, and exhale. Exhaling at this point was not a voluntary response. The weight of the nearly full drum pushed the breath from our chests. We then found ourselves standing upright, our chins at the barrels lip, pulling in another lung full of horrific, contaminated air. Never before had my sense of smell been so brutally assailed.

We shuffled to the edge of the truck, being careful not to drop or spill the shifting contents. The clang of the steel drums on the bed of the truck was a very welcome sound. We repeated the process countless times, making numerous trips to the southern boundary of the base camp. Keeping these drums company on the trip to the perimeter was an equally undesirable task.

We arrived at our destination, emptied the drums into a large trough, poured in a couple gallons of kerosene, and let fly with a lit match. Long-handled rakes and shovels were used to keep the process going. A small western-born breeze picked up in intensity and began to carry the pungent odor back into base camp. "OK, all you shitheads, here comes today's breakfast and last night's brew back at ya," bellowed an anonymous voice, coughing, and choking on his words. When the billowing clouds of malodorous black smoke began to die down, we piled back into our truck and vowed never to shit again. The driver quickly hustled us off because he was late for another detail.

Our just-completed endeavor had left us no time for a shower before dinner, so we headed straight over to join the long line of those waiting for chow. We knew right then that our vow to "never shit again," would be short lived. The line, two to three soldiers wide, with occasional clumps of a half dozen, stretched twenty yards east from the entrance to the tent. Less than a minute after joining the column of culinary connoisseurs, it began to widen and separate around us. I guess we smelled a tad ripe. It appeared to be a long wait, but I was in no real hurry to join those at the front of the line. They were standing over a selection of items, trying to decide which food product they wanted least.

A short time later we stepped just inside the tent where two soldiers were dragging ice off a truck and tossing the huge chunks into large tin bins. There were two PFCs (private first class) hacking away at these miniature glaciers with ice picks. Another guy was scooping up the small irregular pieces in plastic cups and filling them with Kool-Aid.

It was John's turn to take a cup of the ice-cooled drink when I grabbed his arm at the wrist. "Sorry, John, but I don't think you want any of that cherry bug juice today."

"Why not?" he asked, the dripping liquid sloshing on his knuckles.

I pointed to the truck with the hand-scrawled sign stating the contents within as "potable ice."

"Does the number on the side of the truck look familiar?" I asked.

He carefully placed his drink at the edge of the nearest table as if its contents were a cup of nitroglycerin.

Dinner was dry, the air was wet, and my tour of duty was off to a shitty start.

In the Mind of the Beholder

The mind part hasn't even begun
The only true difference is the war
Peace of what?
No other definition is known by man
Tell the Beatles Buffalo Bill doesn't care
But, who does?
Mankind never has
So, why do they call us mankind?
The end is yet to come
But not on this page
Perhaps never
At least not in this world
Is there another?
Eat a peanut butter and cucumber sandwich with your toes,
    sitting on the attic floor
listening to "Does Your Chewing Gum Lose Its Flavor
    on the Bedpost Overnight"
sung off key by Alan Arkin and the Mormon Tabernacle Choir
Make cents?
But what does change?
Surely not this war
The end is yet to come
But not on this page

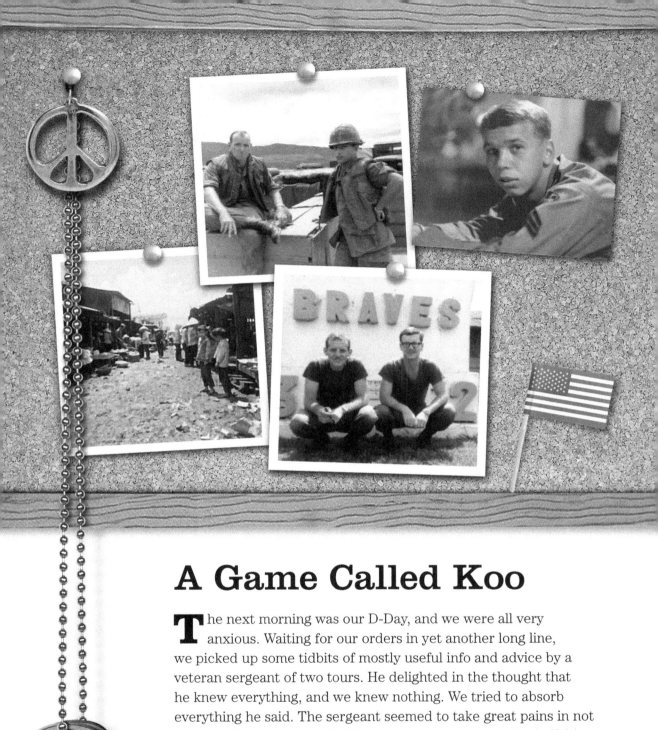

A Game Called Koo

The next morning was our D-Day, and we were all very anxious. Waiting for our orders in yet another long line, we picked up some tidbits of mostly useful info and advice by a veteran sergeant of two tours. He delighted in the thought that he knew everything, and we knew nothing. We tried to absorb everything he said. The sergeant seemed to take great pains in not exaggerating what he said. He didn't want anyone saying bullshit to anything that came out of his mouth.

His advice concerning our immediate situation was to kiss the ass of the SPC-4 on the other side of the door from which we were just inches away. That's right, the person behind that door was not a colonel, nor a major, or a captain, or a lieutenant, or even

CHAPTER 15

a sergeant. The individual who had our destinies at the end of his pen had the low rank of specialist E-4.

"Say the right things, guys, and you're on your way to a year-long R & R; say the wrong things, and you could end up in a body bag," our new mentor advised.

"Bullshit," I thought.

Soon, all that stood between my future and me was that door. Wiping my sweaty paws on the inside of my pants pockets and rocking nervously, I stopped long enough to read a hand-printed note tacked above the doorframe. It read, "Ye Who Enter Here Abandon All Hope." Hope was what I needed and all that I had. I wasn't at all prepared to go one-on-one with a guy who had my balls in his control. Entering in silence, I entertained the thought of saluting him; maybe that would impress him. My next thought was, no, I would be the one hundred and first that's done that before. So I just stood there waiting for him to look up after finishing the paperwork of a very young corporal who was on his way to Da Nang.

The balding spec 4 put down his pen and placed his arm against his forehead to wipe away fresh beads of sweat. When he removed his wet forearm from his face, I came close to losing all my bodily functions. My speech, however, was intact, "Son-of-a-bitch, son-of-a-bitch, son-of-a-bitch, Tim? Tim McAdams?"

Tim was one of the remaining four OCS dropouts that didn't volunteer to train scout dogs on that warm, strange morning nine and a half months earlier.

We shook hands like a pump on an oil rig. "Tom? Wow, I never thought I'd see you again," exclaimed Tim while releasing his grip. He stood, raised his hands palms up, and spun in a half circle. "Can you believe this shit? They discovered my sheepskin during processing and told me to throw my duffel bag in the corner. I've been here ever since. Man, I mean can you believe this shit? I've not been more than a mile from where I got off the freakin' plane."

"Why you don't see me with a four-legged companion: same reason," I said. Top said he needed four with college degrees. There were eight of us, so he used the scout-dog training as a way of culling the herd."

"I guess you could say that a sheepskin may very well have saved our human skins," Tim said while poking the air with his elbow. "Well, let's get down to business. Where do you want to be stationed? And, remember, Germany doesn't count," he said with a straight face while checking over my papers.

"Send me anywhere that's as safe as the gold in Fort Knox," I answered feeling relaxed for the first time since I stepped foot on Vietnam soil.

"This is Nam, man; there is no such place. We even get rocket attacks here." Tim ran his pen up and down the papers in front of him. "Pleiku is the best that I can do at the moment. The action in the highlands has dropped off like the war was being fought with BB guns," he said in an all-knowing manner. Tim told me about it, short and simple—Pleiku was a large inland city in the Central Highlands region, militarily known as "II Corps," home of the Fourth Infantry.

"OK, I'll take Pleiku. Yeah, Pleiku, why not?"

We crammed nine and a half months' worth of "where is" and "what happened to" into two minutes before pumping hands one more time. With great excitement, I looked forward to this place that sounded like a game called Koo. I closed the door behind me and looked hard at the next guy. "Holy shit, man, I hope you do a lot better than where I'm being sent. That guy just signed my death warrant," I said, shaking my head and shuffling my feet.

Life kicked into warp speed. They assigned John to the 545th Military Police Company with the First Air Cavalry in Phuoc Vinh, and a dozen short-term friendships came to a halt. John and I grabbed a moment to say our goodbyes and promised to stay in touch.

"Count all your chickens before they hatch," John said with a straight face.

"Eat as much of the yellow snow as possible," I responded in a manner just as serious.

We then, ceremoniously and facetiously, saluted each other before heading into the unknown.

Just after lunch, all those assigned to Camp Enari near Pleiku, the headquarters of the Fourth Infantry Division, were herded onto a large C-130 transport plane. The first to enter her belly was a corporal, who referred to the craft as a flying, pregnant guppy. A few moments later the four-engine green-and-brown camouflaged turboprop lumbered down the runway hauling forty pieces of human cargo to what was possibly going to be the most memorable year of their young lives.

C-130s had no seats, no windows, and no facilities. They did, however, have two sets of nylon straps dangling from the ceiling: one to hold onto, so one wouldn't roll around when the plane pitched or landed, and a second that had a barf bag attached. I used both. We landed after a noisy, uncomfortable hour. We were then spit from the C-130s belly into the steel bed of a deuce-and-a-half and then to a waiting bus.

An uncomfortable bus trip took us from the Pleiku Air Base through the city of Pleiku. Our final destination was Camp Enari, home of the Fourth Infantry Division, also known as the "Ivy Division." It was difficult to take in much of the local color because the bus had heavy wire mesh covering the windows. The lattice was necessary to keep grenades from being tossed into the bus. A corporal delivered us newbies to the first sergeant at HHC (headquarters and headquarters company), third battalion of the twelfth infantry, the Braves, for our assignments. Disheveled, tired, and still very anxious, a specialist directed us to a one-story, wooden structure located in the compound between the mess hall and a large water tower.

While the others huddled together grabbing a quick smoke, I pulled open a broken screen door and reported in my best military manner. I handed my orders to the large, weather-worn, middle-aged first sergeant sitting so far back in his chair, another inch would have him toppling over. He had barely glanced at them when he spit out his cigar and bellowed, "What shit for brains sent you here? The last thing I need is another 76Y20. I have supply specialists up to here," he said placing his hand at the apex of his balding head. I thought, "Oh no, here we go again."

"What is your secondary MOS?" he asked before I had a chance to respond.

"Secondary MOS? You mean I have more than one?" I said, hoping humor might set a different tone from, "What shit-for-brains sent you here?"

He let out a loud burst of HA, (short for ha-ha) briefly smiled, and then made a short grunting sound while putting his cigar back between his teeth.

My records clearly indicated I was more than qualified as an 11B10, the letter and numerical equivalent of "bang, bang, you're dead." With eight weeks of basic infantry training, eight more of advanced infantry training, and eight weeks of infantry OCS, I was more qualified for the infantry than ninety plus percent of all the soldiers in Vietnam. A few seconds later, he put me at ease with what I was now seeing as a pattern in the military job market, "So you're a college boy."

I was beginning to appreciate my diploma more and more while, at the same time, feeling a little guilty that the more education I had, the better my chances of survival. I wondered how many drafted soldiers with master's degrees were beating the bush for the Fourth Infantry.

Sergeant Max Dole, according to the black letters on his OD-green nametag, put his hand to his forehead and began to massage the wrinkles that apparently formed when he went into concentrated thought. His face lit up as he realized he had a job opening. A job for which he hoped I was the perfect candidate. He removed his calloused fingers from his face and asked, "Specialist Haines, do you have a military driver's license?"

"No, Sergeant, I don't."

"Have you ever driven a jeep?"

"No, Sergeant, I haven't."

He switched the topic to mechanics. "How about engines? Know anything relating to them?" he asked.

A quick look at my mechanical test results would have answered that question. My scores were somewhere between imbecile and moron. "Sorry, Sergeant."

He leaned back in his duct-tape covered chair and chewed on his cigar. "Son, you're not making this process easy," he said as he locked his fingers behind his head. He paused and asked, "OK, one more question. Where do you put gas in a jeep?"

I hit the imaginary buzzer in my head and answered like a confident and proud game show contestant going for the jackpot. "Now, that I know," I said, in a voice full of excitement. "There's a hole on the side of the jeep just to the left and forward of the driver's seat."

"Bingo!" he exclaimed, "Congratulations, you're the CO's new driver. You start tomorrow."

Sergeant Dole then introduced himself, said to call him Top, and welcomed me to the Braves of the Fighting Fourth.

I was stunned as I had just traded my #2 pencil for an ignition key.

Ho Chi's Inferno

Because God has given a choice to man
There must be a place to send the damned
There is a place and it's eternal
The name of it is Ho Chi's Inferno
A sign is posted on the front entrance
Which gives to each his lasting sentence
Written for everyone like a large note
"Ye Who Enter Here Abandon All Hope"

Drawings by Henry Casselli

Drawings by Tom Haines

Bad guy with no fashion sense

Good guy with no fashion sense

"Hey, What's a Sapper?"

I made a quick trip to the motor pool to sneak a peek at my new partner and her gearbox. Copies of the repair manual, operations booklet, and a freshly typed copy of *The Do's and Don'ts of Driving One of My Vehicles* by Motor Pool Sergeant First Class M.L. Yohn were waiting for me. I had always marveled at the combustion engine—never understood it, just marveled at it. Now, in one day, I needed to understand, operate, and repair this complicated piece of machinery. I sincerely hoped my fellow Americans would understand what Tom Haines was going to cost them.

When the sun disappeared behind the tree line, I attempted to settle into my new environment. The walls, floor, and ceiling of

CHAPTER 16

my shared quarters were a mismatch of various types of wood. Sleeping quarters, constructed of one layer of plywood, left plenty of exposed two-by-four studs to hang your stuff. The furniture was sparse and basic. Everything in the room had a look of being purchased in a trailer park yard sale. I couldn't open two of my warped dresser drawers. To make the situation even more irritating, it was the top two drawers.

A siren sounded while I was trying to reorganize my new home. A SPC-4 I hadn't yet met appeared at my door and directed me to grab my gear and head for the compound. Everything was still in its unpacked state, which made this an easy task. I slung the green heap over my shoulder, snatched my poncho from a wooden peg near the door, and went in search of the compound.

The sky was a deep, dark gray. Thirty of us stood checking equipment, fidgeting with M16s, and asking the closest person if he knew what was going on. Our curiosities would soon be satisfied.

An officer who was traveling at double-time, his poncho whipping in the wind as he walked, brought the confused mass to attention. We didn't seem to have it together as we did during our stateside training. Maybe it was because we didn't know each other or because of our preoccupation regarding our mystery mission, but we sure looked like a third-world army at that moment.

"Listen up, gentlemen. We have reason to believe an unknown number of Viet Cong sappers have slipped through the barbed wire at the southwest perimeter of the base camp. Our job is to find them," said the officer holding a clipboard with flapping yellow papers.

"What the hell is a sapper?" whispered the guy next to me.

Not wanting to get into trouble on my first day, as well as not knowing the answer, I kept my eyes to the front, my ears open, and my mouth shut. I was glad I wasn't the only cherry if we were to see action. Then again—

"A sapper is a little guy in black pajamas with satchel charges looking to blow something up," whispered a voice from behind me.

Now I had a question: "What the hell is a satchel charge?" Sappers? Satchel charges? Those words sounded vaguely familiar. I wondered how much more—what I thought was useless information—I may have missed while nodding off during those endless months of training.

There was no time for questions or answers as we were quickly marched out to our defensive/offensive position.

Jesus, Mary, and Joseph—was Tim a son-of-bitch, or was the war everywhere as I'd heard? No front lines, no secure areas, no neutral zones. The dark sky grew ominous as substantial rain clouds continued to move in. The sky was ink-black when we arrived at an enormous, open field. The officers directed us to spread out and hold our position until ordered otherwise. One of them, wearing a full, low-hanging belt and no poncho looked like he was directing traffic, arm up above his head, forearm rocking back and forth. Not having any TV, beer, or soft, round-eyed beauty waiting back at my hooch, I had no problem with that command. Soon the order came in another one of those loud whispers—"Move out!"

I looked to my left and then to my right and saw a line of soldiers at the ready for fifty yards in either direction. We looked like the line of a football team, except that our helmets didn't have face guards. My heart was pounding hard enough for me to be aware of each and every beat. I could feel my shirt move. I began to walk to match those beats.

Then the sky lit up like a Chinese New Year. I started to look skyward when I felt something graze the side of my helmet. *Holy shit, was the end of my tour over on my first day in Nam? Would my parents get a letter explaining the reason my personal belongings, still packed neat and tight, were in that condition because I took one for Uncle Sam before I even got a chance to unpack?* I glanced down and let out the remainder of the air I was holding in and saw what clipped the edge of my helmet. It was the canister shell from a flare that had turned the sky a bright yellowish-white just seconds earlier.

The canister was to my left and behind me, promptly causing me to register another observation. Looking down the field in both directions, I noticed I was the only human in sight. I slowly peered over my backpack. My blood rushed, and my heart picked up a few extra beats. Pulling in another lung full of air I froze like a statue in a park.

The others were still in a straight line, a couple dozen steps behind me. Walking at heartbeat speed was, without question, a mistake. I prayed that those behind me could tell the difference between black pajamas and olive drab fatigues. Above all, I hoped that the other new guy was way down at the other end of the line.

When everyone caught up, I let out the breath I had been holding for a little longer than forever and started forward again at a much slower pace. I wasn't the only one thinking football analogies. "Hey, OJ, do you always go for the goal line with your blockers behind you?" whispered the guy next to me. I was too embarrassed to answer.

No sappers, and a hundred yards later, our new orders came at the same time as raindrops the size of dimes began to pelt us. While we trudged down a dark and muddy road, it became more and more unambiguous that I was not going to enjoy this war. We reached a point where the scenery looked identical in all directions. "All right, soldiers, make yourselves as comfortable as possible on your current hard spot—because this is where we are going to spend the night," announced the lieutenant.

He selected a half dozen for the first round of guard and told the rest of us to get some sleep. No tent, no prepared campsite, no nothing. All we had was Mother Nature, and she was pissed. I pulled my poncho tight around my helmet and lay down in a ditch on the right side of the road so that the water flowed around the poncho leaving only my boots vulnerable to the rushing water. At that moment, my shitty little room back at headquarters seemed like the presidential suite at a grand hotel on a Caribbean Island. Four hours and no VC later, we gathered our muddy belongings and headed back to HQ.

Vietnam—thanks for the invite.

Which Way to An Khe?

2 P6776 was now my responsibility: keep her running, keep her clean, and keep her ready. I slid onto the worn seat of the two-year-old Ford M-151 quarter-ton, slipped the key into the ignition, and eased the gearshift into reverse. The jeep jerked forward, and the engine shut off. A repetition of the procedure produced the same results. Sergeant Yohn, who was closely watching the proceedings from a short distance away, threw down his rag while I ground the gears a third time. Finally, I exited the motor pool in a rapid jerking motion. I couldn't understand his muffled mumblings as they slurred out past his overly chewed cigar, but I had a pretty good idea as to his choice of words.

SNAFU

The captain was waiting for me when I arrived at HQ at the ordered time. I saluted and introduced myself. He was pressed and perfect in his attire. The sleeves of his freshly ironed field shirt were meticulously rolled up past his elbows. One needed sunglasses to look at his boots. I guessed he was thirty-something and Hispanic.

"Pleased to meet you, Specialist Haines. I'm Captain Martinez, and I'm in a real hurry," he said so fast that it was unnecessary for him to add that he was in a hurry. He jumped in, looked at his watch, and said, "Forty-Third Signal Battalion and get me there quick."

"Sorry, sir, I'm new in country, and I don't know where the Forty-Third whatever is wherever."

He took in a deep breath, sighed, shook his head, and said, "You have twenty-four hours to know this camp as if you had built it. You comprende, soldier?" I nodded, muttered "Yes, sir," and started the engine.

We traveled three feet before lurching to a halt and stalling. I quickly started the engine again and reached down to adjust the clutch pedal as if it were at fault. Our new journey took us twenty feet. All right, progress.

"What shit for brains assigned you to me?" he demanded, knowing good and well he was going to have a chat with Top before the day was out. I was beginning to think shit for brains was a regular army description.

"Well, you see, what happened was—" I started to say before he interrupted.

"Are you as new to driving as you are to Vietnam?" He smiled with a smirk, sat back against the worn canvas of the passenger seat, took another one of his deep breaths, and continued. "You have one minute to explain why you are the worst driver in the entire Republic of Vietnam."

In one minute, I took him on a journey from OCS to his front steps. He then stepped out of the jeep and in a very patient but direct manner said, "Well, Haines, you have exactly twenty-four hours to learn the base blueprint *and* how to drive." He took a third deep breath. "If you are unable to accomplish this task, I have another job waiting for you. That job, I must emphasize, you most certainly will not enjoy."

He didn't offer, and I didn't ask, what that job might be. Minutes later he was on his way with a real driver at the helm—one with a license and skills and knowledge, *oh my*. Needless to say, twenty-four hours later I felt confident, if not competent enough, for the Daytona 500. OK, the Daytona 500 at 35 mph. Thank God I was assigned the only stick shift in drivers ed while in high school.

After a day of gear-grinding practice, I became an official wheel jockey and had my first passenger. It seemed the CO had a sense of humor. Leaning against my jeep was a first lieutenant who had been in Vietnam for 364 days. The reason he was using my jeep for support would have been obvious to a blind man.

He was going home the next day and wanted to say goodbye to the entire Fourth Infantry. His knees buckled as he pushed up and off the hood and landed in a crumpled heap in the dust. He mumbled a few unintelligible half-sentences as he struggled to a vertical position. With his hands once again attached to the hood of my jeep, he drunkenly staggered to the passenger door. Once in 2P6776, he grabbed hold of the dash with both hands, leaned over to me, and slurred in the foulest Jack Daniels breath possible, "Move out, *scholdier*."

Oblivious to my still somewhat inept driving, he directed me past group after group of soldiers, as he informed them of his shortness. Most of the time he simply repeated the universally understood word for the countdown of weeks, days, or hours left in country: "Ssshoooort." He spotted a group of strangers and hollered for me to pull over. Like an obedient idiot, I did.

"Hey, hey, hey, you guys, do you knoooow how sh—short I am, am at this very movement—moment?" he asked in an almost inaudible slur. They all looked at him apprehensively and answered, "No, sir," in unison.

"I'm shoooo short I could butt—butt slam a beetle," he said while wiping foam from the corners of his mouth. Everyone gave him a fake laugh and wandered off.

A few seconds later he managed to act—and I mean act—sober, just long enough to allow a major and his SPC-4 driver to pass us in their jeep.

Five minutes into our journey he made the mistake of telling two passing MPs how short he was and waving to them with just one of his fingers. I saw my new military career flash before my eyes. As the MPs began to make a midroad turn, the lieutenant switched into his leadership role and directed me through a maze of lefts and rights that were, in fact, astonishing considering his condition. We lost the MPs. I wasted no time dumping Lieutenant Lush off at headquarters and doing a quick clean up before picking up the captain.

Captain Martinez, arms loaded down with paperwork, maneuvered his way into the passenger seat in one fluid motion, never taking his eyes off the report he was reading. I learned a lot about him in my first week as his driver. He was a career officer who knew his job well and executed his responsibilities in the proper military manner. His five-foot-nine-inch frame was solid and well conditioned due to a strenuous workout regimen. Although he seldom smiled, he had a neighborly friendliness and was an easy conversationalist. No one seemed to know much regarding his personal life. He came across as one whose personal life and military life was one and the same—he didn't offer personal details, and I didn't ask.

For the next three weeks, I crisscrossed Camp Enari running errands and transporting Captain Martinez to his appointed local destinations. At last, twenty-two days after arriving in country, I was going to see something other than this oversized dust bowl, or on rainy days, oversized mud pit. It was a sunny June Tuesday, and the CO, the major, and the first sergeant had a briefing to attend in Camp Radcliff at the outskirts of An Khe, forty miles southeast of Pleiku. Arriving at the motor pool a little early, I was greeted with two—not one—but two flat tires.

I began the changing process swiftly and, to my surprise, adroitly. But I wasn't fast enough.

"HAINES, phone's for you," shouted Yohn.

"Yeah, Haines here, talk fast, I'm changing a couple of flats," I said, talking before the mouthpiece even reached my face.

"Haines. Hines. Your passengers are ready and impatient," said Pete Hines from the COs office.

"Tell them I need all four tires to get them to their briefing. They have to be patient; they don't have a choice. Bye."

Three minutes passed. "HAINES, phone's for you again."

"Yo, talk fast," I said.

"Haines. Hines. Now!" said Pete, who then hung up without waiting for a response.

At this point, I was nearly done. All I needed to do was tighten the lug nuts. The lug nut wrench, however, was nowhere to be found. I did the best I could with a small pair of pliers and made my way to headquarters to pick up three more loose nuts. OK, that's corny, but bad humor is better than no humor. It's a common thread that held our sanity together.

Within seconds, everyone was in place, and we were on our way to An Khe.

The countryside was much less hectic. If asked to describe the Central Highlands of Vietnam in twenty-five words or less, I would use just two words: simple and beautiful. There were hints of modern civilization, but for the most part, the people and their homes, factories, farms, and towns were quaint and primitive. The architecture showed a combination of Chinese, French, and now, American influences. Structures made with thatched bamboo, tin, plywood, stucco, and even Canada Dry Ginger Ale cans appeared scattered across the landscape in hodge-podge fashion.

The most eye-catching structures were the brightly colored, ornate, tiled-roof Buddhist Temples. The only thing that kept them from being postcard, picture perfect was the triple layer of barbed wire fences surrounding them.

A mile into the trip, I began to feel uneasy regarding the lug nut tightening decision. Leaning out of the opening where a door would normally be, I visually checked the lugs as they spun in a blur. I had done this four or five times before anyone inquired relating to this strange ritual.

"What in the hell are you doing?" Captain Martinez asked in a somewhat irritated manner.

"Well, you know those two flat tires I had this morning? Well, after I fixed them, I couldn't find the lug nut wrench, so I ahhh…you know, had to do something, so I… you know, used what I had available at the time…my fingers and a pair of pliers."

"YOU WHAT!" shouted Captain Martinez, "Pull over. Right over there. Pull over. Which tires were flat?"

"Front left and back right," I said, trying not to say anything more that could get me in deeper shit.

We each shared six lugs and gave it everything we had. The sounds of cussing and grunts surrounded the jeep. Once back on the road we took turns leaning out of the open doorway checking our finger work.

A short time later, our concern for our immediate safety switched tracks, from loose lug nuts to the Mang Yang Pass, an infamous landmark twenty miles west of An Khe. I knew straight away we had entered this frightening piece of real estate when we hit the first curve. All aboard locked and loaded their weapons at the same time. The sound of steel echoed in the still air.

The pass was a narrow winding section of Route 19 that snaked through a heavily Agent Oranged, previously green, forest. The sights that appeared at each turn were mesmerizing. It was an atmosphere of total death. Dead trees, dead underbrush, and dead vehicles bleeding rust dotted the brown landscape throughout the pass. Even the air was filled with death. It was very still and had a stench of decay as thick as the history of the pass itself.

A guy in the motor pool told me the French Mobile Group 100 was annihilated there fifteen years earlier to the month. He said at the beginning of a five-day battle, they started with 222 men and had just eighty-four remaining by the end of the fifth day. This battle led the French to end the war with the Viet Minh sometime in July of 1954.

We arrived ten minutes ahead of schedule. The first image to appear was the emblem of the "First Air Cav," the symbol for the First Cavalry Division, painted on the side of Hon Kong Mountain. It was impressive.

I pulled 2P6776 into a parking space sectioned off with chain and let out a sigh of relief. The officers, with big military decisions weighing on their minds, headed straight to the war room; I headed straight to my tires. One glance told me I had maybe a few miles left on the remaining lugs. I tightened them with my fingers and went in search of a wrench, a wench, and an ice-cold brew. Yeah, right. I shortened the list to a wrench and went hunting.

"..."

We gotta get out of this place
If it's the last thing we ever do ...
If it's the last thing we ever ...
If it's the last thing we ...
If it's the last thing ...
If it's the last ...
If it's the ...
If it's ...
If ...

We Gotta Get Out of This Place, if It's the Last Thing We Ever Do

My jeep and I were getting along well. She promised to perform fighting fit as long as I didn't grind her gears. 2P6776 wasn't a fitting name for her, so I christened her with a new moniker.

As a form of morale boosting, the army allowed its drivers to paint nicknames or messages on their vehicles. The highways and byways of Vietnam were by and large two-lane blacktops or one-lane mud paths. I took note of names like Eve of Destruction, Death Machine, and Hellraiser painted bright and bold on the sides or fronts of all types of vehicles.

I found a chewed-up pencil and began to make a list of profound statements. "Eat Shit and Die You Scum Sucking Dogs" was a little long. "Fuck Ho Chi Minh in the Butt" was somewhat crude. After countless rejections, I decided to settle on six letters, that I neatly stenciled in white spray paint on the metal frame of her windshield: Be Nice.

Less than two months had passed since I arrived in the land of devastation, and I was already starting to sprout dove wings. It seemed my fence-riding days were over. Chicken hawk was no longer a part of my resume. I was feeling new emotions, asking questions concerning the war, taking a stand, and feeling good about my recently discovered convictions.

The years of apathy, ignorance, and confusion regarding the Vietnam "conflict" and our involvement in it were quickly changing. The apathy was gone, the ignorance was abating daily, but the confusion was intact and possibly growing. Confusion was a disease running rampant throughout the armed services. Many didn't even try to deal with it. They just did the jobs asked or demanded of them and counted off the days until they could go home. Even though many questioned our reasons for being here, the vast majority were proud to serve their country, confused or not.

A few, to a small degree, myself included, began to acquire a limited knowledge of what was going on behind the scenes regarding the politics of the war. While on a trip to Da Nang, I was enlightened to the small fortune amassed by Madame Nhu, the "Dragon Lady." She was the wife of the chief of the South Vietnamese Secret Police, Ngo Dinh Nhu, the brother of the former President Ngo Dinh Diem. Nhu and Diem were both assassinated in November 1963. Madam Nhu had acquired her riches through bribes and shares in corrupt trade in the early sixties. Then there were the stories of our backing of the idiot du jour.

I had lived in my shared space for only a few weeks before I moved across the road into a room I shared with myself. These new quarters were even smaller than those in my previous hooch. Turnaround space was almost nonexistent.

After dropping my duffel bag in the middle of the floor, I did a 360-degree inspection. The bed had a double layer of mosquito netting draped all the way around it, indicating that the last guy had a big rat problem or at least a big fear of them.

"What a shit hole," I announced to myself. I continued my inspection: patched ceiling, rusted locker, moldy walls. The visual image had an accompanying smell. It defied identity, but I think the mold on the walls had something to do with it. "Geez, unpacking or lunch? OK, lunch it is," I said, continuing my unspoken conversation with myself.

I stuck my head into the attached space and pointed to my open mouth. Rosco, looking up from his letter writing, responded with, "I'll second that." He rolled the manuscript he was writing, stuck it in a helmet hanging on the wall, and grabbed his cap off the next hook.

Robert "Rosco" Creech was a SPC-4 who ran the arms room. He was twenty-four years old, six feet even, and one step away from being described as husky. He kept his reddish orange hair as long as the army would permit and brushed it out of the path of his vision in an endless ongoing ritual.

We were both assigned to the same three-hour detail the morning we had met a few days earlier. A sharp mind, a quick wit, and a wide smile were evident right away—my kinda guy. Twenty minutes into our detail, I discovered that he had a wife and a little girl. He was the only draftee I knew in the army who was married and had a child. It seemed strange and out of place, but it wasn't at all uncommon. By the time lunch rolled around, I knew we would become good friends.

"Writing a letter to Jessica?" I asked while adjusting my cap at the entrance to our hooch.

"No, actually I was writing to my old college roommate. I'm expanding my communication base with the real world," he said, mimicking the ceremony of cap tuning.

"Where did you go to college?" I asked just as we reached the mess hall. I was surprised the subject hadn't come up earlier.

"I spent two years at Western Carolina University as a math major," he said while pulling the screen door open.

He handed me the small, wooden handle that came off in his hand as he flung open the door. "Are you shitting me? I don't believe this. OK, let me hit you with a 'small world' question. Do you know a guy named John Lawson? He was a management major at Western Carolina, graduated in '67," I said, tossing the handle on an empty table near the door.

Rosco thought hard for a moment but came up blank. Lunch consisted of beans and franks and college days revisited.

After lunch, we picked up our mail. Rosco got one letter, while I received three. He ran the envelope under his nose, took a deep breath, and said, "Ahhhhh, Jessica." I ran both of mine under my nose, took a deep breath, coughed repeatedly, and said, "Eeeeeew, swamp-footed John Lawson. Wow, shit, getting letters from John today is eerie, for lack of a better word." I tore off the end of the first envelope, removed three sheets of stationary, and asked Rosco if he would like to meet John via his thoughts and current ramblings.

Rosco nodded in the affirmative, and I began to read aloud.

SNAFU

Well, Haines,

Got your letter today – great to hear from you! I'm a supply clerk in an MP Company, and it's one helluva job. I work 7–5, and that's it! No KP, perimeter guard or anything. I'm really thankful as hell to have it! The guy I'm replacing came over as a supply clerk, and they threw him in the field as a grunt. He had to extend a year to get out of it. So I guess we're both pretty darn lucky.

One rocket attack! Holy shit, we've had 8 so far! Scares hell out of me, too! If you remember, I'm in a place called Phuoc Vinh, 35 miles north of Saigon, division headquarters for the 1st Air Cav. They refer to this place as "rocket alley." I think my living conditions must be very similar to yours. In general, it's a shitty life, but when all is said and done, I'm glad to be here. I really did want to see what it's like. We both have good jobs, so I'm content ... for now!

The thing I really miss is 20th Century living! And girls—I mean real girls—with big tits and everything. I don't think I'll be doing any messing around while I'm here. To be blunt, these girls suck!

I go into the village of Phuoc Vinh every day—it's a dump! It's still my most enjoyable trip, as there is a cute girl (I know I'm contradicting my last paragraph) at the laundry, and she and I sit around and talk and drink Cokes!

Anyway, did you know we're going to break 200 days next week!? So far, this has really proven to be a very unique experience. Write soon! SHORT!

John

"OK Rosco, stay focused; here's his more recent letter. This one he wrote just three days ago," I said as I unfolded three more sheets of crumpled stationery.

Well Haines,

Got your second letter yesterday. You should have gotten my just one by now. Sounds as though they are working the hell out of you! I'm not really surprised that you got lost!!!

I'll bet your Mom will be proud that you volunteered to be an "altar boy," or is that now "altar man," at Mass in the Mess or was it Mass in the Marsh? You did say your boots were completely covered in mud, so I'll assume Mass in the Marsh. Did you remember all your Latin lines, or did you just mumble it?

Hey, remember Joe Sanders, the guy who worked for First Sergeant Rivers at Benning? Got the word yesterday that he was killed when some of our guys fragged (grenaded) him by mistake in a tent thinking that he was the CO. Hearing shit like that makes me sick. He was a graduate of some Ivy League law school—real smart guy.

Speaking of, remember the guy that killed Scharp? All they did was bust him to SPC-4 and fined him. He's working in Bien Hoa. I was told that by Smith last time I was down there. They should have shot the bastard.

I can't remember if I mentioned the racial trouble we're having here, but it's getting worse. Since we're an MP company, we're probably more involved with that kind of stuff than a regular company, as we get involved in every company's problems, black and white. Many of the blacks over here seem real militant, and when you combine that with drugs, LOOK OUT!! We have had only two blacks in our company, and they both wound up going to LBJ. But all the other blacks I've come in contact with are really good guys. One of them is trying to teach me to dap. Haven't gotten it right yet.

On a lighter note, things are going really well. Every time that I see those grunts returning from the field, I'm thankful that I got assigned here. When I arrived, Hamburger Hill was happening, and I almost wound up getting sent there. I later found out that a lot of the new guys who did get sent there lasted only a matter of days. I got to go to Saigon the other day, and there must have been nine million motorbikes, none of which ran without smoking like hell and making lots of noise.

SNAFU

*Well Haines, have you been over here long enough to make
any sense of this stupid mess? Before I got here, I was all in favor
of our involvement in the war. Remember the old "our Country,
right or wrong, but above all, our Country" bit at OCS? I have
since thrown all that junk out the window, and now I'm cynical,
untrusting, and suspicious of any and all politicians. I still
haven't figured out who is benefiting from this war, but it sure as
hell isn't the average soldier stuck over here.*

*Had some fun the other night. I got two other guys to help me in
a prank. I work for a guy that everyone calls "Sgt. Rolling Rock"
because he's always drinking Rolling Rock Beer. The other night, he
was drunk, and he went to the small two-hole outhouse. As soon as
he was in there a minute, we nailed the door shut and proceeded
to rock the thing back and forth until it turned over. Took the poor
guy ten minutes to get out!! He swore that it was me, even though it
was dark, and he was drunk, but I never "fessed up."*

Gotta go! Be bad & remember FTA.

John

"So," I said, "Rosco, this is John. John, this is Rosco."

"Pleased to meet you, John," said Rosco as he extended his open hand to the air
and began to pump.

"So are you going back to Western Carolina to finish up when you get out of here?"

"I'm going back to school, but I'm going to grace the great state of Georgia with
my presence. How about you?"

"Yeah, I'm going back to school, but I don't know where yet. I have to find a school
that starts their semester on or around November 15th," I said with a sigh.

"Good luck with that one, but don't get your hopes up. I'm guessing there are …
ohhhh … I don't know … maybe … ahhh … NONE," he said somewhat sarcastically.

"Hey, I got a school for you to check out, though. It's in Greenville, North Carolina,
called East Carolina University, great party school and very hot coeds, but they also
have some serious academic creds. The school puts out the best teachers in the
state." Rosco continued.

"Holy shit, de-ja-vu. Are you sure you don't know John Lawson? That's the same
school he suggested. Man, all this is just too bizarre. OK … East Carolina … I'll check
it out," I said as I downed the last of the grape bug juice that was beginning to stain
the inside of my glass.

My final correspondence was from a guy by the name of Paul Frank. Here's his latest words on military stationery.

Skinner,

I don't think I told you this story about my induction physical in LA, but there were these inductees that were in handcuffs, escorted by two LA sheriffs. Thru out that day after taking the physical and the oath, two MPs took over from the two sheriffs. I was told that they were gang members. I guess the judge said ten years in the lockup or two years in the army. Anyway, I'm exiting the plane and who is one of the first people I saw? That's right, one of the gang members from the physical. I recognized him because he had a scar that started from the top of his head diagonally down his face to the bottom of his chin. Why do they ask us at our physical if we have an arrest record? Hmmm. More stories later. Stay safe.

Paul

"Damn, can you imagine someone taking two years in the army, then going to Vietnam and ending up dead? That would be like getting the death penalty for selling a couple bags of dope. "Shit," Rosco said while shaking his head. We headed out and saw a guy trying to put a handle back on the door.

The detail Rosco and I were assigned, the morning I painted the Be Nice message on my jeep, was to transport some odds and ends for the CO to An Khe. The June sky was a vivid, bright blue with soft, white clouds strung out like sculptured marshmallows all along the horizon. The air was warm and breezy.

Rosco, sporting a brand-new flak jacket and a freshly oiled M16, swung into the passenger seat. His sleeves were rolled up high and tight, exposing hundreds, maybe even thousands, of freckles. He looked at me with his ever-present broad grin and said, "We're not there yet?"

Driving through Pleiku was always visually entertaining. We passed soggy green fields dotted with oxen-drawn plows and farmers wearing conical hats and black pajamas. We passed a woman with an infant strapped to her back and balancing a large bundle of rice on her head. Just ahead of her was a man sitting on the side of the road trying to fix a bike that any American kid would have discarded many miles of use earlier. Continuing down the poignant string of humanity were three men dressed in bright orange, silk robes walking past a tin shack where women and children were selling film, fruit, fish, black-market cigarettes, and poncho liners. Imagine you could see the stench in the air.

At the outskirts of Pleiku, I became fixated on a very overloaded bus. It was teeming, inside and out, with people, luggage, chickens in small bamboo cages, and personal items too numerous to list. I thought, "There's no way this 1950s heap of metal is going to make it to its destination."

While I was bus-gazing, Rosco was rearranging the back seat. As he shifted items from point A to point B, he inadvertently pointed his M16 inches from my head. When I turned to say something, I found myself looking down the barrel of his weapon. Whipping my head back around to the left, I flung sunglasses from my face in a straight line to an out-of-round telephone pole. It was the demise of my third pair of glasses since I arrived in country, each experiencing a different and unusual termination.

"Oops. Shit, sorry about that," Rosco said with a somewhat nonchalant attitude, "but I'm digging back here for my package … ah, here it is."

"Sorry about that? Damn, I gotta buy—make that, you gotta buy me another pair of sunglasses," I said.

The back of my jeep was in total disarray. Rosco draped over the passenger seat, knees wedged in at the base of the faded canvas, pulled a long, flat box from the bottom of the disheveled heap.

"What is that? Is it yours?" I asked.

"Yep, and in five or ten minutes, you and I are going for a little trip back to America. Sooooo as of this moment, no more questions."

"Huh, what are—" I started to ask, before stopping myself, determined not to press the issue. I could, with ease, contain curiosity for five to ten minutes.

Rosco tried, without success, to return the back seat to a semblance of its former order. He reviewed his final assemblage, snatched a piece of paper from its wedged location between two ammo boxes, and returned to the position of "shotgun." He began to read what he held. The fact was, he read whatever he could get in his hands. This latest acquisition, however, seemed to be entertaining him more than most.

"Bizarre, man. This is totally freakin' bizarre. Check this out. Do you know where they came up with the name Enari for the trash heap we live in?" he asked.

"It was the name of some famous general in the Spanish-American War who died of dysentery—hell, I don't know. Enlighten me," I responded.

"Check this out, check this out," Rosco began. "When this guy, Major General Arthur Collins, our division commander, was moving the fourth to Vietnam, he told a Colonel Jud Miller to name the new base camp after the first man killed by hostile fire after Miller got to Vietnam. On September 3, 1966, PFC Albert Collins was killed in action. Miller, knowing that General Collins wouldn't want it perceived that the base was named after him, suggested to the general that they name the camp after the first officer killed in Vietnam. On November 5, 1966, Lieutenant Richard Collins was killed in action. Can you believe this shit? So anyway, then they decided to name the camp after the first posthumous recipient of the Silver Star. On December 2, 1966, Lieutenant Mark N. Collins—"

Rosco paused, took a deep breath, and started to laugh. "No, I'm just kidding about the last guy. The guy that got the Silver posthumously was Mark N. Enari. He died from wounds received while fighting on Operation Paul Revere IV. Is this story not bizarre?"

"Yeah, but they could have saved themselves a lot of trouble and called the camp … what was that first guy's name?" I asked.

"Albert Collins," Rosco answered.

"Camp Albert. Works for me, and you're right, definitely bizarre," I responded.

"Talk about bizarre, did you hear what happened when A Company went outside the wire last night?" Rosco said.

"Yeah, I heard some poor schmuck got eaten by a tiger. Geez, as if being concerned about the VC isn't enough, now we gotta be concerned about becoming some big cat's dinner."

"What do they tell the guy's parents? Dear Mr. and Mrs. Schmuck, last night your son had an encounter with a hungry kitty, and things kinda got out of hand and he— hey, stop the jeep! Stop the jeep—right over there," demanded Rosco while pointing to a spot just a few feet from a steep drop-off.

I pulled over, leaving the engine running and opened my mouth to speak. But before I was able to get any words out, Rosco said, "Welcome to Augusta, Georgia, home of the Masters." He jumped from the jeep with his long, brown box in tow. He sliced it open with one quick flick of his pocketknife. He threw the lid off into the dirt and removed a tarnished Ben Hogan three iron and twelve range balls with red stripes.

"Holy shit, where did you get that?"

"No time for small talk, Chi Chi. Get your ass to the first tee," he said pointing the three iron to a ridge overlooking a valley of glistening rice paddies stretching for miles below us.

"One of us should stay in the jeep," I said. "You hook, slice, and dub the first six, and then I'll come up and show you how to reach Cambodia from here."

Rosco approached the ridge, stopped to admire the view, and then pushed a tee deep into the soft ground. He placed the ball on the tee, stepped back, and took two practice swings. He removed the cigarette from his lips, put it out, flipped it over the ridge, and approached the ball. Grinding his boots into the dirt started the ritual. He then gripped the club firmly and brought it back slowly. Then he pulled the shaft down fast, caught the white ball solid, and watched it sail high and long while following through with his swing. The ball seemed to hang in the air for minutes. It was a beautiful sight.

Rosco pushed a second tee into the earth. He began to smooth the dirt around the tee. Then, all of a sudden, he pulled up quick, brought the club back fast, and down even faster. No concentration. No style. No form. Before I had a chance to finish, my thought—"boy is he gonna fuck up this shot"—a large snake flipped end over end beyond the ridge, its head almost torn from its body.

Rosco entered the jeep on the run, and off we sped, kicking up stone and dirt as we pulled back onto Highway 19.

"Oh, my God, did you see that?" Rosco asked gasping for air.

"I can't believe you did that," I said very calmly.

"What …"

"OK, I'll say it louder; I can't believe you hit that snake with a three iron—when it clearly called for a pitching wedge," I interrupted, almost not able to finish without laughing.

Rosco joined in with a little nervous laughter of his own and then lit another cigarette. We started to joke concerning how the VC were going to try and disarm our golf ball when they found it. Our humorous banter was interrupted by two low flying planes dropping a mile-long whitish gray fog over the jungle to our right.

"Is that what I think it is?" I said as I stretched my neck for a better view.

"Keep it coming guys; a little annihilation of vegetation to keep our grunts and more from taking an early trip home," Rosco exclaimed while cupping his hands and shouting to the sky as if the pilots would hear him.

"What's with the sea of white? I thought that stuff was supposed to be orange and—" I said as Rosco interrupted my question.

"I think it's called Operation Ranch-hand, or something like that. The spray isn't orange, but the barrels it comes in have an orange stripe around its center. Someday we'll have to write a letter to the company that makes that stuff and thank them for all the lives they have saved."

"You know who I feel sorry for?" I asked.

"Who, Charlie, for having to find another way to hide?"

"No, I feel sorry for the trees," I said as I turned my attention back to the road.[4]

We dropped off our cargo at Camp Radcliff and prepared for our return trip. While refueling, we heard a rumor that all vehicles returning to Pleiku were going to travel in a convoy. Part two of the rumor was disturbing. It seemed the convoy was on a hit list to be ambushed. The word was that some captured Viet Cong, fearful for their lives, had spewed forth information without the usually translated interrogation. Every few minutes we heard the same story with slight variations. Rosco and I weren't real thrilled to hear that our super-great day was perhaps to become the worst day of our young lives.

"Shit, there is no way I'm going to become a target on purpose," I said to Rosco.

"You know what I heard? I heard that drivers have the second or third-highest fatality rate in the Central Highlands," Rosco added.

"Screw becoming a statistic. C'mon, think, think. There must be something that we can do."

We debated solutions. Number one: sabotage the jeep. No, we weren't competent enough to pull that off. Number two, feign illness. Scratch that—the last time I did that they put me in the infirmary for three days. Number three: jump convoy. Yes, that was the obvious answer, especially since we had very little time to be creative. It would be simple, easy, and result in minimal disciplinary action—we hoped.

The plan was simple: when they wave us over to tell us to get in the convoy, we act as if they asked us if we wanted to join the convoy. We approached the slowly forming line at the edge of the camp where two sergeants waved us over. We stopped.

"Destination," demanded the sergeant with a long, brown clipboard.

"Pleiku," we responded in unison, right away realizing solution number four, give a wrong destination.

Too late; we were told to fall in behind a deuce-and-a-half with a bad exhaust. As the truck with a billowing smoke cloud puffing from its rear got everyone's attention, we made our move. Without hesitation, I changed gears, kicked dust, and zoomed past some green and brown targets idling at the ready. We got to the front of the line and saw two MPs with short, brown clipboards. They were talking to a captain, toting his own clipboard, and comparing notes with the MPs. This was our chance. We glided by unnoticed until I changed gears and ground metal for the first time in days. They all looked over and waved their clipboards at us and shouted words we couldn't understand.

"Shit, I can't believe we just did that. Should we turn around?" I asked Rosco, hoping he would say, *"Hell no, don't even think about it."*

"Hell no, don't even think about it," responded Rosco.

We didn't look back until we were clearly out of sight. If there was ever a time I thought I was in a FIDO (fuck it, drive on) situation, this was it. Once we were confident that no one was after us, we slowed down to reinstate the art of scenery appreciation.

The serenity didn't last long, however, because we kept seeing imaginary snipers behind every tree and Devil's Teeth (barbs tossed across the road) at every turn. I pressed the accelerator to the floor. Be Nice was now traveling faster than she'd ever traveled since coming off the assembly line.

The idea of jumping convoy seemed dumber and dumber as we traveled faster and faster. The breathtaking scenery we enjoyed on the trip up was a blur on our return trip. The quiet we enjoyed traveling to An Khe was replaced by a thousand and one noises on the way back. There were fighter planes overhead, helicopters at work in the distance, internal hemorrhaging of my jeep, and thunder from deep in the mountains. Our perfect white clouds turned a dark, sinister shade of gray. I clutched the steering wheel with both hands and pressed the accelerator down another half inch and got her up to her limit of 57 miles per hour. Damn governor.

All kinds of sounds and movement invaded our senses.

"What was that under the bridge?"

"Did you see what was behind that rusted tanker?"

"What the hell was that sound?"

The cracking thunder appeared closer. Our only recourse was to fight sound with sound. Rosco dug around in my tape box until he found The Animals. He put the tape in the deck, ran it to—I swear to God—"We've Gotta Get Out of This Place," and turned up the volume. The clouds got darker, the thunder louder, and the scenery more blurred.

"Rosco, did you just hear and feel something," I said in a panic.

"All I can hear is your imagination running wild. Pay attention to the road and listen to the music." Rosco said. Then he joined The Animals, "We gotta get out of this place, if it's the last thing we ever do."

Rosco winced as he became aware of a burn from an ever-present cigarette wedged between the lower joints of the first two fingers of his left hand. He flipped the nub out of the jeep and watched the sparks dance on the wet, pitch-black pavement. Finally, Pleiku appeared in the distance. However great it was to be home, we weren't home free. When we pulled up to the gate, two MPs with those damn brown clipboards were waiting for us. Questions and answers flew back and forth. Our lies were well collaborated and well rehearsed. No holes, no exaggerations, no unnecessary details. The story must have impressed the MPs, or they didn't want to mess with the paperwork because they waved us on. Just before pulling away, one of the MPs tapped the side of Be Nice with his nightstick and asked if that was a new bullet hole in the back of the jeep.

"Bullet? We got hit by a bullet?" I thought to myself while maintaining an air of knowledge about the alleged attack.

Rosco and I glanced at each other. He leaned over in my direction and cupped his hand to whisper. "Did he say Be Nice took one in the rear?"

With a nod, a shrug, and a "yeah" we pulled away. The convoy, on the other hand, arrived hitless.

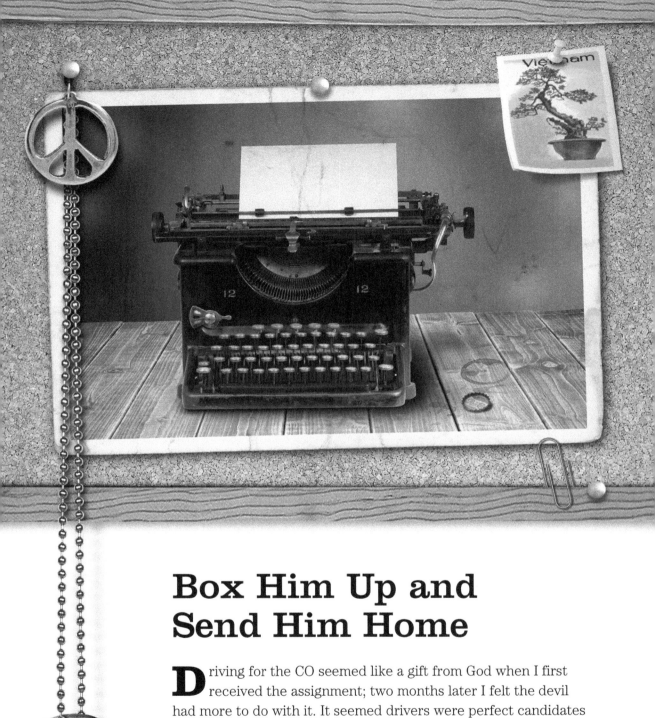

Box Him Up and Send Him Home

Driving for the CO seemed like a gift from God when I first received the assignment; two months later I felt the devil had more to do with it. It seemed drivers were perfect candidates for guard duty, reaction, and antireaction. I began to visit these little trips to hell so often I thought driving was my secondary responsibility. At the end of one long week I was beyond tired—physically numb, mentally numb, numbly numb. When the seventh day came to a close, I had pulled a twenty-four-hour guard, a reaction, an antireaction, and another twenty-four-hour guard. A scorching sun accentuated the agony of that second twenty-four-hour guard duty. We were returning at the end of the twenty-fourth hour of that guard duty back to headquarters.

The heat was so oppressive that I was sure that the thermometer hadn't seen numbers below triple digits since the sun's arrival on the horizon eight hours earlier. When describing the Congo in *Heart of Darkness*, Joseph Conrad said, "The air was warm, thick, heavy, sluggish. There was no joy in the brilliance of the sunshine." If Mr. Conrad had been in Pleiku that day and had written his observations, he would have added a few expletives to his remarks.

The open-aired deuce-and-a-half bounced along slowly, so slowly that the twelve of us didn't enjoy any breeze created by the truck's forward movement. Our green fatigues were a nasty shade of medium brown. Thick dirt rings filled every crevice on our anatomies. The geometry of these lines was broken and muddied by the hundreds of sweat beads that raced down our bodies in continuous streams. Our closeness to each other didn't help the situation. The truck came to a stop.

My shirt and my torso had become one. The air was motionless, which eliminated any hope of being cooled by my sweat. I tried my best to ignore the scratchiness in my throat, the stickiness of skin to skin, and the burn of salty sweat soaking the rash that refused to abate between my legs. My five-day-old growth of facial hair was the start of a beard that I knew was now on the short end of its existence. I was sure the first officer I came in contact with would demand its immediate removal, which would be greeted with immediate compliance, as the constant itching would be one less discomfort I would have to tolerate.

It was midafternoon when we were dropped off at headquarters. No neat footprints trailed in the dirt as I distanced myself from the truck—my boots were too heavy and legs too tired to lift my feet from the earth. I dragged my M16 behind me like a child's pull toy, obscuring designs in the dirt formed by my single, long boot print. The headband inside my helmet liner became embedded in my mud-covered skin. The weight of my steel pot seemed to double every few minutes. My neck muscles ached and throbbed at the slightest movement. I reminded myself: don't look at the ground; don't look at the sky. Glancing in the direction of the sun smacked of insanity.

I rounded the corner of the nearest building and liberated my head from the helmut prison. I flung my backpack down and leaned my M16 into one of the grooves of the corrugated tin wall that surrounded the building. It bounced from groove to groove until it hit the ground with a small kick of dust.

Dropping down, full weight next to my dust-filled weapon, I leaned against the hot tin. An OD green towel and my fatigue shirt gave me limited insulation. My brain fought over the mixed signals it received. I went into circuit overload. The toasted tin burned, but my body was too drained to push away. Tired won out over pain. My body would just have to adjust to the tin that had been baking for hours by unfiltered rays of sun. Alternating feelings of exhaustion and discomfort competed for my attention until a shadow blocked the sun's brightness.

The human shape standing over me was unrecognizable because the sun glared directly between his shoulder and right ear. "Hey, man, can you type?" the shape asked. I couldn't match the voice to familiarity any more than I could identify the form. In my numbness, I didn't realize that by answering in the affirmative, I would be volunteering for yet another detail.

A "friendly mistake" by one of our helicopter pilots killed two of our guys, one whose head was severed from the rest of his body. I was drafted to assist at the clerical end of the bagging and tagging procedure. Seconds later, I found myself sitting before an ancient Remington typewriter first used in North Africa during World War II. Upon closer inspection I changed my mind to WWI. I was in a building I had never been in prior to that moment. I broke military office protocol and shed my shirt. I sandwiched four sheets of paper between three very used pieces of purple carbon paper. At that point, "can you type" meant nothing because I had to hit the keys with a vicious blow, one at a time. The chances of my pinkie imprinting an "a" through all of the rainbow-colored copies in the vintage Remi were the same as getting a long soothing shower before the end of the day. If the shower stall were out of hot water, I would welcome the cold water. In fact, I hoped they would be out of hot water.

They assigned another "volunteer" to box up the personal effects of the still-warm bodies being processed to go back home—not the way they had hoped, not the way their parents, wives, and children had prayed, but the way fate had chosen for them. When you look at a body bag, you almost expect the person inside to start poking at the thick plastic and holler, *"Hey, I'm not dead. It's just a flesh wound. I passed out when I saw the blood."*

"Just go ahead and dump that bag into the middle of the floor," I said to the disheveled looking E-1 while pointing to a muddy, half-filled, green duffel bag. "Put all military items in that box, his personal items in that one," I said. "Then put anything we don't want to send to his next of kin in that trash can," I continued, nodding my head in the direction of each container. The "dinky dau" asshole began to giggle and talk to himself while he tossed a Bible in the trash and a Playboy magazine in the box labeled to his parents.

"Excuse me, pond scum, have you ever eaten a typewriter before?" He looked up and just stared at me. "I'm serious, you shit-for-brains dirt-bag; reverse those items."

He did as I demanded. I guess he didn't want my nasty ass all over his nasty ass. After hitting the last key, I sat back for a break. I checked on the contents of the boxes going back to America to make sure Private Dirtbag got it right. He left before I finished my paperwork. As I was checking the boxes, I saw movement out of the corner of my eye. I looked up and cried out, "Holy shit; what the hell." One of the bags was moving. I ran over to check to see if we still had a live one. I got to the bag, and it was still. After a little inspection, I spotted a string attached to the bag at the far end and immediately went in search for Private Dirtbag. He was nowhere to be seen. I changed his name to Private Asshole Dirtbag.

I then shuffled through an open drawer and fished for something to read while downing a warm Pepsi waiting for the bagging crew to show up. I came across a letter from another soldier that I assumed didn't make it into a box to his parents. It was written to his mom, dad, and little sister; it was badly smudged and not in an envelope. His handwriting, however, was painstakingly neat. It read:

Dear Mom and Dad,

Eighteen days and counting. I really appreciate the welcome home party. I've missed all of you, and I can't wait to see you and Becky and Bill and, of course, Mandy. Tell her I'm looking forward to seeing the banner she and her friends made for me. Tell her I'll keep it forever and that I expect everything to be spelled correctly, haha.

Anyway, things have been quiet lately. Thank you, Lord. Sarge says we may see action this week. But I sure hope not. I sure hate this war. I wish they would turn us all into Peace Corps workers. That way we could help these people instead of killing them. Jack, Morgan, Franklin, and I helped pull a farmer's cart out of a ditch today and repaired it for him. It sure did feel good, especially almost nailing my first dap from both Morgan and Franklin. Well, everybody give each other a hug for me, and I'll see you in three weeks.

Love, Tim

P.S. Eighteen days to clean sheets!

Without reflecting on why, I made a copy of his letter. Not in the mood to do any heavy reflecting regarding the war, I stuffed the copy in one of the oversized pockets on my fatigues. I then dropped off my chair and stuck my head in a bucket of water sitting by the door. I had no idea why it was there and, at that point, didn't care.

I looked up fast as a shadow appeared in my path. Large drops of the bucket water broke the even layer of dust on his boots. It looked to be the same shape I had encountered earlier. When he spoke, my fears were confirmed.

"Is your name Haines?" he asked. I nodded in the affirmative.

"Drop whatever you're doing and report to the CO immediately. He says he has another detail for you."

"Whatever the old man wants to be done, he can damn well do himself because I'm not interested," I said to both the messenger and myself.

He reached down and wiped the combination of dust and water from his boots. "You can damn well tell him yourself because I'm officially off duty," he responded while rotating to leave.

Grabbing my cap, the one green item I had in my possession, I stormed up to HQ. As I huffed the hundred yards to headquarters, I was consumed by just one thought—what the hell was "off duty?"

There would be no prepared speech because my brain cells were no longer capable of coherent thought. I reached the CO's door, half-heartedly tucked in my shirt-tail, pounded on the doorframe with my palm, and flung open the door. I'm not sure if I heard him say enter. At that point, I didn't give a shit. However, he received a salute in the proper military manner.

"Sir, I respectfully decline to perform, partially or completely, the detail or details to which you desire for me to perform or do whatever task you or others that you may have in mind for me to do whatever needs to be completed … what I mean is, that whatever detail that it is that needs to be done …," I stopped babbling and tried to gather my thoughts.

The captain just sat and stared at me, apparently trying to figure out how long it had been since I drove him anywhere and what the hell I was babbling. With a five-day growth on my face, it was obvious we hadn't been in each other's company in at least four days.

He broke the silence with an abrupt "OK" and dismissed me. "Thank you, sir," I responded while saluting and turning to leave. My mind tried to digest what had just occurred. OK? He said, "OK." There were no outside interfering noises. There were no choppers whirring overhead. It was very clear. He simply said, "OK," and dismissed me. Had I missed something during basic training? Could we get out of details by exhibiting arrogant behavior or babbling like idiots when dealing with our commanding officers? I think not. Something wasn't right. Curiosity replaced relief.

Removing my hand from the doorknob, I wheeled around on my heels. In as sheepish a manner as I could muster, I asked a question to which I wasn't sure I wanted to know the answer. "Sir, may I be so bold as to ask what it was I just refused to do?"

He answered without looking up from his paperwork. "Oh, nothing important. It's just that Miss America and six other beauties from other states are coming here to put on a show for the troops. You might have heard about it. One of the girls is from New York. I knew that you were from New York. She needs an escort while she's here, so I thought you might want the detail. You know, take a walk around camp, talk about home. You know silly stuff like that. But as you've already made yourself perfectly clear, you are not interest—"

He didn't finish his sentence because his capacity for compassion was stronger than his capacity for torture. I'm sure I must have looked like a puppy left gazing through a screen door as his entire human family prepared to leave for a vacation without him.

Captain Martinez put down his pen and began to grin. He leaned back in his chair and locked his fingers behind his head. When the front legs reached six inches from the floor, he said, "OK, the detail is yours, if you'll consider changing your mind. If you do change your mind, then finish what you were doing and take the rest of the day off. In fact, take tomorrow off as well and, for Christ's sake, spend part of it shaving."

I thanked him two or three or nine times and began preparations for my respite from insanity.

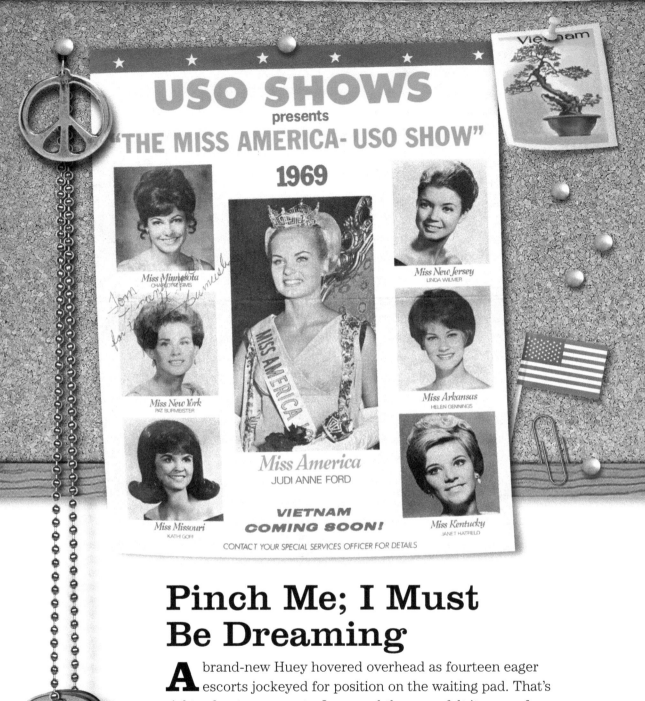

USO SHOWS
presents
"THE MISS AMERICA- USO SHOW"
1969

Miss Minnesota
CHARLOTTE SIMS

Miss New York
PAT BURMEISTER

Miss Missouri
KATHI GOFF

Miss America
JUDI ANNE FORD

MISS AMERICA

VIETNAM
COMING SOON!

CONTACT YOUR SPECIAL SERVICES OFFICER FOR DETAILS

Miss New Jersey
LINDA WILMER

Miss Arkansas
HELEN GENNINGS

Miss Kentucky
JANET HATFIELD

Pinch Me; I Must Be Dreaming

A brand-new Huey hovered overhead as fourteen eager escorts jockeyed for position on the waiting pad. That's right—fourteen escorts. I guessed the army felt it was safer and fairer to have an enlisted, low-ranking GI, like myself, and an officer, like Lieutenant Peckerhead (a nickname I silently bestowed on him that would stay within the confines of my mind) act as co-escorts. While the chopper jockeyed for a touchdown, I paced back and forth, hoping a tall, gorgeous redhead would appear from the swirling cloud of dust. Lieutenant Peckerhead had the edge on me with his officer status. If she was tall, maybe my six feet three inches, versus Lt. Pecker's five feet nine inches, might even out the odds a little.

When the red dirt settled back to earth, activity began to take place on the landing pad. I could feel my body temperature rise as seven of God's finest creations began to exit the chopper. At the same time these visions of loveliness closed the distance between the chopper and our pad, I noticed their chaperone was still taking care of details while crouching under the spinning blades of the big OD dust-kicker.

Now just a few feet away, it became apparent that there were no plans regarding introductions. No problem. I looked at my watch and noted it was 0859 hours. With only twenty-three hours, fifty-nine minutes left as their escorts, no time should be wasted.

I extended a slightly damp hand to the first female to arrive while holding onto the bill of my cap with the other. "Welcome to Pleiku and the Fourth Infantry Division. I'm Specialist E-4 Tom Haines. Which Miss State are you?" I asked, in as loud a voice as I could without actually shouting. The noise level picked up even more as a second and third chopper prepared to land.

"Excuse me, but what do you mean which mistake am I?" she responded in bewilderment with a sweet southern drawl.

"No! No!" I answered, trying to be louder than three sets of chopper blades, "Which Miss State are you?"

Her hair slapped her face. She placed her hands, one on either side of her mouth, held her hair flat against the side of her head, and squinted to the point that you couldn't see her eyes. "Ohhhh, Arkansas. And where are you from?" she said, with a smile that replaced her expression of confusion.

This time I had enough sense to keep it short: "New York."

She reached out and took hold of the arm of a beautiful redhead. "Tom, is it? I'd like you to meet Patty Burmeister, also from New York. And believe me, she is no mistake."

"Hi, Tom, I'm Pat. What do you say you, the lieutenant, and I try to get as far away from these helicopters as fast as possible," she said, trying to hold a scarf in place.

Twenty-one introductions later, we gathered suitcases, matched up girls and guys from Minnesota, New York, Missouri, New Jersey, Arkansas, Kentucky, and Illinois, and headed out. Patty was from Portsville, New York, and the lieutenant was from a town just outside of Albany.

I was two for three regarding my wishes. Patty was gorgeous and redheaded but only about five feet six inches tall. I needed to find another edge over Lieutenant Peckerhead. I discovered it as we piled into Be Nice. A wonderful, although stupid, "Funky Fourth" rule did not allow officers to drive military vehicles in war zones. I drove; Patty sat next to me while Lieutenant Peckerhead kept the luggage company in the backseat. My new edge—a driver's license. I was back in high school as a second-semester junior, with my sophomore brother in the backseat.

A dog and pony show was the first item on the agenda. I did my best to steer Patty away from embarrassing sights: the guy shaking off after using an open-air piss tube, followed by a soldier returning from the shower, removing and rewrapping his towel low on his hips, made our task a real challenge. Navigating a sea of testosterone, the tour of the base camp was becoming a parody of a silent-screen comedy. Patty turned a lot of heads. Guys walked into each other, a jeep almost ran off the road, and catcalls came from far and near.

Ten, long minutes later we arrived at headquarters. "Boy, that was fun, and definitely different than a tour of upstate New York, huh guys?" Patty said.

"Oh yeah, I can say for sure that I've never seen anyone walking down Washington Avenue in Endicott with no more than a towel wrapped low on his hips," I said.

"Well, we arrived safely at headquarters, but we can't guarantee to keep you healthy two hours from now," I added.

"Aaaaand why is that?" Patty inquired.

"Because according to my schedule, we're picking you back up in ninety minutes for an encounter with—um, drum roll, please—theeee mess hall," I said, cupping my hands around my mouth for the last three words.

Lieutenant Peckerhead, who turned out to be a really nice guy, showed up right on time. Showing up on time proved to be quite a miracle, considering my watch was ticking off minutes as if they were seconds. At least the process of wardrobe selection didn't slow us down.

Lieutenant Paul Simmons, Lieutenant Peckerhead's real name, was pressed to the max. I could see my reflection, as clear as a mirror, in his polished brass. The creases on his fatigues could cut through paper. His baby face glowed under the bill of his stiff new cap, emblazoned with a shiny, new, gold lieutenant's bar.

"Excuse me, Sir, but can I ask you a question?"

"Sure. I'm twenty-three, though I look like I'm sixteen. Isn't that what you were wondering?"

"No, actually, I thought more like fourteen."

He laughed, then promptly turned serious. "From the day they gave me this bar it's been a real problem trying to get the men to give me any respect. Looking pubescent is a major curse for me. I guess I'll appreciate it when I'm in my sixties, but right now it sucks."

We crammed a lot of conversation into five minutes, but just as he was about to tell me what he was going to do when he returned to the world, the girls arrived.

Patty's appearance was a complete sensory experience. I took her arm as she descended the stairs. She looked stunning, smelled fabulous, and felt divine. However, her clothes were another story. She wore a conservative red and white checkered sleeveless dress with a little less than zero sex appeal. It wasn't long before we found out the other six American goddesses were wearing the same dress. I guess the brass felt that all they wanted to see raised was our temperatures. We filled a small convoy of jeeps and headed to chow.

"Holy shit!" I blurted out as we rounded the corner into the mess hall. "Excuse me, sorry about my choice of words, but this is, this is—"

"Lovely," said Patty finishing my sentence for me.

I panned the room and snapped mental images to pass around later back at the hooch: table cloths, flowered centerpieces, and food I had forgotten existed.

At that very moment, a realization hit me like a dog peeing on an electric fence. These girls did not see the real Vietnam. They were shuttled around from tablecloth to tablecloth. Every face they looked into had a smile on it. I was cleaned, pressed, freshly shaved, and doused with cologne. Two days earlier, I was brown, sweaty, and smelled like a crate of broken eggs left out in the midday sun.

At that moment, I wanted to take Patty aside, hand her some C-rations, some powdered milk, and a canteen of warm water. I would then instruct her with the command, "Come with me later tonight to the base camp perimeter, where we can sit in a bunker, stare out across the barbed wire, and imagine every tree and bush moving toward us. Better yet, we'll chopper out to an isolated artillery fire base twenty miles from nowhere and listen to the alternating sounds of blasting M155s and croaking frogs. Even better, let's read Tim's last letter home." Instead, an imported form of reality had us pulling up chairs to a four-course meal from the "real world." Everything was pristine and perfect.

The food turned out to be edible but hardly worthy of the setting. If reviewed by the food editor of the Sunday edition of any stateside newspaper, our culinary delight would have received two and a half stars, or maybe three because we were being served in a war zone.

The conversation was light and friendly and free of horrible anecdotes of death and bloodshed. At one point a quiet set in. Although the silence was no more than a few seconds, it seemed to last minutes. A very attractive blonde, Miss Kentucky, broke the silence as she addressed Major Sanders, sitting at the head of the table, who I guessed wasn't looking forward to becoming a colonel. "What is it that you do, Major?" she asked. The major, the only one at the table in dress khaki, complete with a chest full of colorful ribbons, responded without hesitation. He expounded that he was in charge of X number of men, in charge of X number of thises and thats, as well as being in charge of a few of these and those. He was essentially in charge of being in charge.

After his oratory ended, silence again settled in. Patty turned to me. "What about you, Tom? What do you do?" she asked sweetly.

"Huh, who me? Why, I'm in charge of a jeep," I boasted, just before sticking a fork full of salad into my mouth.

The sounds of stifled laughter came from up and down the table. Lieutenant Simmons excused himself to clean up the iced tea coming out of his nose. I glanced over at the major and removed the fork from my mouth, checking to see if my boot was attached. A stare from Sanders and meaningless chatter monopolized the remainder of the festivities.

It soon became time to take our Cinderellas back to their "castles," so they could get plenty of rest before their afternoon rehearsals. I headed to the duty board before returning to my little "castle."

I stopped off at the latrine. It was medium dark, but clean. In about thirty seconds I had company. Mama San, the "senior" hooch maid, joined me a couple of seats down. We made for some small talk. She finished and started to leave. She got to the door and asked if there was anything I needed. I said no but followed that with, "Wait a minute—would you track down Miss New York and tell her I would like her to join me for a minute."

Mama San, looking very confused, said, "What you mean? You want me to—"

I interrupted her and said, "Never mind. I'll catch up with her later."

Mama San left with that same confused look, and I started to snicker like a little kid. I guessed her age previously as somewhere in her early seventies. I was later informed that she was forty-five. Her teeth were decayed and stained from years of chewing areca, a betel nut opiate that deadens the pain of decaying teeth. I finished and headed to the duty board.

I couldn't believe what I was reading. Then again—yes, I could. There was my name: Haines, Thomas L., E-4, guard duty, bunker 68 at 1800 hours. Showtime was at 1900 hours. I was going to miss the wet dream of a lifetime because of fucking guard duty. I was pissed.

My first thought was to take away Lieutenant Peckerhead's nickname and give it to the major in charge of the war because I was sure he had something to do with this. Instead, I concentrated on reversing my assignment to hell. A hurried plan immediately went into effect. Time was short, and obstacles needed overcoming, expeditiously.

Step one: infiltrate forbidden territory—the officers' barracks—where "The Seven American Goddesses" set up house, albeit temporary. Step two: track down a pretty redhead and plead with her to intercede with the higher ups to release me from whatever silly duty they had assigned to me because my attendance would mean a great deal to her. Step three: pray that she could pull it off.

Armed with forged papers and a pocket full of lies, step one was accomplished with ease. OK, Tom, turn up the charm for step two.

"Patty, I need a major, ahhhh, make that a large, favor."

"Sure, what's up?" she asked.

"Well, I want to see your show."

"Of course you can see the show; I'm expecting you to be there," she said, befuddled.

"Well, you see, there's a problem. I just found out I was assigned to guard duty at the same time your show takes place, and I thought that maybe if you asked the right officer, I could get out of it."

"Give me a name, and I'll see what I can do."

Damn, what I thought would be a difficult scam turned out to be a cakewalk. At 1400 hours, I was released from guard duty.

At 1900 hours, brightly colored props decorating the stage competed with a cornucopia of colorful costumes. There wasn't a sign of olive drab anywhere in front of the first row of soldiers, of which I was one. Singing, dancing, and corny jokes were the order of the day. God, how I hated to see that show come to an end.

The next morning, I wasn't able to bid a fond farewell because someone else escorted Patty to the chopper. I was unable to perform that task because—son-of-a-bitch—I was on guard duty. I looked out over a field of barbed wire and gave no thought to the war. All my thoughts were locked and loaded on the weekend pass I had just spent back in the good ole US of A.

Me: "Hey, Ed, would you take a picture of us?"

Ed: "Sure, no problem."

Me: "Do you know how to use an SLR camera?"

Ed: Absolutely. Piece of cake." ... Click.

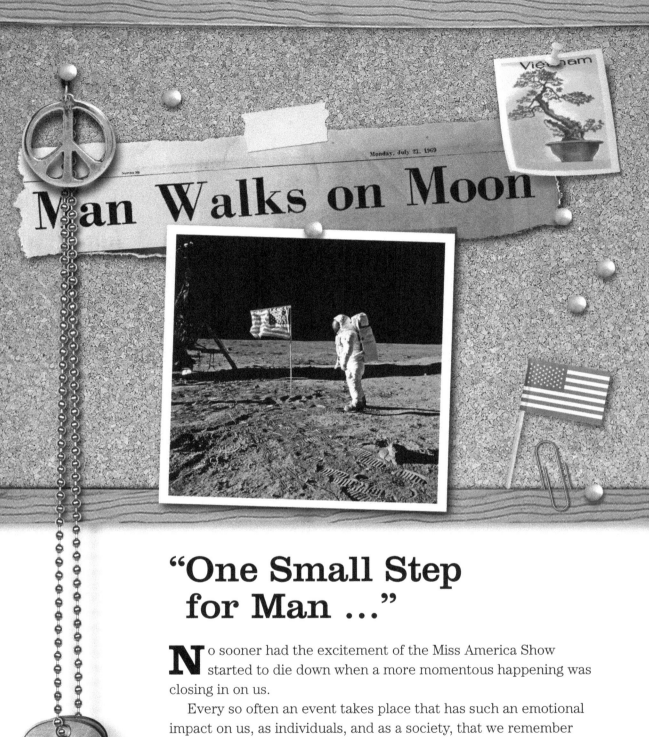

Monday, July 21, 1969

Man Walks on Moon

Vietnam

"One Small Step for Man ..."

No sooner had the excitement of the Miss America Show started to die down when a more momentous happening was closing in on us.

Every so often an event takes place that has such an emotional impact on us, as individuals, and as a society, that we remember where we were and what we were doing at that precise moment. President Kennedy's assassination was one such event. Almost anyone over ten years of age in 1963 can tell you where they were and what they were doing and probably in great detail. I was agonizing over an upcoming algebra exam in the study room of

SNAFU

Wehrle Hall at Gannon College at a table with two other guys. I was facing the door. David, the dorm doofus walked in and very calmly announced that the president had been shot. He then did an about-face and left the room.

Not until July 20, 1969, did I experience another memory-etching moment. Where were you and what were you doing when man first set foot on the moon?

For most at Camp Enari, the day started with the spacecraft already on the moon. It landed sometime around 0415 Indochina Time (ICT). Everyone was talking about the landing and the walk. The war seemed to take the day off. The most important item on everyone's agenda: find a radio and be near it at 1030. Back in the States the nation would be gathering around TV sets at 2230 EST. It was one of those moments when we were made aware of the vast time differences between the East Coast of America and the East Coast of Asia. I was feeling good about catching the walk because I didn't have guard duty, and the CO wasn't going anywhere for rather obvious reasons.

A kind of party mood was settling in. We had acquired a case of beer, some assorted junk food and, from God knows where, a bag of balloons. Everything was on schedule, and the countdown was on. With a red balloon a breath away from bursting, I noticed a human shape through the hazy, stretched latex. Squeezing the tip, I pulled the expanded bubble from my lips and greeted First Sergeant Harris.

"I'm sorry that I have to be the one to pop your bubble, but you and I are hitting the road," he said. "You have to give me a ride to somewhere I can't even pronounce," he added. I let go of the balloon and watched it fly briefly around the room, imitating my feelings at the moment. "I'm going to look for a radio. I'll meet you at HQ in ten minutes," he said, letting the door slam when he left.

Minutes before we were to leave, Sergeant Harris arrived, grinning ear to ear and sporting the largest, ugliest, most beautiful radio I'd ever seen. It weighed ten pounds and was a strange combination of black and olive drab. Some of the knobs were missing, others jerry-rigged. The radio had no space not covered by chips, cracks, scratches, and gray duct tape—but it worked. We immediately found AFN (the American Forces Network). The sound that emitted from this chunk of junk was slightly scratchy and uneven, but it was music to our ears.

The day was clear and sunny. Be Nice had just had a tune up and was purring like a kitten. Soon we were moving along nearly deserted mountain roads at a steady pace. A package from home sat in the back seat. It was full of chocolate chip cookies, crushed almost beyond recognition, but still edible. Also in the box, equally crushed, was a pair of sunglasses my mom had "carefully" packed for me. I didn't give it a second thought; after all, it saved me the trouble of breaking them myself.

As time closed in on America's moment of pride and accomplishment, Sergeant

Harris turned the radio to every conceivable angle to achieve the best reception possible. We were now in the thickest part of the mountains of the Central Highlands and not able to pick up diddly. We were climbing fast and receiving and losing the signal at every twist and turn of the road and radio. I downshifted while praying my way through a particularly sharp curve. At the end of the curve Sergeant Harris suddenly commanded, "Pull over! Pull over! Pull over! Pull over!" Dust flew, and stones spit out across the shoulder as we came to a jerking halt. "I got it! I got it!" he exclaimed while he jumped from the jeep and double-timed to the edge of the road.

I hoped he was talking about the signal and not a Ben Hogan three iron. He placed the radio firmly on his broad left shoulder, with his M16 gripped firmly in his right hand. I joined him, placing my ear just inches from the dust filled speaker. The sound was clean and sharp. It was as if the signal tower were at the top of the mountain we had so vigorously navigated.

Moments later we heard Neil Armstrong proclaim, "That's one small step for man, one giant leap for mankind." Goose bumps rose on our exposed arms as Sergeant Harris lowered the radio and looked over at me. Both of us registered the other's expressions. We didn't need words to know what we were each feeling at that moment. Refocused on the living portrait displayed a hundred yards below the ridge, we were witness to a throwback image from the Stone Age. A dozen or so Montagnard villagers were gathered outside of their thatched bamboo huts doing what they needed to survive.

Naked, malnourished children played in the Earth's dirt while silver-suited men kicked up the moon's dust while planting an American flag. A bare-breasted woman in a black wrap-around skirt was preparing to roast a rat while lab-coated assistants in Houston operated sophisticated computers directed to a destination 240,000 miles away. Two men in loincloths struggled with a broken wheel on a flimsy, makeshift bamboo cart while two of their brothers sent back high-tech video images from the super sophisticated Eagle module.

We were experiencing sensory overload—ears tuned to an amazing feat of man's ingenuity and resourcefulness, eyes fixed on a scene of man's struggle to exist, hands clutching instruments of destruction. None of it made any sense. What the hell was I doing here?

Top broke the silence. "Bullshit! What did he just say? A giant leap for mankind? More like a shitty little step, if you ask me. Redirecting our misguided energies and snuffing out this shit would be a pretty big step for mankind," he said, pointing to the scene below with his extended M16. "And then let's see if we can fucking coexist with each other with a little dignity and respect. Now that would truly be a giant fucking leap for mankind. Come on, Haines, let's get the hell out of here." If you threw out the cuss words, Top's statement on the world condition would have been considered pretty profound by most anyone's standards. I think he and Abe should get together and enjoy a waxing poetic moment.

We drove in silence for most of the remainder of the trip while I struggled to understand what we had just witnessed. The morning was over, but fortunately—or unfortunately—our dreams would continue.

APO San Francisco

For many of us, our first letters were not much more than instruments for passing information. "Dear Mom and Dad, I'm here. I'm safe. I'm stationed in Pleiku. This place sucks."

However, as time went on, letters took on different meanings. They became our only daily link to the outside world and kept loneliness from smothering us. Letters reminded everyone, and in some cases told us for the first time, how much we cared for each other. Family, friends, and lovers aided us in maintaining our hope and sanity. San Francisco, the conduit for all mail to Vietnam, was becoming everybody's second favorite city and APO (Army Post Office) everyone's favorite three letters.

Mail call was the most anticipated and anxious time of each

day. During this daily ritual, the air became supercharged with emotion. Some took their envelopes and put them in oversized fatigue pockets for private readings at a later time. Others ripped into their mail with a vengeance, devouring them as they walked, totally oblivious to obstacles that might lie in their paths. Once settled in at the end of their journey they would then reread everything, a moment's escape from our world, a world filled with hate, confusion, indifference, apathy, anxiety, fear, and a hundred other emotions that would permeate our existence, possibly for the remainder of our time on Earth.

One particularly cool rainy day, I received four pieces of mail, all dated Monday, August 18, 1969. One was a small package wrapped in brown paper and covered with scotch tape. The second was the standard blue airmail envelope with the red and blue border. The third was a large brown envelope stamped, "Do not bend or fold." The fourth was a letter from in-country. I was about to experience my most unusual mail call since arriving in Pleiku. I ripped open the small brown package with my bayonet.

After sending a dozen or so letters to Mom and Dad, we switched our method of correspondence to audiocassette. For me, tapes were easier, more fun, and I didn't need to refer to my pocket dictionary for correct spelling. During one audio communication, when I was feeling the weight of the war pushing me to the earth, I let loose with a ten-minute diatribe about "The Vietnam Conflict."

My parents received the tape on the same day they were entertaining guests at a dinner party. After the meal, they played the tape at the request of their guests. What I cradled in my palm was a ten-minute rebuff to my antiwar ramblings, courtesy of my parents' guest of honor, retired Army General Albert Wilson.

"Tom, my name is Albert Wilson, retired general of the United States Army. Your mom and dad just played a tape from you. They are a little concerned about your morale, so they asked me to say a few words. Tom, I would like for you to try and not be distracted from your mission by the sometimes confusing and sometimes misunderstood things that seem to be changing the way you perceive this awful but necessary war. If we back out of Vietnam now, our position as a world leader will be severely damaged. We are committed to Vietnam in their effort to shed themselves of communist control from the north. But we are also committed to other nations around the globe who are watching to see how reliable we regard those commitments. Give my words some thought, and you may change your mind regarding the bigger picture. I wish you luck and God speed." There were no movies on the agenda, so the general's tape would supply the evening's entertainment or maybe alter the thinking of some that listened.

With an upward snap of the wrist, I opened the large manila envelope and slid out its contents onto the worn, wooden, wobbly table in front of me. I removed the protective cover sheet and gazed in disbelief at a most incredible sight. Laid out before me was a detailed, eleven-by-seventeen-inch watercolor portrait of "The Midnight Skulker." Brian Sullivan, a SPC-4 from Massachusetts, had acquired the nickname Midnight Skulker, most often shortened to Skulker. What made Brian stand out from the rest of the military population was the smile that never left his face. Someone could tell Brian he was going to pull guard duty for six straight days, in the rain, and have to fill 3,000 sandbags, and he would need only a few seconds to find something to smile about. When it got to the point that I had heard Skulker so often I forgot his real name, I grabbed a moment and wrote a letter to Johnny Hart, who drew the comic strip *BC*. The Skulker was a character that appeared occasionally in the strip. I asked Johnny if he would sketch the Skulker for Brian. What adorned the table before me was far beyond a simple sketch. It was a work of art filled with bright yellow, red, green, blue, and purple wash. What a wonderful contrast to its surroundings of olive drab, brown, olive drab, black, olive drab, gray, and olive drab. This gift would surely widen the already widest smile in the camp.

In all the excitement surrounding the first two openings, I had almost forgotten about the two regular letters sitting crumbled on the edge of my camouflaged quilt. I picked up the one on top. It was an in-country letter from my junior year college roommate, Joe Heimbold. He was a second lieutenant forward observer (FO) with the Twenty-Fifth Infantry Division, stationed in Cu Chi. My mom had mentioned in her last letter that he was awarded a silver star, three bronze stars, a Vietnam Commendation medal, and recognition as the best FO in the Twenty-Fifth. Not bad for a guy with a bachelor's in English whose main interest in college was seeing how many rules he could break. As editor of the school newspaper and president of the Young Democrats, it was easy seeing him as an officer, but the rules—I just couldn't see him adhering to a lot of rules. His twin brother, Jim, was killed in action a couple years earlier. The rule was, if Jim was killed, Joe couldn't be drafted. So he enlisted.

Skinner,

Check this out. Jeff O'Hara was reading a copy of the Twenty-Fifth Division's newspaper and saw my picture on the front page. I'll tell you the story about that later. So without warning he decides to fly the 80 miles to show me the paper. He's flying a Huey at 100K northwest of Saigon. O'Hara finds my radio frequency and requests permission to land. Of course, I called him off having no idea who this pilot is. Plus, I'm in the middle of nowheresville, and there's nothing worse than having a helicopter flying in circles telling the world, "Hey, there must be something in that bush." Oh well, after clearing who he was using old fraternity pass codes, I gave him permission and security coverage to land. After he landed he approached us with his patented, wide, Irish smile, gave me the ΠΚΑ handshake, then reached for and handed me beers for me and my FO team. How he found out where I was in the boonies? To this day I'm still in amazement.

So keep your eyes out, you may be O'Hara's next visit ... or is it victim?

Joe

The final envelope, from Bill Conner, one of my best friends from home, was the smallest and lightest. The entire content of the letter was about a wild three-day concert he had attended, just under a two-hour drive from Endicott, 8,800 miles from where I stood. He said the parking was so bad that he should have left the car in the driveway and walked to the concert. I had never heard the name of the town he referred to, so I pulled out my dog-eared map, unraveled it, and covered what remained of the exposed area of the table in front of me. I immediately found it, just off the New York Turnpike—a place called Bethel. He said the concert was called Woodstock.

Peace—It's Just a Symbol

While lying in bed and staring at a large split in my plywood ceiling, my thoughts traveled back in time. As a child, many hours had been spent playing with hundreds of little, green, plastic army men. They were all so perfect. No tears in their clothing, no missing limbs, no blood squirting out of their eyes, no looks of fear on their faces. Some stood tall and proud, marching with rifles resting on their shoulders. Some kneeled. Others lay flat, their weapons aimed at the enemy. And little, green, plastic soldiers did not come with body bags or laid out unnaturally twisted with their intestines hanging out of their bodies—those pieces didn't exist because playing war is supposed to be fun.

As new stories of the fresh death filtered in from the demilitarized zone to the Mekong Delta, and on the coast of the Pacific to the borders of Cambodia, I became more and more obsessed with the peace symbol. I wore one high around my neck, another drawn on the worn canvas that covered my steel pot, and a third decorating a lighter. Etched on the flip side was the quote, "Fighting for peace is like fucking for virginity."

I needed a much more dramatic statement. While returning from another encounter with the culinary delights at the mess hall, I saw my jeep in an entirely different perspective. Seen from head on, the shape of the "snapper," a booby-trap wire catch welded onto her grill, was a perfect reproduction of the peace symbol. Early in the war, the Viet Cong would stretch wire across roads and decapitate unsuspecting jeep drivers. The US government thwarted this practice by fixing a four-foot bar, supported by two extension legs, to the front of jeeps. The design was crude but effective. The only thing missing was the circle.

The search for a metal ring to complete my new find was easier than I thought possible. There was a large pile of metal objects from a variety of sources behind the motor pool. A two-foot-wide ring was lying on top of the pile. It was slightly too large and a little rusty but was otherwise perfect. Within an hour, I was the proud owner of the only rolling peace sign in Vietnam.

Unfortunately, I was only able to parade my handiwork around base camp for a few short minutes. In that brief time, I received a couple of military salutes, a bird salute, and at least a dozen peace salutes. I stopped at the canteen for a Coke to the cheers of a dozen or so carrying their purchases back to their hooches. On my way back to my jeep, I ran into Captain Martinez, who informed me that my invention was not acceptable to military regulations and demanded its immediate removal. He was shaking his head and smiling as he turned to leave.

Pulling into the compound, I hit a full sandbag lying at the edge of the road. The ring jarred loose and began to roll at an incredible rate of speed past a hooch and then another. It slowed and came to a halt in the dust next to the third hooch. When I got to the ring, I dug my heel into the dust just inside its upper lip and made a trail to the other side of its perimeter. Making miniature ditches on either side of the center line, I turned to my hooch and began to execute my next "peace plan."

Plowing through my duffel bag, I found my poncho and laid it on the table. I fished out my magic marker, swimming in a school of pencils in a coffee cup, and enthusiastically went to work. In less than an hour, the art of the day was complete. On the back of the poncho, I drew, in great detail, Snoopy lying on his doghouse in his usual relaxed, "I don't have a care in the world" pose. His house, surrounded by barbed wire, M60s, claymore mines, and rocket launchers, was ready for inspection. A peace symbol dangled from his collar. The cartoon balloon over his head read, "Fuck it … just plain fuck it." This one lasted considerably longer than my oversized peace symbol on wheels. I had worn it selectively for a week before the order came down to dispose of it.

My efforts didn't bring the war any closer to an end, but it seemed that my poncho, plus a design for a "short calendar" that was in wide use throughout the Fourth, put me into contention for an open slot as a combat artist. There were four of us vying for the position. For a brief moment, I thought I was going to trade in my ignition key for an artist's brush. My dream, however, was short-lived. A left-handed artist with ten times more talent in his right hand than I had in my whole being was selected.

So I kept my ignition key and my M16 and continued to "fight for peace."

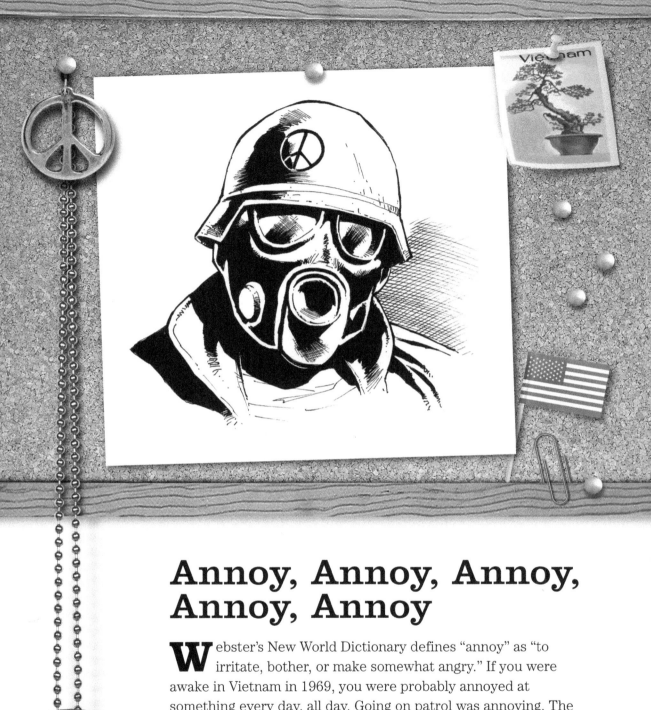

Annoy, Annoy, Annoy, Annoy, Annoy

Webster's New World Dictionary defines "annoy" as "to irritate, bother, or make somewhat angry." If you were awake in Vietnam in 1969, you were probably annoyed at something every day, all day. Going on patrol was annoying. The food was annoying. The latrines were annoying. The monsoons were annoying. Almost any assignment was annoying. Lines were annoying. Many of the Vietnamese were annoying. Americans were often more annoying. The war, in general, as well as the generals in the war, were annoying. Life in Nam was almost totally opposite of life in the real world, therefore, making annoyances more

CHAPTER

24

prevalent. In one week, I was annoyed ninety-six times. I think this qualifies me for AA, Annoyed Anonymous. Part of the twelve-step program is to bitch about your annoyances while you get shitfaced.

It started on a Monday when we were out of water for showers but were being rained on by one of the heaviest downpours I'd ever witnessed. My matted, damp sheet felt sticky and nasty as I listened to the raindrops pelting the tin roof of my hooch like a staccato machine gun until I couldn't take it anymore.

I jumped up, stripped to my birthday suit, and stood under nature's giant showerhead. The only thing missing was a hot-water handle. I took a step back under the protective lip of the hooch and slathered every inch of my lily-white body. Then, without any warning, Mother Nature decided she was through for the evening and called it quits. There was no tapering off to a drizzle. She simply came to an immediate screeching halt. Bitch!

Tired, sticky, itching, and annoyed, I went in search of clean water. After a long thirty minutes, I was back where I started, between damp, matted sheets, dreaming of a hot bath with steamed-up mirrors and sweating porcelain.

On Wednesday, our water supply was back to normal. I had just finished with the longest, hottest shower I'd had since arriving in-country when I lost a flip-flop on the way back to my hooch. The narrow walkway that took bathers from the shower to a row of huts twenty yards away was extra slick.

My flip-flop slipped and sailed out over the monsoon-mud lake to my left. It skidded for six or so feet and came to rest in the middle of the thick, brown pond. I had to get it. Stepping off the worn, wooden walkway, I tested the mud in much the same manner people test the temperature of the water in a swimming pool in May.

My first step went a few inches into pure mud. I could feel the cool liquid earth ooze between my toes. After hitting bottom, I tested my weight by holding my other foot in the air to see if I'd sink farther. I didn't. As I searched for my next step, I sunk deeper. My sandal was only inches away, so there was no way I was turning around. While stretching, straining, and grunting, I fell forward into the murky brown gunk. Both my arms sank into the depths of nature's pudding halfway between my wrists and elbows.

Agility and coordination were never strong suits for me, and I failed the test once again. As I tried to get up, I slipped, twisted, and turned until I was completely covered in mud from my mashed down hair to my flip-flopless feet. I snatched my flip-flop from the surface of the chocolate-colored pond and began to plod back to the gangplank. There was my other flip-flop, still clean and dry. I slipped and slid back to the shower where a snickering mail clerk informed me that there was no hot water—none, nada, zilch. At that point, ice-cold water would have been fine, which was a good thing because that's what I got.

*****

Tuesday, my buddy Shade and I were on our way to the mess hall, in itself a daily but necessary annoyance. We encountered a loud, obnoxious grunt taking any and all bets regarding his expertise with throwing his bayonet. The corporal stood in front of a makeshift target fixed to a sandbag on the other side of the road. A small stack of MPC (military payment certificates) sat neatly piled next to the bayonet.

After ingesting the culinary delights of the mess hall, I saw that he was still there. Apparently many dollars richer, he continued to carry on, louder and more obnoxious than before. An instant brainstorm filled the void of my thoughts, or maybe it was just part of the daily gastronomical annoyance that followed dinner. I took Shade aside and explained what I had in mind. I pulled out my wallet and fished through a pile of three kinds of money: US greenbacks, MPC, and Vietnamese piasters. Jeez, even the money was annoying. I separated three George Washingtons and laid them down on the pile of sandbags next to his knife.

"Hey, dude, can my man give it a try?" I asked putting my wallet back in my lower fatigue pants pocket. This is Shade. His nickname used to be Blade. Still wanna bet?"

"Sure, sucker, I can spend your money, Shade's money, or Blade's money just as easy as the bucks I've already plucked from the other chumps populating the Funky Fourth," he responded. Nice guy.

I pulled his miniature "Excalibur" from the sandbag and pointed it toward an aluminum pie pan tied to a string flopping in the breeze at a distance of seventy-five to a hundred feet and handed the bayonet to Shade. I whispered to him to throw the blade as far as he could in the direction of the pan. I wouldn't miss the three dollars because possessing greenbacks was illegal in Nam anyway. They were part of my winnings from a wager earlier in the week. Maybe this asshole would get caught with them.

Shade placed the blade cutting edge out, in the palm of his hand. "Is this how you hold it?"

"Like it's going to make a difference," the corporal said shaking his head.

Flipping the knife in the air, Shade caught it by its handle; this was no ordinary military-issued bayonet. It was light, polished, and beautifully balanced.

Giving a quick 180-degree glance of our immediate AO (area of operations), Shade determined the area to be secure. Drawing the blade back to his ear, Shade asked, "That pan is my target, OK?"

"Huh, what?" is all the corporal was able to get out before Shade let the blade fly.

Quickly turning around, we shrugged our shoulders and started to walk away. We heard the back-to-back sounds of the hit and a gasp from one of a half dozen who stopped to watch the festivities. Corporal Obnoxious was stunned. Slowly turning back around, I spotted the knife stuck just off center in the pie pan jammed to the wall of sandbags.

"Shit, I missed dead center," Shade said. The corporal said nothing because he had nothing to say. He was also too embarrassed to try and top Shade's lucky toss. I grabbed our winnings and walked briskly away. It occurred to me, upon picking up the pace that, the owner of the heavily damaged pie pan might be annoyed at Shades knife throwing abilities. I handed the winnings to Shade and asked, "Was that a lucky toss?" He responded, "From that distance, yes. But I've thrown a blade about, oh, I don't know, maybe aahhhh—a thousand times. I have two trophies and one invitation to become a Vegas act," he said with a huge grin. We then saluted a captain who was walking towards the crime scene. We truly hoped the corporal's valued Excalibur would be confiscated while his enterprise collapsed.

*****

On Wednesday, I had the bad luck of being in the wrong place at the wrong time. However, I did find a small amount of comfort in the fact that I wasn't the only person occupying this unwanted space. Along with me; two others were "volunteered" to help move an ammo dump. I was assigned to drive someone else's vehicle. No one seemed to care at all that I ground the gears at each shift. For some reason, it was apparent that this was a very expendable deuce-and-a-half. If not for the invention of duct tape and the welding torch, this clunker wouldn't have made it out of base camp. We shook, rattled, and rolled to an isolated area where dozens of boxes of ammunition awaited our muscles.

At a point of visual safety, the private first class (PFC) sitting next to me pulled out a joint the size of a small cigar. "This ought to make them ammo boxes a lot lighter," he declared. The other PFC giggled in response. Without asking my permission (sometimes there's just no respect for higher rank), he lit an oversized match and held it at the tip of the oversized "doobie" and drew heavily. We weren't heading for guard duty or to some other possible life-threatening detail, so I didn't object.

"Hey, man, you want a hit?" he asked me.

"No thanks, I—"

"Man, pass it over here. I'll take his hit, Westmoreland's hit, LBJ's hit, and then I'll finish it off with a few hits of my own," interrupted private first class number two.

You do know that LBJ's not the president anymore, right?" I asked PFC number two.

"Really, who is the president?" he inquired.

"Nixon is our president," I said.

He and his buddy proceeded to pass the joint back and forth until it disappeared.

When we arrived at the dump, the two guards on duty grabbed their stuff and headed out with the words, "Adios." We found the ammunition stacked neatly—high and wide. My back began to throb as I surveyed the stacks and rows of boxes.

We slipped on our work gloves and rhythmically grunted as we moved our cargo. I just discovered a new meaning for Wednesday being declared hump day. After ten minutes or so, we noticed a strange noise coming from a distance. It was a very loud buzz hum, for lack of a better description. As the sound grew louder, we became more curious about the sound's origin. Simultaneously, we jumped up onto one of the stacks and witnessed an impressive sight of nature—a huge swarm of bees.

"Holy Mother of God, would you look at that," said PFC number one, throwing his hands high and wide and bringing them down on top of his head.

"Man, we need to get the fuck out of here, either right now or sooner," said PFC number two.

"I can't tell. Are they heading toward us?" I asked.

A second or two of mathematical calculation determined that we were definitely in the path of these angry, four-winged, hairy insects.

We began to unintentionally mimic "civilized" man's greatest trio of bumblers—the Three Stooges. Larry and Curly, at this point, were pretty much wasted. Their first move was to turn into each other and crack heads. Curly fell from the stack of sandbags and landed hard onto the red clay, face down, with a thud.

"Oh shit, I think I'm hurt. I think I'm bleeding. Hey, you guys, how bad am I bleeding?" Curly asked while rubbing his eyebrow.

His sweat-covered face imprinted into the red soil.

"Get your ass up, dimwit, that's just red mud mixed with your nasty sweat," said Larry, jumping to the ground.

We picked up our pace and began to screw up at every turn. There was flying sweat, red and regular, everywhere, and the buzzing was getting louder and nearer. Each box slammed into place caused my sunglasses to shift to the end of my nose.

We were down to our last box. I turned loose of the rope handle attached to the end of the rectangular wooden box, slipped off my gloves, removed my glasses, and put them in the only remaining slot. Grabbing two rope handles, I began to shake off like a bird-dog exiting a pond. I wiped the last of the sweat from my eyes and heard simultaneous sounds of a thud and a crunch. Larry and Curly had deposited the last eighty-pound box of ammo in the only remaining slot, oblivious to my gloves and new aviator sunglasses.

My anger was nothing compared to the fury of the swarm. It was now only a few yards away and approaching fast. I wedged my butt between broken springs trying to escape through a thin layer of canvas and cranked up the engine. The tailpipe was scarcely above the ground as we coughed and bounced away. Boisterous cheering arose as that dilapidated bucket of bolts got us out of the dump.

Curly rubbed his brow and kept repeating variations of, "Whoa, man, what a trip, man, oh shit, man, can you believe that shit."

A quick check indicated that we suffered only one sting, and that was to my wallet for the purchase of my sixth pair of sunglasses.

*****

Thursday brought on a twenty-four-hour guard duty. An hour into our countdown, a loud explosion, chaos, confusion, and panic fused to create a sense of doom. A figure appeared in the doorway of our bunker talking loud and fast in short sentences.

"Put on your gas masks, y'all. Seriously, this is for real. No shit, seriously, the captain just confirmed it. Said a heavy dose of gas is coming our way." He pulled the mask that was sitting on top of his head down over his face and left.

There were three of us in the guard bunker. I had been playing cards with a clerk from HQ while a guy from the motor pool was taking his turn watching for Charlie. We got the word after the explosion that we might be under a gas attack. Mr. Y'all was the confirmation. My guard mates retrieved their masks from rucks sitting in a far corner. I wasn't diving into mine because I knew there wasn't a mask inside.

Panic set in; I felt helpless. As the others pulled masks over their faces, tightened straps, and checked valves, my heartbeat quickened, and I began to spew incoherent babble. "Awww shit, I didn't bring a mask. I don't have—hey, anyone know if there are any extras?" Flitting from one to the next and talking to no one in particular, "Damn, hey, you guys know if there are any extra masks anywhere? Shit, I gotta find a mask. Shit, damn it, shit."

Flashbacks to basic training flooded my head. "What is it? Mustard? Tear? Fuck, nerve? Oh, God please make it CS or tear. Does anyone know what kind?" I switched back to pleading. "Are there any extras? Does anyone have—does anyone know if there are any extras." I moved in a jerky manner, not knowing where to go, what to think. The guy I was playing cards with said he'd see what he could find. I couldn't hear him clearly through his mask and my panic. The other guard soaked the corner of my poncho liner from his canteen and handed it to me. "Man, am I gonna fucking die? Am I?" He didn't answer. I never felt so helpless in my life. Basic training consumed my thoughts. I didn't think CS or tear gas because they are pretty innocuous; damn, who doesn't think the worst during a crisis? A vision flashed in my head; a sergeant, holding up an open hand and folding in a finger as he listed the effects, "Mustard: inflamed eyes, vomiting, then blistering of the skin, blindness, followed by death within twenty-four hours if chemical or bacterial pneumonia sets in." When he finished, his fist sprung open again, and he displayed a second hand to reinforce his digital explanation points. He continued, "Nerve: painful breathing, coughing, sweating, vomiting, cramps, followed by loss of bowel control, convulsions, and then unconsciousness and death." Bringing back these worst-case scenarios sent me into a deeper sense of terror. I was paralyzed by fear when my card-playing buddy entered the bunker with the ugliest, most beautiful gas mask I'd ever seen. "Thanks, man, thanks. Thank you, thank you, oh man, thank you," I repeated while fumbling through the mask donning ritual.

We sat in silence looking out over the concertina wire for the next few minutes, fidgeting with our masks while waiting for the arrival of the gas to raise the hair on our arms. Another minute later, the call of all clear echoed up and down the perimeter. The SPC-4 who told us to put on our masks returned to give us an update.

"Lightnin' hit the fougasse and CS way on down the line, so relax y'all and change your drawers," he said. While continuing to giggle, he left to pass on the same info to those in the next bunker. His visit was for his entertainment because as he was informing us of the situation, the same info, minus the changing our drawers reference, was coming over the bunker's field phone. We went outside and caught a whiff of the pungent fragrance. I forgot to ask the king of hearts where he got the mask because I was so embarrassed. If this is what Monday through Thursday laid on us, I didn't even want to think what was in store for us on the weekend. Then I remembered—oh shit, the next day was Friday the 13th.

Give Them the Finger

The war plodded on, the monsoons relentlessly attempted to wash away the continent, time away from my bed continued into the second phase of forever, and personal hygiene ceased to exist.

Rosco and I were driving back to headquarters, returning from a fire base twelve clicks from nowhere when we spotted a couple dozen or so new recruits huddled close against the side of a long hut waiting to sign in. Shifting, shivering, anticipating, observing, and daydreaming, they stood patient and ready to serve. You might have noticed, after the word "ready," I left out "willing and able." They were "TBD." There was just enough

CHAPTER 25

room between the end of the roofline and the side of the building to keep their crisp and shiny uniforms dry, clean, and green. Rain fell heavy and steady. All these fresh cherries needed to deal with was mud stuck to the soles of their new boots and on the bottoms of clean, still-stiff duffel bags. The usual pile of sandbags stacked high around every building in Enari was missing. I had a good idea what these unsuspecting "volunteers" would be doing as soon as they signed in if the rain let up. If the rain continued, then the sand would be waiting at 0630.

Glancing at each other with heads down and eyes up, Rosco and I came to the same quick and obvious conclusion. No question about it—they needed to be messed with before the second hand met with the next minute on my watch. They were pristine, while we were rancid—they deserved it.

"OK, OK, I got it. Let's scream incoming at the loudest level that our voices could command and watch them dive into the mud," Rosco suggested.

We quickly tabled that idea when I pulled my hand from my pocket, clutching the ace of pranks.

"Rosco, dear fellow, I do believe Cousin Doug has given us the answer to our demented dilemma," I declared in my poorly performed aristocratic voice.

Nestled full in my hand was an old wooden chest the size of a watch box. Doug's gift from a friend in Hollywood had arrived late in the previous week. The only thing interesting regarding the box was its ornate oversized latch. The brass had deteriorated into a moldy green, crusty assemblage. I remembered opening the box and flushing as I studied its contents. What brought Rosco's eyes to attention was a very realistically detailed, fleshy, rubber finger lying on a bed of cotton, stained with red Karo syrup. It had become my entertainment for the week, thus why I had it with me.

After poking it a couple of times, Rosco hastily developed our one act play. We rehearsed it once and then gave each other thumbs up as we prepared for scene one.

"God, Rosco, all our time together, I'm just now finding out about your bizarre sense of humor. You had me fooled with that dry, sophisticated wit of yours," I said of Rosco's ever-emerging and complicated personality.

Once in place, Rosco put his hand inside his shirt Napoleon style and said, "You know, Haines, we are perfectly cast for the parts of two deranged soldiers who play pranks to ebb the endless boring days that permeate their existence—sooooooo let's get those cherries." His aristocrat impression was far superior to my feeble attempt.

I put the jeep into first gear, quickly threw it into second, and then pushed full weight on the accelerator. Shifting into third gear and turning the wheel hard we slid sideways across the soaked metal tarmac. Hitting the brakes brought us to a jerking halt just a couple yards from the line of figurative and literal green grunts. Glad my intuitive timing was dead on, or else I would be reporting to Top that I just ran over eight new FNGs (fucking new guys) sideways.

Springing from the jeep—our ponchos flapping in the wind—we made our way toward the huddled mass. Rosco, while traveling at double-time speed, turned his M16 upside down and pounded it hard on the tarmac to regurgitate the mud from the barrel. We were soaking wet and filthy dirty. Our faces were sporting a four-day growth. Droplets of rain dripped in unison from the steel lips of our helmets as I stretched out my hand to Rosco. He dug deep into the lower pocket of his fatigue pants and ceremoniously handed me the worn wooden box. Gripping the miniature coffin like a baseball, palm up, I paced back and forth in front of the line of newbies and rambling about just coming in from a firefight.

"We had six confirmed kills," said a very animated SPC-4 Creech as I waved the box at them. "You cherries need to be officially introduced to the war first hand," he said. *"Pun intended,"* I thought. He stuck out his lower lip and blew a raindrop off the end of his nose. "Y'all are in Nam, like it or not, and you need—note, I said need—to know what it's like out there in Charlieland."

I released my grip on the box, cradled it in the palm of my hand, reached over the top, flipped the latch open, and lifted the lid for a full inspection.

"Here's one dead VC that no longer needs this to pick his nose," Rosco said in his best macho voice.

One guy gagged, a second begged for a closer look, and a third repeated over and over what sick sons-of-bitches we were.

These three totally different reactions made Rosco and me realize how complicated war can be. Not only do we, as a nation, have to grapple with the moral justifications of war and how we deal with them, but also as individuals, we have to come to grips with our set of values, virtuous beliefs, and philosophies regarding war and how we must handle those decisions that could lead to death and destruction. Naaaaaaah, actually, we didn't think about any heavy-duty philosophical stuff at that moment because our prank was not quite finished. Philosophy can wait; pranks can't!

I closed the creaky lid with a snap and jumped into Be Nice, which must have seemed like an oxymoron to those we had just introduced to the facts of war as we saw them. Rosco snatched the box away from me, opened the lid, removed the finger, and stuck it, thumbnail first, in his mouth like a cigar. "Welcome to Vietnam, ladies." We spun off, spitting water and wet sand in all directions.

I think the third guy was right—we were sick sons-of-bitches. But, hey, you know—it don't mean nothin'.

Barry and the boys

The ginger ale house

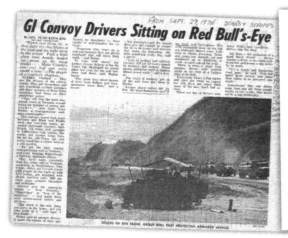

A September 1970 Stars & Stripes article about Highway 19, which runs between Pleiku and Qui Nhon, considered the most dangerous road in Vietnam.

3rd of the 12th

Adventures in a Borrowed Cream Puff

At 0900 hours on a Thursday in early September, I was traveling alone, unless you counted Otis, Jim, Janis, Jimmy, John, Paul, George, and Ringo, who were all sitting stacked neatly on end in a makeshift tape case. The only item on my agenda was to deliver some crates to LZ Action, a fire support base near the entrance of the Mang Yang Pass. When I arrived at the gate, a well-pressed MP waved me on.

The war seemed to be on hold: helicopter noise was minimal, night-time artillery shelling had come to a halt, and reports of fighting had ceased. I pulled away from the camp without the usual nervous stomach caused by fear and an uneasy sense of the unknown. But I didn't have to drive very far to be reminded of the war zone without boundaries. A detour around a blown-up bridge, a burned-out truck rusting in a ditch, and a forest leveled by Orange were all reminders that I wasn't on a leisurely drive for a day at the beach.

The most unusual aspect of this journey wasn't that I was driving fearlessly, but that I was driving someone else's vehicle—a brand new deuce-and-a-half. The odometer on this cream puff was still in double digits. When I ground her gears as I headed through Pleiku, I—without question—felt guilty.

The trip went smoothly, the day warm and breezy. The soft-blue sky was uncommonly clear. It was the kind of day I wanted to bottle up and save for the first wet, depressing, gray afternoon that was sure to darken the calendar before the week was over.

Rounding a curve on Highway 19 through the Mang Yang Pass, I spotted a red sign that proclaimed in bright yellow letters, "LZ Action—home of the famous Billy G Action—next right—food—lodging—fire support." Directly across the road from Action sat the burned-out rusted hulk of an M42 Duster. I unloaded my cargo in record time and, without the temptation to visit, started on my return trip. With a large chunk of the clock to kill, I decided to take my time and a detour. I drove past a brick factory and took a couple of pictures without coming to a full stop. The word was out that a bus station of sorts, out in the middle of nowhere, had fresh American submarine sandwiches. There was a rumor of real ham, roast beef, and turkey. After a short drive, my hunt was over. I pulled into this strange oasis on a hilltop and followed the smell. There were two jeeps in the parking lot. Moments later, spread out before me on a makeshift picnic table, was a big, sloppy sub with a variety of fresh produce hanging out from between two pieces of a newly cut wheat roll. The smell of the freshly baked bread brought an instant feeling of homesickness.

I took a large bite and chewed for a long time, allowing this fantasy feast to caress my taste buds. Each chew was a slow-motion grind that gave all the parts of my anatomy involved the time to enjoy the sensual pleasures of real food.

Washing down the first half of the sandwich with a large swig of an ice-cold Coke, I watched a large, old bus maneuver through the unpaved parking lot. The gravel crackled under the weight of its over-capacity cargo. All the nearly bald tires needed air. Each shift in direction created different sized rubber bubbles. The front end of this mass of rusted metal just missed the rear bumper of my borrowed cream puff.

The guts under the hood sputtered, wheezed, shook, and popped as it came to rest under a makeshift tin canopy. The gray monster fell quiet, its door squeaked open, and the first of its human cargo tumbled onto the gravel. A body, which I couldn't discern to be male or female, looked at me as it pushed itself into a wobbly standing position. I felt embarrassed as I caught myself staring. I felt like a five-year-old at a mall, pointing at a one-legged man. But a child would be curious and inquisitive. I felt pity and revulsion.

Before me stood, with the help of makeshift crutches, a rag-wrapped man I guessed to be middle aged, with open sores, white scaly scabs, and stubs for hands and feet. His hair was wispy, dull, and patchy, not at all like the full, shiny black hair of most Vietnamese. I lowered my eyes and gathered the remainder of my sandwich as more heart-wrenching examples of nature's cruelty began to regurgitate from the bowels of the big, now-silent bus. Montagnard men and women in various stages of disease began to fill the lot.

I clutched my sandwich in one hand, my Coke in the other, and slid along the picnic bench toward my truck. I reached it without making additional eye contact with those in the parking lot and flung open the door, almost hitting a teenage boy who was asking me to buy some souvenir trinkets. While pointing to some plastic jewelry I didn't need, I asked him about the people on the bus. I handed him a handful of "Monopoly money" (what we called MPC) and looked at him for the first time since we started our transaction. He was thin and dirty but quite handsome. He smiled at my overpayment of at least a hundred P (piasters, Vietnamese currency) and answered my question with one word, "Lepers." I responded with a simple "oh" and stepped into my truck.

I drove off into Mother Nature's contradiction. The sky was blue, and the air was warm, but much of her human landscape was decaying. War and disease, two of the ugliest realities of mankind, seemed to be flourishing in the year 1969. I thought how short a distance we'd traveled in such a very long period of time.

The main gate of Camp Enari had just come into view when I spotted a small, shoeless boy in very oversized clothes limping down the road. He had a long cord wrapped around his tiny fist. Attached to the twine, dragging in the dirt behind him, was a small wooden box. Glancing at my watch, I realized I still had a couple of free hours.

Down-shifting quickly, I stopped and jumped to the ground, landing evenly on both feet in the dirt at the edge of the pavement. My appearance had startled a teenage girl who was straddling a ditch. With one foot planted on the top of each ridge, she was in a full squat, peeing, when she spotted me. She sprang up like a jack-in-the-box and ran off with her pajamas at her knees and a look of panic on her face. What caused her to run was one of the sad asides of war. All too often, the women and children of the "host country" become tragic victims of sexual and physical abuse. Many of the Vietnamese regarded everyone as the enemy: the

Viet Cong, the Americans, the NVA, the ARVN—everyone. I felt really bad that this frightened child thought that I had stopped to molest her. I shouted again and again that I didn't want to hurt her, but that just made her run faster. If she didn't understand English, which was more than likely the case, her imagination probably translated my shouts into some terrifying command from the enemy.

When she disappeared into the tree line, I turned my attention to the real reason I had stopped. I squatted and began the ritual of trying to communicate with my new little friend. I guessed he was nine or ten years old. He was still giggling at the sight of the girl running across the field pulling up her pajamas as she ran. He stopped giggling when our eyes met.

"Do you speak English?" I asked. He held up his hand, created a space of an inch between his forefinger and his thumb and thrust this measurement of his English-speaking skills within two inches of my face. I fell back, landing hard on my butt. My sunglasses slid to the edge of my nose. He grinned and giggled in response. His face was as dirty as his clothes, but in the middle of that dirty face was the whitest, most perfect set of teeth I'd ever seen on a Vietnamese. He covered his mouth as he continued to giggle.

Introductions seemed to be in order at this point. I pointed to myself and said, "Tom," and then pointed at him and asked, "What is your name?"

"I Little Shit," he answered without hesitation and with great pride. I guessed this was a name given to him affectionately by a GI friend.

"Well, Little Shit, do you want a ride?" He recognized the word "ride" right away and began to repeat it and the word "yes" over and over.

When I looked at his feet, I noticed some blood. "Hey, little buddy, how did you hurt yourself?" I asked pointing to his right foot. Instantly, he dropped to the ground, spit on his ankle and began to clean it with his oversized shirttail. My guess was that he thought I wanted him to clean his feet before getting into my nice unsullied truck. "No, no, no," I said while waving my hands in front of his face.

As he pushed himself up, I put my hands under his armpits and sailed him through the air to the passenger seat. He was so light I flung him higher than was necessary. It was like picking up a milk carton that you thought was full but actually was empty. I interpreted his giggles as a sign that he was enjoying the flight. I picked up his little wooden box and put it on the floor in front of him. It also was surprisingly light, almost as if it too was empty. Making a U-turn in one full sweep, we were on our way.

I pushed the play button on my recorder and turned up the volume. The Beatles were now rockin' and rollin' down Route 14. I looked over at my small friend, saw those big white teeth, heard that ever-present giggle, watched his little fingers tapping on his leg out of sync to the music, and once again felt good about my day.

A minute into the trip he became fixated on my paper-wrapped package. He carefully tried to lift the corner of the paper to see what was inside, watching to see if I noticed his curiosity. I did.

"Have you had lunch?" I asked while pointing to my open mouth. No response. "How about—do you want something to eat?"

His eyes lit up, and he repeated the word "eat" while he nodded his head "yes" in a rhythmic, jerking motion. I tossed the sandwich in his lap and watched him tear into it with delight. He was obviously very hungry, and the fact that the sandwich was half eaten made no difference to him whatsoever.

A short time later we arrived at the outskirts of Pleiku. I asked him where he lived and received a blank look. He watched my mouth with great concentration hoping I would say something he understood. Pointing at him I asked, "Where your house?" I think he understood "house" because he immediately pointed down Route 14 in the direction we were traveling. A minute later he pointed to our left and said, "House."

There was a sign on the corner, which read something to the effect of "No U.S. Military Personnel Beyond This Point." I read the sign to him, but he kept repeating "house" and pointed with a thrust. His face was pleading. I guessed he would be the big cheese in the neighborhood if a big, new military truck dropped him off. The event would be similar to us Americans being delivered to our favorite restaurant in a chauffeured limousine. I should have also considered the very real possibility that, depending on his neighborhood's political orientation, he would be an even bigger cheese if he handed over an American soldier to the VC.

The war seemed to be on hold, and of course rules were meant to be broken, so I swung a left and headed down the nameless narrow street into the unknown. Two turns later, I was in no-man's-land. The streets were full of holes filled with standing brown water. The side of the road was a curb of garbage for as far as the eye could see. The Vietnamese cared for their own space but had little regard for the cleanliness of their country in general. After four hundred years of war, this was somewhat understandable.

There was minimal electricity and no plumbing. Dingy clothes that looked as though they'd never been clean hung on lines to dry. Children, naked from the waist down, sat on the hips of older brothers and sisters. Except for the elderly—somewhere in their fifties for Vietnamese—there were few adults within sight.

As an old man attempted to cross the road, I slowed to a crawl. He was beating the backside of what appeared to be a cow. I glanced out the window to my left as we inched forward, nodding hello to a man standing on the side of the road left of my front bumper. My little friend rapidly dropped off the seat onto the floorboard and hollered in a whisper, "VC-VC-VC!"

I coolly and calmly asked him, "Where? Shit! Where? Oh my God! Who? Where? Fuck, I'm dead! Oh my God! Hey, Little Shit, answer me, where is VC?"

He looked up through arms draped over his head and pointed at the door on my side of the truck. I looked out the window and again saw the little man on the side of the road. He was now directly to my left.

At five feet tall, wiry, and clean, he was well-dressed in simple peasant clothes. Little man's expression was blank, and he held a small rectangular package. I blinked my eyes many times, scanning from the little man to the road and back at each blink. Checking to make sure my M16 was at a snatching distance, I forced a smile as I nodded "hello" to him once again. I prayed that his package was a present for his girlfriend and not an explosive device. Little man stared at me; I nervously stared back. The truck inched forward. The peasant and the "cow" had traversed the road. A few seconds later I glanced at the little man in my side mirror, and he was still staring. I wasn't. I was visually fixed on the road straight in front of me, clutching my M16. I grasped it hard and took a deep breath. As the man on the corner became a speck in the distance, my heartbeat returned to normal—sorta. I released my white-knuckled grip on my M16.

A couple of blocks later Little Shit hollered stop. "Thanks boocoo, number one GI," he said, without his ever-present grin, as he jumped from the cab clutching his still-unfinished sub. He ran limping into a shack that was leaning badly to the left. I swung around in another giant loop but was unable to turn around in one move. Pulling hard to the left, I stopped and then backed up until I ran into a pile of garbage. There were children hanging all over my truck. I hollered for them to turn loose and stomped on the gas. From my rear-view mirror, I made sure that a little girl about twelve, with very uncommon, almost blond hair, an obvious product of an indiscriminate French soldier, had landed safely when she leaped from the running board of the truck.

My stomach was now in a knot, and my mind was in the same state. "Please God let me remember the proper turns in reverse and please don't have ole Charlie crouched in a doorway somewhere in sniper position staring in my direction." I was talking out loud to myself.

The trip back through the off-limit slum was mostly a blur. I had the pedal to the floor and hit most of the potholes without concern. Brown water flew everywhere. The engine roared; my heart pounded; civilians fled.

Route 14 appeared at last. I let out my long-held breath, eased my foot off the gas, and rounded the corner. Flipping the tape in my recorder, I ran it to the song I was looking for and listened to John, Paul, George, and Ringo sing "Penny Lane."

I arrived back at the motor pool late and turned in my slightly tarnished cream puff. The brilliant sun was just beginning to set as I prepared to leave the compound. The sergeant in charge hollered, "Hey!" I thought, "Oh shit, I screwed up his pristine new truck. I grimaced and slowly turned to see that he was holding a small wooden box. "Is this yours?" Returning to the truck, I took the box and thanked him.

Sitting in my jeep with the box nestled in my lap, I tugged at the twine that was tightly protecting its contents. I snipped the cord with my pocketknife and removed the lid. Firmly stuffed inside was a fluffy, chocolate-brown teddy bear. The bear's paw had a tiny label sewn onto it. It read, "Hug Me."

I never saw the little boy again.

Mang Yang

SNAFU

Drawing by Henry Casselli

Pleiku

REMFs in the Field

My day on the loose proved to be an isolated incident. The next two weeks were nonstop details and guard duties. I was living in my hell on earth. Did I finally drive (pun intended) Captain Martinez crazy with my gear-grinding style of shifting, leading him to find a replacement with a softer touch?

After a twenty-four-hour guard, I discovered "reaction" on my list of up-and-coming activities. If anything happened after dark, we were the unit assigned to "react." Cussing and grumbling, I grabbed my gear, which was always in a state of readiness and headed to the reaction barracks.

After the mess hall closed, the barracks filled with REMFs—rear-echelon motherfuckers. Mail clerks, drivers, arms

CHAPTER 27

room personnel, and various other members of Remington's Raiders gathered for an evening of close confinement. Loaded rucks sat at the foot of each cot in the large, open room, and weapons were at the ready. Chatter was louder than usual at this dusk-to-dawn pajama party.

Reaction and antireaction were duties everyone hated but tolerated. They gave everyone a chance to catch up on reading or letter writing. It was also the perfect detail for anyone in pursuit of a good game of cards or friendly conversation.

I wrote a couple of letters, read a couple of comic books, and called it an early night. I fell quickly into a deep sleep despite the decibel-charged atmosphere. The previous twenty-four-hour guard had included the filling of countless sandbags. I could have fallen asleep at full attention with a full sandbag under each arm.

"Let's move it! UP! Up! Up! Let's get it in gear, ladies." Three human alarm clocks roused everyone from various stages of sleep. I wiped my eyes and tried to focus on my watch. It appeared to be 0415. I blinked and wiped my eyes again and saw that I was correct. What a stupid time to have a drill, I thought. However, that thought only lasted a fraction of a moment as I found out it was not a drill; it was the real thing.

Seconds later we were outside, in formation, being briefed. The VC had kidnaped the chief of one of the local Montagnard villages. Our mission, even if we chose not to accept it, was to go on a hunt through the jungle, find, and return this local dignitary to his people. None of us thought to inquire how we were to accomplish this task. After the briefing, we piled into a deuce-and-a-half and headed out of base camp.

I'm not sure where all the time went, but at the moment we were organized and ready to move out, the sun was up. "Breakfast time; let's go home," announced a voice from the back of the truck. No such luck. A brief, bumpy ride later we arrived at our destination.

A Lt. Marval, whom I guessed was not looking forward to becoming a captain, gathered us together for another short briefing. His fast-talking, no-nonsense demeanor worked well with his six-foot-four-inch, lumberjack-like exterior. Dan, as someone had called him, carried himself with authority and confidence. I felt pretty good about him being in charge.

As I surveyed the area, I tried to get a fix on where we were. Generally speaking, we were in the jungle, the boonies, the field, the bush; more specifically, I had no freaking idea where we were.

For most of us, this was our first experience with being a grunt. New encounters came at us in rapid succession. The consumption of C-rations was also a first for most of us in a real field situation. There were a dozen meals to select from, all edible but most unappetizing, such as ham and limas. I played it safe with peanut butter on crackers.

The sun was cooking by midmorning. Sleeves were rolled up past the elbow, shirts unbuttoned, and towels draped around necks. Some of Remi's Raiders complained early on about sore feet and bad backs. By noon, my respect for the infantrymen had increased a hundred fold and would continue to grow with each grunt and groan.

What we had to endure for a day, grunts had to live with for weeks on end: dirty clothes, wet feet, heavy rucks, hot sun, no latrines, no showers, no hot food, no time without fear, and no end to this list.

Besides lugging our gear, we helped each other by taking turns carrying the extras. My placement was behind the M60 machine gunner, so my extra weight came in the form of bullet belts. These belts consisted of dozens of 7.62 mm rounds of ammunition strung side by side and hung diagonally across the chest. Every time I saw a war movie, I thought the guys wearing the crisscrossed belts of ammo were the most macho, macho enough even to squeeze off those rounds with their bare hands. Now I was the guy with the crisscrossed belts, and I didn't feel macho at all. What I felt was uncomfortable—very, very uncomfortable.

After a mile of meandering through the boonies with the weight of a steel helmet pushing down on my head, a flak jacket wrapped around my chest, and a full rucksack clinging to my back, I began to fade—just a tad. Adding on a disoriented couple hundred more yards to our trek, my body became painfully aware that there was a bandolier of extra M16 magazines and three belts of M60 ammo draped over my shoulders, a belt supporting a full canteen, two frags, a bayonet, and other assorted items hanging from my waist, and an M16 gripped tightly in my hands. I continued to fade—just a tad more.

My six-foot-three, one-hundred-sixty-five-pound body sent me many messages. My muscles told me I was sore all over, head told me it was throbbing, sweat glands told me I needed salt tablets, mouth told me I needed a couple of slugs from my canteen, and bladder told me I needed a tree. Also, my soul told me I needed to suck it up because there was someone out there who needed our help, but my body simply didn't give a shit at that moment.

Just as my message center went into overload, and my body was to shut down, we came to a halt. The lieutenant told us to take a break as they surveyed the field in front of us. My first objective was to lighten the load and respond to a couple of my body's messages.

Ten minutes later we were again on our feet and on the move. The lieutenant had determined, with an amount of certainty, that mines covered the field in front of us, so we were redirected to walk through the tree line to our left. One glance at the jungle, and I thought, "Hack through it, maybe; crawl through it, maybe; Orange through it, maybe; walk through it—I don't think so. As we gathered together in groups of four, the lieutenant designated the route and pointed at the entrance with his machete. A snag, a snap, and a grunt accompanied each step. I thought I had just figured out how the infantryman got his nickname. We went over rocks, around trees, and through the brush. We imagined all kinds of exotic snakes and deadly booby traps with each step into the thick, low-growing underbrush. A rusted-out can of Tiger Paw Beer stuck between two branches of a tree was the only indication that any form of civilization had ever seen this spot before.

The sun rose, peaked, and began its descent as we realized that all the action we were going to see that day was water buffaloes swatting flies off their butts. After a short conversation on the field phone, Marval changed our position and soon had us back on trucks facing Camp Enari. I thought the least they could have done was to pick us up in choppers.

We didn't accomplish our mission that day. No one told us what happened to the Montagnard chief, and sadly, I don't think anyone cared. However, we did get something from the experience. For the first time, many of us partially understood the daily plight of a soldier in the bush. Even though we didn't make contact with the enemy or have to spend the night in the jungle in a torrential downpour, our respect and empathy for the ground-pounders of Vietnam couldn't have been any higher. As we boarded the truck that would take us back to purgatory, I knew that those in the field occupied the real hell on earth.

Pooch in a pouch

"Sir, I Respectfully Quit, Sir!"

Our hands were one with the worn wooden benches as the truck came to a jerking halt. I had to bend at the waist when I stood and waited for the tailgate to drop. A corporal pulled the pin to allow the heavy steel gate to slam against the rear frame of the truck; the sound echoed far into the distance. Fourteen of Remington's finest began to spew out and into the dust of a small, open field. We had launched ourselves with what little energy we had left. Mentally and physically spent, some simply fell off the edge of the truck.

SNAFU

We stretched our arms, scratched our fresh insect bites, shook our legs, and took inventory of our belongings. We rolled down our sleeves, that annoying ritual that took place every night at 1800 and were dismissed without a formation. Most of us headed to our respective hooches to dump gear before showering, eating, or checking mail. Everyone had his set of priorities. Mine was showering and then sleeping. Everything else could wait.

On my way to the shower, I stopped by the headquarters information board and checked the duty roster. Everything on the board had a thumbtack at the top and bottom of the paper and somewhere around the center, requiring a flattening process. You had to use both hands to read the probably-useless contents. But a neatly typed single sheet, secured to the well-worn plywood at all four corners, stood out. I ran my fingers down the sheet and stiffened when I saw my name. I stared in disbelief at the words printed next to "SPC-4 Haines, Thomas L."—twenty-four-hour guard.

I slammed my bar of soap to the ground and watched it ricochet three or four times before coming to a halt at the edge of the walkway. Letting loose with a soccer style kick, I sent the brand-new bar of soap sailing across the compound. As I cursed louder and stomped harder, I caught the approaching figure of Captain Martinez in my peripheral vision. When we made eye contact, he hesitated between words as he inquired about the source of my distress. He didn't seem to want to know what was causing my anger, but I believed, as the CO, he should have felt compelled to care.

"Mr. Haines, what—is—your—problem?"

"Sir, I respectfully resign as your driver," I proclaimed, without hesitation, while still maintaining eye contact.

I stopped with no further details because I wanted to see his immediate reaction. Plus, I had not prepared to make such an outrageous demand. What was I going to say next?

"Excuse me?"

I repeated my very emphatic statement. "Sir, I quit. I'm no longer driving a jeep. I'm turning in my notice. I'm hanging up my keys."

He looked bewildered. "You can't quit. This is the army, not Sears."

I changed tactics. "Sir," I repeated and was prepared to repeat again and again, "I respectfully request to be transferred to a position that matches my MOS, sir. You don't need me, sir. In fact, you haven't even seen me in eleven days."

The corners of his mouth turned down, lips pursed, eyebrows raised, and a "hmm" rolled up his throat. He realized that I was right; it had been eleven days.

Without giving him a chance to expound on the "hmm," I went a step further. At this point, I was so frustrated that I had no control over the ill-conceived and utterly stupid statement that came next. "Sir, I would be willing to trade places with someone in the field. Find a guy who's been beating the bushes a little longer than eternity. You know, someone who deserves some back time and can be brought in to replace me, and if necessary, I'll replace him."

As soon as this statement, full of words but void of thought, was out of my mouth, a word began to flash over and over in my head—retract, retract, retract. After all, I was asking to change jobs because I was continually pulling guard duty, so without thinking, I asked to trade guard duty for full-time bush beating—I think not.

Captain Martinez simply said, "OK, I'll see what I can do." Volunteering for permanent ground pounding must have helped in driving home my point. "I'll find a short-timer, but forget about going into the field," he said. "You'll be much more valuable in the rear." I wasn't going to touch that line with a six-inch pole.

I was numb. I couldn't believe what had just happened. I had quit my job. I half expected Captain Martinez to turn and say, "By the way, Miss New York is coming back through the area. Guess I'll have to let the new driver be her escort."

A few days later, Martinez handed me papers and wished me a very sincere "good luck." Just outside the door to headquarters, I read my new assignment. "Wow, An Khe. I'm going to Camp Radcliff," I announced out loud to myself. Radcliff was the main base camp for the First Cavalry Division and the 173rd Airborne Brigade, with the Fourth Infantry a big presence there as well. The captain had one more chore for me. I had to drop off a box to Landing Zone (LZ) Action on the way to An Khe.

Not driving on that trip would give me the opportunity to actually *see* what I had been driving through those past few months. I had my Kodak point-and-push at the ready.

After twenty minutes of packing, I was ready to go. A mental inventory of personal belongings was last on the agenda: portable cassette recorder, check; ammo box filled with comic books, check; one civilian T-shirt, check; one dusty, unused beer mug, check; a recently purchased, still-in-its-box, portable black-and-white TV, check; eight *Playboy* centerfolds, otherwise referred to as wallpaper, check; and a brand new pair of sunglasses, check.

With a duffel bag over each shoulder, an M16 in one hand, and a wooden box containing a small, brown teddy bear in the other, I ended one chapter of my military career and prepared to begin another. The keys to 2P6776 were now in the hands of an elated Corporal Carl Dubail, and I was on my way back to #2 pencils. Rosco jumped up on the bumper of the deuce-and-a-half as it pulled away; we exchanged handshakes and promises. The handshake would last a couple of seconds, the promises a lifetime.

An Khe, Vietnam

Sixty Miles and a Click

It was strange traveling those forty miles between Pleiku and An Khe; I wasn't behind the wheel. Someone else handled the delivery of this cargo, human and otherwise, safely to its destination. Now I know how others must have felt with me behind the wheel—petrified.

I used the time to observe the country whose fate was in the hands of the US military. It was hard to see through the war, past the destruction, beyond the reality. The mountainous countryside was wide open, often beautiful, and very simple.[5] The land looked a lot like my home in Endicott, New York. My village is nestled in the Susquehanna Valley where the Catskills, the Adirondacks, and the Appalachians come together. However, the topography was the only similarity between these two places on opposite sides of the globe. America—a technologically advanced culture of glass and steel high-rise superstructures, unlimited food-choice supermarkets, and multimillion-dollar Super Bowls. Vietnam—a poverty-ridden, third-world nation of mostly grass and tin one-story huts, diets consisting mainly of fish and rice, and low-piastre sports like kickball.

Many well-intentioned politicians were trying to impose our culture, our beliefs, our politics, our economic goals, and our worldly possessions on a people whose culture was best described as delicate. Americans were never very good at the understanding of delicate or being subtle and efficient in their generosity. Ignorance, greed, and mismanagement had gotten in the way of many good intentions throughout the war.

Another pothole jarred me back to reality as we approached An Khe. My thoughts switched from the politics of war to curiosity about a new job and home. Hon Kong Mountain came into view, followed by the eighteen-kilometer-long barrier protecting the base.

The truck pulled into Radcliff around midafternoon on what turned out to be a scorching-hot September day. The first order of business was to ditch my sixty-pound flak jacket and accompanying gear and find an ice-cold anything. Ultimately, military obligations took precedence.

Reporting to First Sgt. Charles Robert Chambers, I was directed through the various chains of command. It was always important to know whom to report to in any given situation. Within an hour, I met almost everyone I would come in contact with on a daily basis. It took less than a week to figure these guys out. Two of them made an unusually strong first impression.

Chambers, without question, was a lifer. He was forty-something and a man with a mission: do as little as necessary and not make waves. He had rugged good looks and cut a very military figure. My guess, he weighed what the chart said for a six-foot soldier. The word was, don't mess with him, and he won't mess with you. Right or wrong, do it the US Army way. If it requires work, look for the shortcut as long as your superiors approve or don't find out. Need to trade for a favor, his slogan was "talk to me." Above all, if you have a complaint, keep it to yourself. His philosophies might seem contradictory, but not to Chambers.

Lt. Bill Hatcher was cut from a different military mold. He was a ninety-day wonder who was marking time until civilian clothes, once again, hung in his closet. He was twenty-three years old, five feet ten inches, about 180 pounds, with very round eyes centered on a very round face. He had an olive complexion and a short smile that disappeared into dimpled cheeks. He was conscientious, organized, and "by the book," as long as "by the book" worked. If it didn't, he wasn't above improvising. He was quiet and laid back and expected everyone to work as hard as he did, but he didn't work all that hard. He knew what it would take to get the job done and keep his superiors happy. He was a smart guy.

After introductions, I was directed to my hooch. It was the second building in a long row of tin-roofed, wooden structures. My new home was surrounded by sandbags piled four feet high and wrapped in steel tarmac sections held up by metal posts, which were buried three feet into the hard, reddish-brown soil.

My room was the first door to the left. Slinging my gear into a corner, I hollered out the standard, "Hello? Is anyone here?" There was no response. The space was sparsely furnished with a chest of drawers and a simple wooden table with two straight-back wooden chairs. Keeping these items company were a regular army-issue footlocker and a slightly sagging single bed. The mattress was thin and worn, but the drawers on the dresser opened and closed, a nice change from the garage-sale reject back in Pleiku. All of this was arranged logically on a warped wooden floor. As the inspection continued, I kept noticing one thing—cleanliness. Everything was neatly arranged and pristine. "OK, Mom. Mom?"

The heat of the day was beginning to fade. I hung my flak jacket on a hook, removed my shirt and draped it over the jacket, kicked off my boots, and dove into my duffel bag. The neatness of the room compelled me to separate, fold, and put items in their proper places. This task took more time, but time was in abundance. Reporting to supply wasn't on the agenda until 0730 the following morning.

As I pulled open a drawer, I heard someone clear his throat in an attempt to get my attention. Spinning on my heels, I began to introduce myself to an individual I thought must be one of my hooch mates. I was wrong.

The last word I uttered as I made eye contact jammed in my throat. I froze for a long moment—a moment that became a permanent image carefully sculptured on the invisible walls of my memory. I believe God allows each of us a small number of sensations that have strange effects on us physically, spiritually, emotionally, or maybe even sexually, then allow us to remember, cherish, and relive them many times. I was experiencing one of those moments.

Before me stood a vision that was nothing short of angelic. She appeared to be around eighteen years old, five feet five inches tall, with long black shiny hair that hung a few inches past her waist. She had a very soft, shy smile that could melt ice cream buried in a glacier. Her femininity contrasted sharply with the surroundings. A bright, flowered blouse hung loosely over black silk pajamas. Her flawless skin was slightly lighter than most Vietnamese, and her large black eyes seemed to float above her high cheekbones. Both of her hands loosely clutched a small feather duster.

"Hi, my name's Suzie," she said turning that old saying "soft as an autumn breeze" into a reality.

"Hi, I'm Tom, and … ahhh … umm … so Suzie is it? What is it that you do here?" I was struggling to regain my composure.

"I your hooch girl," she explained in broken but well-pronounced English. I felt like I had just won the Irish Sweepstakes.

I was trying to put everything into perspective, whatever that might be. Suzie, still standing in the doorway, reached out to her left, while maintaining eye contact with me, and appeared to grasp something. With a quick tug, another vision of Asian loveliness appeared in the doorframe. Firmly held in Suzie's grasp was a young girl, maybe sixteen or seventeen. She pulled long black hair from her face and shyly giggled as she was introduced.

"This my cousin, Mia. See you tomorrow, GI Tom," she said in very fast English, followed by even faster Vietnamese. They scampered off.

Suzie and Mia were quite a contrast to the hooch girls of Pleiku. Our maid in Enari was good ole Mama San. She cleaned as well as she spoke English, as did most of the women hired in Pleiku. Those hiring in Pleiku and An Khe used totally different criteria when making their decisions.

Only a few seconds had passed before the building echoed with human voices. This time, basses and baritones filled the air. The first guy appeared and leaned in, feet still in the hallway. He held onto the door frame and stretched out his hand. "I'm Grounder. See you in a few," he said and quickly exited.

The next visitor stayed a little longer and was soon joined by two others. I met "Grease," "Big Red," and "Shade" and was compelled to introduce myself with my college nickname. I dealt all my name cards with "Hi, I'm Specialist E-4 Thomas Lewis Haines, but just call me Skinner."

In the mess hall the introductions continued. By the end of the day I had also met Funky Fred, Ace, Cross, Booney, Doc One, Recall, Jackfruit, Doc Two, Spanky, Rat, and Jim—good God, how did someone ever get a nickname like Jim?

Ready, Aim, Fire

By week's end, I was up to speed with my job and the names of my coworkers. Since everybody had a nickname, it made the task easier.

Lieutenant "Hatch" Hatcher and I saw eye to eye on almost everything. Staff Sergeant Daniel "Fred" Frazier and SPC-4s Phil "Grounder" Lindsey and "Chico" Fernandez were all good guys. They worked hard. Their goals and those of the army may have been miles apart, but when something needed to be done, they did it.

Except for Lieutenant Hatcher and Sergeant Frazier, all of the men in supply had joined the army or been drafted right after high school. There were no troublemakers in the group. They were, however, a mischievous and playful bunch. Practical jokes were abundant. There wasn't a lot of planning that went into their shenanigans, and details were minimal at best. The pranks were mostly fun little fillers to break the monotony of tedious days in a hot, woefully underequipped office.

On one balmy day, I discovered a baby python had replaced the Cokes and beer in the refrigerator. I retaliated by placing a pound of homemade confetti on the blades of a ceiling fan in the center of the office. When Sergeant Frazier hit the switch one hot morning, small flakes of artificial snow rained down on his head. The following day, as I tried to type my first report, nothing appeared on the forms. With a new ribbon in place, I crunched the keys—*a s d f*. Again, no imprints. Chico was at his desk trying to stifle a laugh. Upon closer inspection, I discovered the keys had been meticulously covered.

The "Gotcha Award" for tomfoolery took place early on a sunny morning during my third week in An Khe. I got hung up in the mess hall and arrived late to work. Individual projects had Grounder and Chico fully engrossed. Baby-san, the nickname of the company office girl/hooch maid, was busy cleaning coffee cups on a makeshift stand in the corner. Her nickname fit her well. Not more than a child herself, probably fifteen or sixteen years old, she had just recently given birth to her first child. I think it was a girl.

"Good morning, Mr. Skinner," said Baby-san.

"Good morning, Baby-san. What's with everyone's noses in typewriters? We got an inspection I don't know about?" I weaved my way through the maze of desks, rusty file cabinets, and freshly emptied trash cans.

"The lieutenant has a job for us this afternoon that comes with a ton of paperwork, so he's got us humping these reports before lunch," said Chico as he handed me three forms.

"Oh great, my favorite thing in the world to deal with—stress." I rolled up my sleeves, rolled three sheets of paper and alternating carbon into my typewriter, and rolled my chair to a comfortable distance from my desk. The clatter of the Remingtons harmoniously filled the air.

A minute later I felt a drop of liquid fall on my cheek. With no concern for its origin, I wiped it dry and continued to type. Again, two or three drops appeared on my report, and an equal number dispersed on my desk, my arm, and my big, black Remi. I glanced up at the ceiling and then around the room. Everything appeared to be normal.

"Is anyone else in here getting wet?" I asked.

"Huh?" responded Chico, never looking up from his typing.

"What are you talking about?" said Grounder while slamming closed a broken file cabinet drawer. Sergeant Frazier didn't respond.

One by one, I glanced at everyone in the room. The detective part of me deduced that someone had a squirt gun and was waiting for the right moment before firing and then quickly disposing of the evidence. My concentration shifted. Typing took a back seat to locating the perpetrator. I would accomplish this with swift body movements. I was prepared to turn my head, my body, and my chair in the direction I believed would put me face to face with my prankish antagonist. Rolling my chair back into position, I began to peck at the keys randomly. Fifteen or twenty seconds into my stakeout, a steady stream hit me full on the side of my face. I whipped around and jerked to a halt. There I was, not face-to-face but face-to-tit with a double-barrel-firing, milk-packing mama—Baby-san. "Hey, OK, OK, stop. All right already, stop. Take a break and reload," I shouted while holding my hands out to block the fixed stream flying on target from around six feet away.

Baby-san released the double grip she had on her rather large and obviously full breasts, allowing her white blouse to drop over her still-dripping weapons. She had been hiding behind a filing cabinet. Sarge was holding onto the side of his desk with one hand and slapping a pile of paper with the other. He was laughing so hard he quivered. Grounder and Chico stood and raised both their hands, thumbs up in triumph. Giggling, Baby-san went back to her coffee preparation chores.

"OK, OK, we're talking major payback here," I said.

"You should … you should … have … seen the look … look on your face," gasped Sergeant Frazier while he wiped away tears.

With frivolity out of the way, we settled into a day of non-stop reports, inventories, order forms, requisition sheets, and other assorted pieces of bureaucratic bullshit.

Lieutenant Hatcher arrived midafternoon with more paperwork, which in the bureaucratic double speak of Uncle Sam needed completion sooner than before the last that was unfinished and redone on top of what had been partially completed and transferred to be denied for further alteration and approval. Make sense? No, but then neither did half of what we "accomplished." Most of our completed tasks seemed either redundant, unnecessary, or overkill of what was necessary. Everyone from the lowest E-1 in basic training to the highest five star at the Pentagon was aware of the incredible waste of time, money, and resources that the armed services generated at its every move.

One of the most poignant examples I came across involving gross waste and stupidity came in the form of a letter I had received the previous day. Sam was a college buddy who spoke fluent German without an accent. Naturally, when he joined the army, he asked to go to Germany as his "destination request." His letter arrived from Fort Bragg, where he was spending his time stoking fires and painting rocks pink. He had never been in any trouble and had no security problems. But transferring to Germany was out of the question because he was too short, so they were sending him to Vietnam. Excuse me. Knock, knock, is anyone home?

SNAFU

With the day's duties completed, the trash cans full to overflowing, and the humidity dropping a bit, we brought our day to a close. Lieutenant Hatcher gave everyone verbal congratulations on a job well done and quickly exited to the officers' club. I tossed an empty Coke can into the trash and watched it hit the floor as it bounced off the crumpled mound of papers spilling over the top. Chico grabbed me by the collar and said, "Let's book." We picked up our mail and reluctantly made our way to the mess hall for the day's third ingestion of our daily sustenance. Just outside the long wooden building, we caught a whiff of what to expect and were pleasantly surprised when we entered. Although we couldn't quite put our finger on the source of the aroma, it was still very inviting.

Two of Chico's buddies caught his attention just as we got to the door. They exchanged details of the day's events as they related to each other.

I turned my attention to the elevated grassy area to our right and greeted the company's pet monkey, Judy, and a dog we called Mr. Chips. A heavy-duty wrestling match kept Judy and Chips entertained. The dog was a medium-size mutt with off-white hair and large brown spots covering 40 percent of his body in no particular pattern. Judy was a macaque. She had short, chestnut brown hair. Although Mr. Chips thought he was winning this playful encounter, it was Judy who was in control.

I had my camera and snapped a quick shot of them in a death grip. Upon hearing the click of the camera, Judy looked up at me as though to say, "You had better have gotten my good side." The two combatants took a break from jumping, rolling, and playfully soft-biting at each other to come over and inspect my clicking chunk of plastic.

I couldn't resist the opportunity. Sliding my sunglasses to the edge of my nose, I dropped down on all fours and aimed a stare at Judy.

"Hey, Judy," I said, "Do you think you can outlast me today?" She walked over, got into position, and began to stare back. We locked into a visual close encounter and held our respective ground. Neither of us flinched. Neither of us blinked. Neither of us seemed to be breathing. Four cold, staring eyes locked into a psychological form of combat. Soon, I could feel her breath, as I'm sure she felt mine. Then in a swift, clean movement, Judy reached out and snatched the glasses from the edge of my nose and ran off with her trophy. Shrieking with glee, she celebrated her victory, swinging the glasses in a circle.

"Judy," I said, "I know a python who hasn't eaten in a week." In response, she snapped the glasses in two, tossed half in the direction of Mr. Chips, then walked over to me, and placed the other half delicately in the palm of my hand. "You're a sore loser and a communist sympathizer," I said while picking up the remains of my glasses. I then added the purchase of sunglasses number seven to my list of items to get on my next trip to the PX.

Gone with the Fucking Wind

It was 0900 hours on a Wednesday when Lieutenant Hatcher arrived with a day's work cradled in his outstretched arms—a day's work for a battalion of clerks that he wanted the four of us to accomplish in the same amount of time. We settled in with pens, pencils, typewriters, and shovels at the ready. The day progressed fluidly with everyone working at a comfortable pace.

When the afternoon began to wind down, I started to make my plans for the evening. I no longer had to pull guard duty in my new position; however, I often found my name next to other chores

SNAFU

I was "volunteered" for by Chambers. My assignment for the evening: designated theater operator.

Lieutenant Hatcher arrived with a basket in tow to pick up our reports—the perfect opportunity to make my move. My hands began to shake, my mouth became dry, my heartbeat quickened, and I started to sweat profusely. I handed the lieutenant a handful of reports, placed a small stack of forms on top of the disheveled heap, put a pen in his hand, and directed him to place his signature next to the lines bearing red *X*s.

"What am I signing for this time, Haines?" he asked.

"Just the same ole same ole that you always sign for, sir," I responded.

He read the top one, recognized it as a form he needed to endorse, and scribbled his signature. He then proceeded to do the same with the rest of the stack, sans the reading.

When he got to the line marked with a red *X* at the bottom of the sixth form, my heart picked up an extra beat. He pulled his pen from the paper, after semi-neatly signing it. I mumbled the word "bingo" to myself a little too loudly.

"Excuse me?" he responded while holding his pen at the ready for the next form.

"I said, 'I gotta go.' Sir, I'm showing tonight's movie."

My heart continued to pound, and beads of sweat collected in uneven rows across my forehead. "Oh yeah, I forgot. What's showing?" he asked.

"I haven't a clue, sir. Do you want me to save ya a seat?" I asked, knowing his negative response before he even said anything.

"Thanks, but I think I'll pass, but you have a nice evening."

After he signed three or four more documents, I sprinted out of the room, this time talking at a level only I could hear. "A nice profitable evening, thank you, sir." I removed paper number six, an authorization for the acquisition of six cases of beer for some bogus function for the brass and tossed the remainder in my outbox. My heart rate returned to normal, and my hands stopped shaking as I left the building.

The PX, crowded as usual with soldiers purchasing everything from chocolate bars to chocolate-colored cars, was a dangerous place to frequent because it was the closest reminder we had of the real world. It was all too easy to spend entire paychecks in a matter of minutes. I glanced around at the overflowing shelves, spotting one soldier looking at diamond rings, another listening to a portable cassette player, and a third smelling different scents at a perfume counter. The sights, sounds, and smells of America were brought right to our doorstep in a war zone, courtesy of the entrepreneurs of our wonderful capitalist system. And I thank God for that system because I was in need of another pair of sunglasses and six cases of beer.

With my ill-gotten booty in place, I sprinted to HQ to pick up the evening's entertainment. I signed my name on a ledger, grabbed the shiny, black-plastic handle of the package in front of me, and began to exit. The SPC-4 behind the counter hollered a loud "HEY" at me just as I reached the door. I spun around on the heel of my boot and focused on the shiny, black-plastic movie reel he was holding at shoulder height.

"Are you planning on showing just the first half of *Gone with the Wind?*"

"*Gone with the Wind!*" I said in disbelief. "Are you shitting me—*Gone with the Fucking Wind!*" Damn, I didn't get enough beer.

I arrived at the "theater" at 1900 hours to begin the ritual of the makeover. The "all purpose" room had been in use for a briefing earlier in the day, so very little rearranging took place. Reggie Ford, the assistant "volunteer" was already half finished with arranging chairs and benches when I arrived.

Although I rarely saw Reggie except on assignments like this one, it was always a pleasure to be in his company. He had a great sense of humor, a keen sense of doing things right, and more common sense than most. He was from South Central Los Angeles and had joined the army after dropping out of trade school. His family was poor, so he'd planned to learn a trade courtesy of the United States Army. He was a mechanic in the motor pool with a specialty I didn't understand—no surprise there. He was also one of the few people I knew who had taken President Kennedy's physical fitness program to heart. He was six feet even and weighed 190 pounds—all muscle, no fat. His skin was ebony, and he had a wide, bright smile that lit up any room he entered.

As soon as the movie was over, he would join a dozen other black soldiers in Franklin "Rumor" Gray's hooch for an evening of wine, talk of women, and song. As you walked by any hooch, you could tell who was inside by the music coming through the walls. You could be sure when you walked past Rumor's, it wouldn't be Creedence Clearwater Revival or the Beatles. What you heard, however, would change the way you would walk by because Rumor had the best collection of R&B east of Cambodia.

There was a kind of self-imposed segregation of blacks and whites during their off time in rear areas. There were many exceptions to this unofficial segregation, but most blacks and most whites formed bonds within their race, quite often creating unintentional racial tension. For the most part, there seemed to be a "don't fuck with me, and I won't fuck with you" attitude that existed between the races. But, in combat, everyone was the same color.

Reggie and I had no problem with the color of our skin. What we did have at that moment was a problem with the projector. The elevator screw at the front of the machine was jammed—permanently.

"Hey, Skinner, hand me those operations manuals under that chair," Reggie said pointing to a bent aluminum chair in the corner. After turning pages, he got it to the best height possible; problem solved.

Reggie then unraveled the extension cord while I wrote the name of the movie on a small, cracked chalkboard. The small piece of chalk became my weapon of sarcasm that I executed in a crude form of calligraphy in large letters, "Gone with the Fucking Wind." I placed the board on an easel by the door.

Reggie untangled the last knot and glanced at the board. "Ohhh, maaan, so much for hangin' with the bros in here tonight." He grabbed a cloth off a hook, wrapped it around his head, and bugged his eyes out. "No, ma'am, I don't know nuthin' 'bout birthin' no babies," he said, nailing a dead-on perfect impression of Prissy.

Upon completion of my bout of laughter, I placed my arm around Reggie's rock-hard shoulder. In my most aristocratic clenched-teeth voice, I said, "Reggie, ole chum, how would you like to engage in a most profitable endeavor that would involve a minimum of effort and a maximum of financial reward?"

"Speak to me, ole boy," Reggie responded, power-slamming my much softer shoulder with his forearm.

I directed him outside to a jeep containing six cases of warm beer and a tub of ice. He gave me wide eyes and a wide smile and initiated the ritual of "the dap," an elaborate synchronized handshake. I had made it half way before my whiteness caused me to screw it up.

We unloaded the beer and set up our concession stand at the rear of the room. We surrounded the medium-size chunks of ice with eighteen cans of beer.

"Snatch one of those for me, will ya?" said Reggie.

"Reggie, they've only been on the ice for eight seconds. I think you might want to give it a few more seconds, like maybe two or three thousand."

"How long have you been in Nam? Didn't anyone show you any survival tricks, like getting warm beer cold real quick? Toss me a—I mean, hand me a can and watch the master of instant cool," he said with an air of authority.

Reggie placed the can of beer on its side on top of the ice and rapidly spun it for thirty seconds. He removed the can, popped the tab, and took a large gulp. "Aaaaaah, refreshing and ice-cold." OK, maybe not ice-cold, but cold enough. Thirty seconds later I joined him with one of my own perfectly spun cans.

The room was almost full by the time 0730 rolled around. There were approximately thirty-five guys spread in a haphazard fashion around the room. The chairs filled up first, floor space directly in front of walls went next while planks set across barrels finished up the seating process. A few brought pillows to sit on. Reggie pulled the cord on the light in sync with the starting of the projector, and we were rolling. Hoots and hollers echoed throughout the room. These guys were "hornily" ready for an evening of gawking at Vivian Leigh.

Everything was going great. Beer sales were brisk, the sheet on the wall beautifully reflected the burning of Atlanta, and Reggie was mouthing all of Rhett's famous lines on cue.

Somewhere around eighty minutes into the movie, a PFC with a can of beer in one hand and a hairbrush in the other squatted down next to me. He waved his beer hand in front of my face and pointed over my shoulder with his brush hand. He stood up without saying a word and made his way back to his nest.

I turned my head and felt my heart pick up an extra beat. Twice in one day—jeez, I didn't need this shit. I hit the off switch and yelled for some light. When Reggie hit the toggle, forty heads turned at the same time and let out a collection of short "oh" phrases. There were some "oh shits," a few "oh fucks," and a handful of "oh nos." Personally I was saying all three minus the "ohs."

The reason—a giant heap of shiny black celluloid piled almost three feet high and squirting out in all directions, the film from the front reel. Upon inspection, it was discovered that the take-up reel was inoperable. The rubber band that turned the reel had dried up and broken. We had spare bulbs, but my guess for the closest place to get a spare band was Adolph Gassers Camera Store in San Francisco.

Reggie put his face to within a couple of inches of the projector and, once again, gave me the Prissy bug eyes. "Lawdy, lawdy, massa, whathcu gonna do now?"

"I've got three cases of beer left, so what do you think I'm gonna do? I'm gonna finish showing *Gone with the Fucking Wind.*" I hollered out, "Beer and piss break," and began to rewind the shiny black mountainous mess while Reggie took care of suds sales.

A short while later we were ready to roll again. I positioned myself behind the projector with a finger on either side of the take-up reel turning it ever so slowly by hand. The reel was sharp, the projector hot, and I was miserable. When that glorious moment arrived, when the words "The End" appeared on the screen, I dropped off my stool and began to blow at the quarter inch grooves in my fingers.

While I was still blowing on my dented digits, a very large figure appeared over my shoulder. I glanced up and could only see the outline of this massive structure because the light bulb in the ceiling appeared at the edge of his right ear. My first thought was there was no way I was going to be able to type anything at work with these fingers, so just go away. I shifted slightly to my right to position the bulb directly behind his head.

Standing before me was a sergeant from an infantry line unit that had just arrived from the field. He was still clutching his M16 and wearing his ruck. He had obviously been in the field awhile. His fatigues were solid brown, and he smelled a tad ripe.

"Hey guys, I know it's kinda late, but our company just came in from the field. Some of our boys—four of them from Georgia—heard about tonight's movie, and we were like, you know, wondering if there was a chance of a late showing for them," he said in a voice half exhausted and half pleading.

"Sorry, Sarge, but the projector's rubber band on the take-up wheel is broken; the only way to show the movie is by hand," I said.

"Oh, that's a shame. Well, thanks anyway," he said as he dropped his head and started to leave.

Reggie and I exchanged looks. "What the hell," we said in unison and called the sergeant back. Upon hearing the good news, he smiled broadly, exposing a large gap where two teeth should have been. He promised to return with a roomful of very appreciative grunts and permission for Reggie and me to show up very late for work in the AM.

With no sensation in my fingers, no evening with the Temptations for Reggie, and no beer sales for either of us, we still managed to feel good. Reggie rigged a device to help turn the take-up reel while I solicited a couple more "volunteers." Reggie and I took turns catching some Zs. A few of the grunts curled up in fetal positions and cut a few Zs as well.

It was so late when Reggie and I left the "theater" that some would have referred to it as early morning. A few of the grunts had fallen asleep and resembled small children curled up in front of a TV on a Saturday night, trying desperately to stay awake. The ones who went first were those who had grabbed a quick, warm shower before heading to the show. We hit the lights. Those that didn't respond to the shiny tubes of light, we shook awake, and then all of us headed out.

At three hours and fifty-three minutes, we wrapped up a second showing of *Gone with the Fucking Wind,* and frankly my dears—we didn't give a damn.

AAAAAAUUUUUUGH!

The final order of business before calling it a night, or in this case, a morning, was a quick trip to the latrine. We walked past Rumor's now-quiet hooch and then past another half-dozen dark and silent huts. The air was heavy with humidity but with a touch of coolness to it. The only sounds were the crickets and frogs performing their nightly concert.

The latrine came into view as we rounded the corner past the last hooch in a row of five, bathed in a soft light from a street lamp positioned to its right. The steps and the door creaked at the slightest touch. The spring, attached by a bent nail, slammed the door shut behind us.

Reggie and I groped in the pitch darkness, hunting for the thin, white cord attached to a ceiling light fixture located somewhere near the center of the room. We sliced at the air. Reggie glanced against the cord with the back of his hand.

"Got it," he proclaimed as he gave it a tug. "Oh, man, it's burned out."

Matches weren't an option because neither one of us smoked. Nature was calling a little too much to consider hunting down a flashlight, so we decided to answer her call with the hunt and feel method. We ran our hands along the plywood that had butt-size holes cut every couple of feet, feeling for loose rolls of toilet paper. I hollered, "Bingo," at the same time Reggie announced, "Found one."

We "dropped trou" and began to feel again for a proper hole to occupy. The smell became our topic of conversation.

"Man, it stinks in here. I wonder how long it's been since they burned shit around here?" I asked.

"I don't know, but judging from the smell, I'd say sometime during the Korean War," Reggie replied, then added, "Damn, this hole is huge. Mama Cass would fall through this thing."

When my laughter stopped, silence set in. The crickets entertained us through the walls. Just as Jiminy's choir took a break from their never-ending, monotonous antimelody, Reggie let out a blood-curdling scream. He continued to holler as my ears followed his distress through the dark towards the door. I took a quick swipe with a wad of course paper and followed him outside.

I pushed open the door and saw Reggie, pants at his ankles, shooting his moon to the moon in the sky. He was still making noises in a low muffle and was brushing his hands at lightning speed across his butt and legs. The cause of his distress—maggots. They were setting up house on Reggie's ass. I guess the shit was piled high, and his ass was settled low. A few seconds later, an inspection of his butt, legs, and scrotum showed that he had removed all of them, somewhere between six and twelve.

We hunted down a flashlight and returned. What we discovered made Reggie's comment about the Korean War seem like the truth. It appeared that covering the shit with lime at the end of each day was easier than burning it. However, the hole Reggie settled into was lacking lime and was filled with hundreds of squirming maggots. Reggie's ass was just a small fraction of an inch from the top of the city of maggots.

At lunchtime, we took our demands to Top. We arrived exhausted and in foul moods. Chambers was alone when we entered HQ.

"Top," Reggie said before we even came to a halt, "have someone burn the shit in the latrine closest to the mess hall, or we will have someone burned. We're serious—burn before sundown, or we will demand a full inspection. And I'm sure no one around here wants an article 15."

Even though Chambers had already heard about our nocturnal experience, he turned red because he didn't like being threatened. It was the only time either one of us ever "ordered" a superior officer to do something, and frankly my dears, we didn't give a shit ... so to speak.

Burning Shit

We lifted the drums of retching vapor
Filled with shit and toilet paper
Placed them on trucks in rows of five
Then held our breaths to stay alive

The barrels shifted hard to the right
Launching their contents into noble flight
Piss and puke and all kinds of crap
Landed, full and heavy, in the center of my lap

We arrived at the perimeter at quarter to three
Where we burned tubs of turds and vats of pee
We arrived again at half past four
Ready and willing to rejoin the war

We finished our last run at ten minutes to eight
And watched the fetid smoke drift back to the gate
Then it was off to the mess for a bite to eat
Then off to the latrine to ...
AAAAUUUUUUUGHBLUBWOOOOG

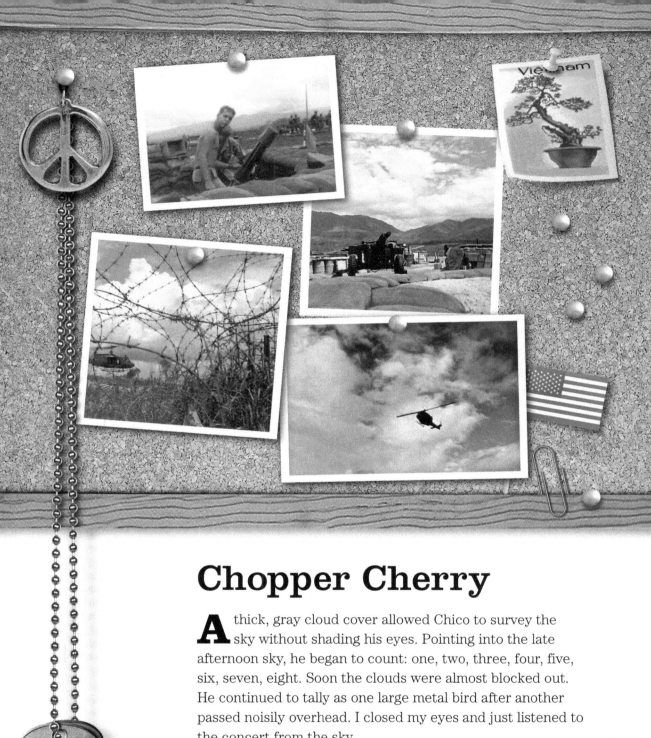

Chopper Cherry

A thick, gray cloud cover allowed Chico to survey the sky without shading his eyes. Pointing into the late afternoon sky, he began to count: one, two, three, four, five, six, seven, eight. Soon the clouds were almost blocked out. He continued to tally as one large metal bird after another passed noisily overhead. I closed my eyes and just listened to the concert from the sky.

Think of Vietnam and sound; think of the helicopter. Hueys, Loaches, Huskies, Cobras, Chinooks, Tarhes, and Sneebs all sang that same powerful melody. The sound, which I won't even begin to try and phonetically mimic, was a source of excitement to some, while instilling a numbing fear into others. The noise was part of a constant choreography of precise movement in the humid air overhead. Transporting troops, engaging in battle, moving supplies, and picking up the dead and wounded kept these vertical-flying birds crisscrossing the landscape from early morning until late into the evening.

Like all other gravity-stricken ground-hounds, these creatures and the stories they held fascinated us. It was the third Tuesday in September, and everyone in the supply room traded tales, embellishing, exaggerating, and in some cases, out-and-out lying to top the previous yarn.

Sergeant Frazier finished the day with the final "flying fish" story.

"No shit, guys, there was this corporal who was blinded in a firefight; they were evacuating him to the hospital when the chopper pilot and copilot were hit. He was directed by a wounded sergeant to take over the controls from the dead pilot and fly it out of the hot zone. The sergeant then got on the phone with HQ and walked the blind corporal through his moves. He was badly wounded in both legs and one arm—the sergeant, not the corporal. The only thing wrong with the corporal was that he was blind. Anyway, he lost consciousness just before touchdown—again, the sergeant, not the corporal. The corporal knew he was close, so he set the chopper down right where he was. It landed on the roof of the HQ that was giving him direction. And that's the honest to God's truth." He told his tale so well that we all decided to play along and pretend to believe it.

When I completed my final task of the day, Sergeant Frazier called me over to his desk. I responded with a great deal of enthusiasm because Frazier didn't like asking people to do stupid things for him, and sometimes he had to do just that. I felt that if I sounded like I didn't mind, it might make him feel better asking.

He handed me a piece of standard, white typing paper with a short, handwritten list of equipment scribbled on it. He then directed me to hunt this equipment down and match the serial numbers with those on the paper. Yep, I had just gotten one of those stupid assignments.

Jeez, first I had to act like I believed his chopper story, and now I had to act excited about a dim-witted assignment.

"OK, Sarge," I said, "point me in the right direction."

"Just follow the flying fickle finger of fate," he said while he beckoned me outside with a come-hither forefinger. He handed me some orders, realigned his finger skyward, and pointed to a Slick flying overhead. "Get on one of those and tell the pilot to take you to Firebase Melissa, and that's where you'll find the equipment." Looking at me out of the corners of his eyes, he grinned and winked.

I gave him my best military salute, something most noncommissioned officers disliked receiving, and added a very loud and sincere, "Yes, sir," another gesture most sergeants hated. Chico, Phil, and a handful of others gathered behind me making chopper noises and announcing to the compound that I would no longer be a chopper cherry.

This great detail carried a bonus with it. Not only was I getting my first ride on a chopper, but the journey would also deliver me to the doorstep of Sergeant Scott Simmons.

Scott was a platoon leader for an artillery team at Firebase Melissa. He was in his early twenties but looked younger, dark-complexioned but had sandy-brown hair, and stood five-ten but looked taller. Tanned and wiry, he went shirtless as often as he could. "Born Leader" was written all over him. I never met another individual who cared more for the men under his command than Scott did. This trip was perfectly timed because Scott was going with me on R&R to Singapore. It was an ideal time to nail down details.

Suzie made a checklist of everything she thought I'd need. I took everything she had written down in surprisingly accurate and legible English but hoped I wouldn't need the rosary. I arrived at the chopper pad right after lunch the following day, hoping I wouldn't regret it, considering my history of motion sickness. I was traveling light: M16, poncho, an almost empty rucksack, and of course, a brown clipboard containing a piece of paper with a lot of numbers on it. The day wasn't pretty, but it wasn't raining—yet. Alternating white and gray clouds almost completely covered the sky. If you looked really hard, you could spot a speck of blue peeking through.

Activity was hectic at the chopper pad. The wind generated by the helicopter blades blended with the swirling air created by Mother Nature. I was the last to board. "Hey, Spanky, save the best seat for the cherry," came a voice from within. Great, the word had filtered down to complete strangers.

I stepped up onto the skid, tossed my belongings inside, and threw myself in behind them. The spot they so graciously saved for me was called "riding the door." "Hey, thanks for saving me a seat with a view," I said, spinning around on my butt and dropping my legs out the door. Instantly and without warning, the chopper rose like a fast elevator. It went straight up and out into a banking climb. We were now fully racing the wind to Melissa. My knuckles instantly turned white from the death grip I had on the chopper's doorframe. Even though the laws of physics kept me from being sucked out, I maintained a modicum of security by keeping my fingers one with the metal.

The ride was exhilarating. The powerful drone of the chopper's blades monopolized our sense of hearing while the wind delivered a nonstop thrashing to our sense of touch. However, our sense of sight was treated to a cornucopia of nature's finest. Checkerboard rice paddies, virulent rolling hills, and chocolate-colored rivers came and went as we whirred by at speeds between ninety and 115 miles per hour. At 1,500 feet, the war appeared peaceful.

Activity aboard the Slick picked up as our LZ appeared in the distance. Firebase Melissa was a conglomeration of sand bags, large rocks, tents, 105 mm howitzer emplacements, 81 mm mortar positions, wooden ammo boxes, underground bunkers, and telephone poles supporting a network of netting. Massive rolls of triple-dannert barbed wire totally surrounded the firebase. It was an island of brown in a forest of green, except for the first few rows of trees and brush that had lost their life to Agent Orange.

We pulled in fast. A CH-54 Tarhe helicopter had just dropped off a few thousand pounds of cargo by sling. She pulled away just as we landed. The Slick didn't kick up much dust because the monsoon rains had the earth's cover holding wet and heavy.

Scott was waiting, shirtless, as I expected, with a mortar part in hand. I grabbed my M16 in one hand and my rucksack with the other and jumped to the ground. He held a mortar part high over his head and waved it at me. "OK, Mr. Remington, let's get those goddamn numbers, so we can get down to some goddamn serious visiting," he said.

Twenty minutes later I had all my numbers. The list showed no items missing. I did notice, unfortunately, that not all the equipment was in working order, so I made notes of those items, just in case that was part of the detail and I didn't know it. The rains played havoc with the serviceability of the equipment during the monsoon season. Nothing was ever really dry; it only became a little less wet.

With serial numbers out of the way, we concentrated our energies on a different number—six. We popped the first of our half dozen after its roll on the ice and began our plans for a little R&R in Singapore. Scott's fire mission, scheduled well after dark, gave him a few hours of downtime.

The day went fast, and the dark appeared early due to large, dark, ominous, gray clouds replacing the few remaining white ones. You could smell the rain approaching. The evening's fire mission was definitely going to be a wet one.

Scott and I propped up against a fresh pile of sandbags and ate a combination of Cs and sweets from a care package from Minneapolis. I had taken a large swig from my canteen when I heard, "Fuck you," coming from a short distance outside the wire. I was 99.99 percent sure it wasn't Charlie coming up to the edge of the perimeter to verbally harass us. My guess was that

I was hearing the sound of a gecko lizard for the first time.

"Is that what I think it is?" I asked Scott.

"You got it, buddy. That's the sound of the most obnoxious creature on earth. A friend of mine from the Twenty-Fifth said the only time it didn't sound obnoxious was when it was around that crazy bird that says nothing but 're-up.' What a great concert they make. Re-up. Fuck you. Re-up. Fuck you. Re-up. Fuck you. God, I could listen to that for hours," Scott said laughing while throwing a stone in the direction of the sound.

After finishing all the crumbs left of homemade, chocolate chip cookies, eight of us retreated into an underground bunker, home to Scott and three others. The bunker's air was thick with the odor of rifle oil, sweat, wet boot leather, damp canvas, and mold.

Huge raindrops had begun to pound the camp like miniature mortars. We shook off like dogs leaving a pond and searched for a comfortable spot to roost. I tried to fluff up a flat, heavy, musty-smelling pillow while I stuffed my rucksack in the corner of a bunk. I laid the pillow over the ruck and swung myself into a horizontal position on top of a camouflaged poncho liner and picked up bits and pieces of different conversations.

One discussion concerned a rumor that the firebase was going to be noteworthily short of manpower, not just for a few hours, but for days. Only a handful of soldiers would be left to man the fire missions as well as guard the perimeter. The higher ups were gambling that Charlie wouldn't discover the change in security.

I reached into my rucksack and pressed the record button on my Sony just as the news filtered into the bunker—click.

Morgan: "Before you go to bed tonight you better get down on your knees and pray."

Pierce: "It's going to be a nightmare."

Rivera: "What I'm gonna try is to get off with fourteen days left in the Army. I'm gonna …"

Pierce: "Yeah, I'm gonna ask him to pull me the next fuckin' day I'm in."

Haines: "You mean Bravo's leaving, and Recon is going to be gone at the same time, and that will leave you guys alone here to guard the perimeter for—"

Simmons: "What's Top say about that?"

Haines: "—for four days?"

Simmons: "Well, possibly we'll have one guy—one guy in operations to gun the fire missions."

Rivera: "For just four days?"

Simmons: "Yeah, four or five days."
Morgan: "OK, first squad will volunteer to be in operation."
Simmons: "Man, that's five days too long for Bravo Company to be gone."
Click—silence.

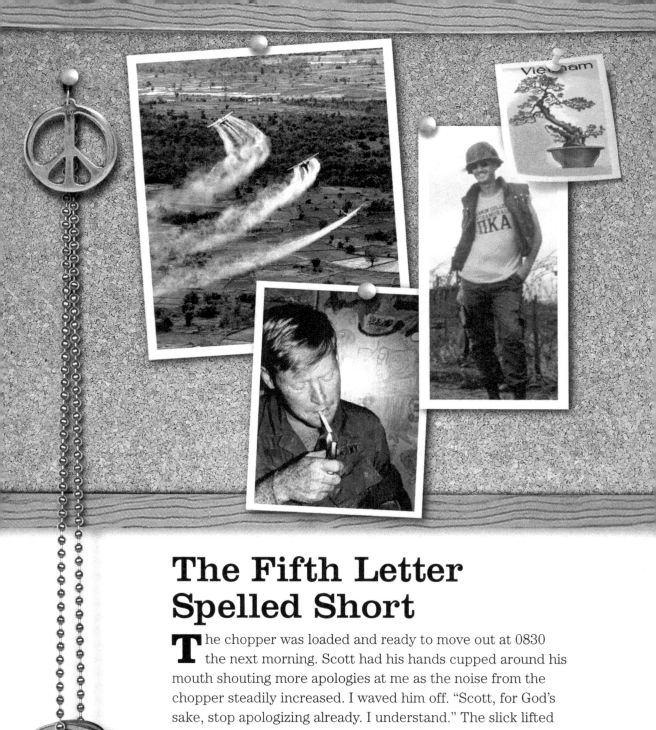

The Fifth Letter
Spelled Short

The chopper was loaded and ready to move out at 0830 the next morning. Scott had his hands cupped around his mouth shouting more apologies at me as the noise from the chopper steadily increased. I waved him off. "Scott, for God's sake, stop apologizing already. I understand." The slick lifted and turned into the brisk morning air. We watched Scott's shirtless body become smaller and smaller as we rose to 1,500 feet and drifted away.

Scott was apologetic because he had bowed out of our planned R&R due to the newly discovered security situation. Our R&R and the days of Bravo's absence coincided. There was no way he would leave his men hanging on their own. I knew that. Scott knew that. His men knew that.

Someone had cranked up Hendrix on an oversized cassette deck strapped to the wall at the same time the blades whirred into action.

The return flight was no less exhilarating, possibly because I didn't maintain a death grip on the door frame. I sat in the open doorway with my feet dangling and the fingers on my left hand playing upside down on an imaginary guitar. Hendrix's guitar and chopper rotor blades, a combination that could only be described as far freaking out. Helicopter rotor blades, Hendrix's guitar, rotor blades, guitar, rotator blades, guitar. I put my helmet-covered head into my hands and drifted off to San Francisco. The journey back didn't have the peaceful feel of the trip up. There was troop activity on the ground, and the sky looked like a busy highway during rush hour in Atlanta. However, the ride was without event, and we landed safely and on time, dead center on the "golf course."

I delivered my report to Sergeant Frazier and thanked him again for the experience. He looked at me like he had a burned-out light bulb over his head and then winked. "You're welcome. See you tomorrow, bright and early."

I took a deep breath, held my finger up, and said, "Tomorrow? What about the rest of ... oh, yes, sir, Sergeant, I'll see you tomorrow, bright and early." That's the second time in two days I called him sir. I hoped it didn't piss him off too much.

I had no idea what to do. Suzie also had the day off and was going to visit relatives in Kontum. I felt lost but only until I entered my room. Neatly piled in the center of my bed was the largest stack of mail I had ever received, here or at home.

Pulling off the rubber band, I picked up the stack and began to count. There were eight envelopes, four from in-country and four from the world. There was also a note from Suzie:

Dear Tom,

You have many people that love you. Cherish this great gift.
You beaucoup number one, Tom.

Love, Suzie

P.S. Chico helped me with some of the words. In fact, Chico is the kindest, nicest, coolest, most wonderful American GI that I ever met. In fact, he is so nice you should offer to loan him twenty dollars until payday.

It looked like Chico had helped her with all the words in the P.S.

I separated the envelopes into two stacks, in-country and the world, and began to read.

Envelope one: Endicott, New York (home). Mom, Dad, Steve (brother), and Mopsey (dog) were all doing fine. Main news—Steve set his wedding date to coincide with my returning home at the end of January. Main advice—stay safe.

Envelope two: Poughkeepsie, New York (Vassar). Lucia was doing great. Main news—she just returned from a trip to Europe. Florence was her favorite city. Main advice—stay safe.

Envelope three: Erie, Pennsylvania (Gannon College). Barry Procacina and the eleven other residents of the Pi Kappa Alpha House were doing well at balancing academics, sports, and partying. Main news—the Pikes at Gannon were selected to represent Duke Beer for free kegs. So much for that balance of academics, sports, and partying. Main advice—stay cool and safe.

Envelope four: Greenville, North Carolina (East Carolina University). Main News—Thomas Lewis Haines has been accepted to attend the East Carolina University School of Art for the second quarter beginning December 1, 1969. Main advice—please pay fees on time. That news put me in a state of euphoria. East Carolina University had just subtracted two months and ten days from my military career. I had an emotional orgasm that left me light headed. A month earlier I had visited a very small Quonset hut that contained more than 300 college brochures. I flipped through them in rapid fashion, checking one item only: start dates. I found three that were on the quarter system, which would allow me to get almost all of my early-out days. There was one in the Dakotas, one in Missouri, and East Carolina University (ECU). The selection was a no-brainer. John and Rosco were due thank yous.

I tossed all the letters, except the one from ECU, in a pile in the middle of my bed and raced outside to announce my news to the world. When I reached the entrance to my hooch, I leaped into the air as high as I could and landed on a small pile of busted sandbags.

"Hey, buddy, do you know how tall I am?" I asked the guy who was working on the sandbags.

He looked up at me with a bewildered look. "I don't know—six-two, six-three," he said.

I pointed with extended index fingers to the step from which I had just jumped. "No, no, no, I'm much shorter than that. In fact, I just became so short, I would need a ladder to climb back up that step."

I abandoned the puzzled stranger and started to make lighter-than-air strides toward the supply room when I remembered I had the day off. Running around telling everyone that I just became two and a third months shorter while I was pulling some unwarranted downtime would be the ultimate in obnoxious cruelty. So back to reading round two of my letters.

Envelope five: Phuoc Vinh, Vietnam (First Air Cavalry). John Lawson was pulling time and counting days. Main news—he'd positively decided not to get an early-out to return to school. Advice—I should do the same. I couldn't believe the timing. Here is what John neatly printed on First Cav stationery.

Well Haines,

>*I just don't want to get an early out for school! It's just not me! I want you to think about it also. I'm grateful to have come over here short, and I just don't want to leave until I'm all finished. If I were gonna be here a full year, then I would definitely try for the early out! But such isn't the case, and as corny as it may seem, I feel obligated to finish this thing—to see it through. Think about it, and I think you may see my point, and feel the same way yourself!*
>
>*Anyway, do you know where Vung Tau is? It's the in-country R&R center. A friend of mine with the military police recently got his wish and got transferred from here to there. He figured that was the safest place over here. Within a week, some guy who was AWOL killed him. He was killed in an alley chasing one of our own guys. Damn!*
>
>*Well, we finally got our contest going. Every time you kill a rat, you get a free beer. Winners would be declared on a monthly basis. Sounds sick, but it's kinda fun, in a weird way, and boy what a party at the end of the month.*
>
>*Almost got in real trouble the other day. A full bird Colonel showed up and demanded that I open a certain Conex container. When I did, and he found it almost full of typewriter ribbons, he really came unglued. He said I had all the ribbons in the division, and he gave me two days to get them all back to division headquarters. Just killed me; I could trade ribbons for anything this company needed. Oh well!*
>
>*Along the same note, several weeks ago the CO came to me and said that we were getting ready to be inspected and that we were three Jeeps short—someone had stolen them! He told me to*

take anyone that I wanted, and not to return until I had stolen three Jeeps for our company! Can you believe this shit—a supply specialist for a Military Police company being told to steal three jeeps! Anyway, he said that he would cover our asses once we got them, and sure enough, he did! Just another day at the office. I didn't already tell you that story, did I?

John—SHORT

P.S. This fucking rain is driving me nuts!

Envelope six: Pleiku, Vietnam (Fourth Infantry). Robert "Rosco" Creech was not a happy camper. After reading Rosco's letter, no question, he and John needed to meet.

Skinner,

Boy, have I got a story to tell you. Remember my telling you about the missing TVS4 Starlight Scope. After you left camp, I spent several weeks finding another one to cover the missing one.

You won't believe the amount of trading, swapping, "borrowing" my boys and I had to do to have a big enough barter bag to interest the ones who had one to trade. I could have "bought" all of II Corps for much less. If I were the type of guy to do so, I could have purchased a string of girls and made a fortune easier than I got that scope.

I popped off the serial & plate and scratched 1031 on it, and then all was well on the property books. Wrong!

I received word that we were having a "surprise" IG inspection on Friday morning. Got the word on Wednesday, so all was well with the world. Again, wrong!

Late Thursday afternoon I received a piece of equipment from Div. Maint. Guess what? It was the original TVS4 #1031. It had been shipped back to the world to be repaired, and now, of course, it had to show up. Aw hell! What to do with two scopes. Too big to hide. When I checked it out, I found that the guts of the scope were still smashed beyond repair. It even still had the original bullet hole in the case. It was of no use to anyone and only served to cause us more hassle. Ain't it always the same SNAFU! It took me weeks to replace, and now I only have hours to make it go away. No sweat! When I see you eyeball to eyeball, I will tell you how I made it go away. But I will tell you this. If I had been like some we know … but you know me, keep it in the Army and use it for the men in the field, they deserve it!

Man, bring your butt on back or hold still until I can get there. We are the best "crooks" in this man's Army. With your talent and my nerve, we can turn this screwed up place around.

Later, Rosco

P.S. Maxed out the IG under stateside conditions. Boy, if they only knew! Long Bihn couldn't hold us all! They say I'm going to get a certificate for doing the best in the entire Division. How do you figure it?

Envelope seven: Somewhere, Vietnam (196th Infantry Brigade, part of the American Division). Frank Zedar, my best friend while growing up in Endicott, New York, had come a long way from our days of playing cowboys and Indians. Main news—he was now a platoon leader attached to the "4/31" Fourth Batallion, Thirty-First Infantry. He was mainly with I Corps in the mountains west of Da Nang to help the Marines, as a covering force, to get them out of Khe Sanh.

Envelope eight: Somewhere else, Vietnam (199th Infantry Brigade). D.J. Thompson was feeling really low. Main news—Al Rhoades and Pete "Quiet Man" Pitofsky were killed in action. Bobby Lane lost a leg, and Dean Barlow might lose both of his. Advice—stay safe.

I sat down hard on my bed and stared at the dirty, wrinkled envelope for a long time.

Frank Zedar

R&R in a Sling

Singapore—even the name sounded exotic. Preparations were complete. I was going to meet Rosco, David Lowe, and Eddie Jennings in Pleiku at noon on October 6th to leave for a week in paradise. David was a friend of Rosco's, a lifeguard from King of Prussia, Pennsylvania, and a drop-dead good-looking dropout from Penn State who would surely turn a lot of female heads in Singapore. Eddie, on the other hand, must have just made it on the weight restrictions when he entered the army. He was at least twenty-five pounds overweight with curly, red hair, a ruddy complexion, and a heart of gold.

Snapping the latch into place, I threw an overstuffed bag over my shoulder and headed for the door, where I encountered a slight delay. Suzie, taking up as much of the doorframe as possible, wanted to say her … hmmm … ah … goodbyes.

"You got lots of rubbers for boom boom?" she asked with a large dose of sarcasm in her voice.

"Hey, Suzie, I've told you at least a hundred times I am not going to Singapore for boom boom."

"I only say that to setup you."

We both laughed, mine nervous, hers sarcastic. I placed my hands on her shoulders and said, "That's upset, not setup, and I don't boom boom; I make love. And to make love you should be in love, and I doubt that I will fall in love in Singapore."

I then rambled on about needing to take a break from this God-forsaken insanity, and that's why I was going to Singapore.

Suzie walked with me to a waiting truck for the trip to Pleiku. I squeezed her hand, kissed her on the top of her head, and left. Once in Camp Enari, Rosco greeted me with a squeeze of the hand and a clap on the shoulder. "Are you ready to put your ass in a sling? A big, red Singapore sling that is."

"Ready, willing, and more than able, my dear fellow," I responded while handing him a fresh cup of hot coffee.

We made a quick stop at the "post office" to drop off a cartoon for the *Steadfast and Loyal* or *Ivy Leaves*, both Fourth Infantry Division publications. I didn't get the combat artist position, but I did snatch the runner-up prize: division cartoonist. Worked for me. Then we picked up our paperwork at HQ, Eddie and David at the mess hall, and a ride at the motor pool. The journey would take us to Camp Holloway for the flight to Cam Ranh Bay and then to Singapore. I studied my pay voucher on the trip to the bay. My basic pay as an E-4 was $190.20 a month. Added to this princely sum were foreign duty pay of $13 and hostile fire pay of $65. Then there were the subtractions: $18.75 total allotments, $2 for insurance, $2.72 subsistence/leave rations (whatever the hell they were), $1.20 for Soldiers Home (wherever the hell that is), and of course, the ever-present FICA tax that came to $9.13. The net amount was $234.40. I had an entire three months of pay with me, hidden deep within my socks.

A few long hours after leaving Cam Ranh Bay, we landed in Singapore and headed straight to our R&R orientation. The room was big and comfortable, as well as crowded and noisy. We had received an R&R information booklet on the flight that contained our processing paperwork and information, hotel accommodation, money exchange rates, shopping areas, activities and clubs, and churches. The booklet kept me occupied while waiting for the orientation to begin. On page 39 was a listing of hotel costs. The average was $6 a night. That, I could handle.

The noise subsided when a captain wearing dress greens arrived. He headed straight to a podium at the far end of the room and started in on a speech the captain most definitely had delivered many times before.

"OK, gentlemen, settle down. I know the last thing you want to hear is a lecture, so I'll make this as short and painless as possible. You should be out of here in a couple of hours. There are, as you probably have guessed, some rules, regulations, and laws that you need to become familiar with. There are also some warnings, cautions, and advice that the Department of Defense would like me to pass along."

He spent a few minutes explaining some of the local laws and reminded us that we were guests of another country and to conduct ourselves like the fine examples of American soldiers that we were. He then explained that the army had six hotels on its recommended accommodations list, all of which provided girls who were checked weekly for diseases by army doctors. After a lecture on infection, personal hygiene, and common-sense behavior, we were turned loose on the gracious city of Singapore.

We selected the Imperial Hotel because it had the classiest-sounding name. Twenty minutes later, gathered in the lounge, we set up a game plan. The main event on my agenda was to inform Guinness of the new record for Singapore sling consumption and then, of course, the mandatory trip to Tiger Balm Gardens. And the week-long adventure had to include an excursion to downtown Singapore for the biggest shopping spree of my life. With $600 in my sock and a two-page list of items in my wallet, I was ready for action.

Rosco and David were seated at the bar when I entered the brightly decorated room. The overhang at the bar sported two dozen hanging paper lamps, alternating red, orange, green, yellow, and blue. Soaking a cardboard coaster next to an empty chair was a crimson-colored drink in a tall, sweaty glass with an umbrella floating on the surface.

"Your inaugural sling awaits your approval, sir," Rosco ceremoniously announced. We found ourselves sucking down number two within minutes. Number three came, at which time we changed gears and slowed it down. Number four would be "TBD."

The room had filled with soldiers and "hostesses." I leaned over to whisper something clever to David about the mating ritual unfolding before us, but his seat was abandoned. I scanned the room and found him by the exit, talking to the prettiest girl in the lounge. Rosco and I watched as the men and women traded repartee.

"Where you from, GI?" one woman asked, directing her question to no one in particular.

"New York," responded a young man wearing glasses, a grass-green Izod golf shirt, and dungarees.

Many of the women, we were told, study the geography of the United States to bridge an obvious cultural gap and also to remind the GIs of their most treasured memories—home. "City or upstate?" she added.

He appeared a little miffed that anyone would even think he might be from anywhere north of the Tapenzee Bridge. He again answered in two words, "The city."

"I'll bet you're from the Bronx," she said, going for broke.

"Yeah, how did you know?" he asked, using enough words to form an entire sentence.

"Because all the best number-one looking guys are from the Bronx," she responded. A couple of minutes later they were on their way to Mama San's table in the far corner of the room near the kitchen. Mama San was a very short, round women in her late fifties. She took care of the financial dealings of all the girls in the room.

The scenario was, to say the least, extraordinary. Most of these guys never paid for sex before coming to Vietnam and probably never would again once they returned home. But on R&R, it was not only accepted but also expected. And this included all groups: married, single, and celibate. The army did absolutely nothing to discourage it; in fact, I believe they encouraged it as a means of boosting morale.

I set down my glass and held up two fingers to the bartender but changed my mind and waved him off. I turned around on my bar stool and continued to observe the soldier birds and the Asian honeybees.

Rosco and I soon found ourselves face to face with three young ladies in very short miniskirts.

"So, GIs, you shy or you funny boys?" one asked while another put her hand on Rosco's knee, or mid-thigh I should say.

"Neither, I'm just not interested," I responded.

"Unless, of course, you girls can come up with enough money, and then he might be interested," Rosco interjected.

Picking up his cue for a little deceptive give and take, I shot back, "Shit, Rosco, you promised not to tell anyone. I volunteered for Nam just to get away from that lifestyle."

"What you two talking about? You telling me we should pay him for sex?" the spokeswomen of the group asked Rosco.

"Well, no, we're not asking you to pay. You obviously can get all the sex you want. However, …," he said placing his hands palm up at shoulder level and tilting his head sideways.

"You mean women pay you money for sex?" she asked, directing her question to me this time.

"Yeah, and lots of it," I responded.

The oldest of the three, maybe in her mid-twenties, spoke for the first time. "You fooling us, right?"

"Come back with a hundred dollars, and I'll show you how much I'm fooling," I said as serious as I could. They looked to Rosco for affirmation, and he again gave them his palms up, head tilt, gesture. At this point, they switched to their native language and wandered off to spread the news throughout the room.

The girls went to the table where David, with his new best friend, Kim, were making plans for the week. They had switched to speaking English, so David could hear what they had to say. He listened for a while, figured out what Rosco and I were up to, and then broke into the conversation.

"Would you like to know what Tom's nickname is?" All heads turned to David in eager anticipation. "In the States, he is known as Goldenrod," David said with an air of authority. This revelation caused a combination of gasps and giggles.

Rosco and I gathered up our change, left a hefty tip, and headed to another bar for another round of slings and lies. We got to the exit and saw a bar named The Umbrella Lounge. Wouldn't take a rocket scientist to figure that one out. We had enough sense, however, to quit way before the Guinness record, whatever it might have been.

The following day we all made our obligatory trip through the tourist attractions. Our main stop was Tiger Balm Gardens, which we found to be both bizarre and fascinating.

Once the sun met the horizon, David and Eddie were nowhere to be found, and Rosco was spending the evening in his room recovering from the dry heaves. Experimenting with a local food cart gave his digestive system a fit. That combined with a little bit of a hangover, which we shared, kept him in the bed, unless he needed to sprint to the toilet.

At 1900 I was back at the bar, perched on my anointed favorite stool and ordering another sling. I had just removed the submerged umbrella and slung the excess liquid from my fingers when I heard, "Easy there, mister. Drink it; don't sling it."

I turned around and apologized to the gorgeous young lady brushing the red liquid from the front of her miniskirt.

"No problem, Mr. Goldenrod. Or is it Tom, or Skinner, or Specialist Haines?" she said smiling.

"The answer is … all of the above," I responded. And boy was I impressed with her homework.

"May I sit down?" she asked.

"Yeah, of course," I said. *"But in that dress, I doubt it,"* I thought.

"My name's Stacey," she said extending her hand. "I couldn't make it to work yesterday because of some personal business, but I heard you created quite a commotion in here last night."

"I guess I had my fair share of fun," I said trying to maintain an air of coolness. "Would you like a drink?" I continued.

"Yes, white wine. Thank you." Her looks, mannerisms, and English were all a full notch above the other girls under contract with Mama San.

After a half hour of conversation that covered a dozen or so topics, I asked if she was allowed to go to dinner. She apologized and said that it was against the rules and that she needed to go shopping for her sister tomorrow.

Uh oh, I thought—she said the magic word—sister ... err ... ahh ... I mean shopping. I seized the moment. "Shopping is one thing I'm not real good at, especially in countries where you haggle over the prices. Here, look at this, and tell me how much it'll cost," I said handing her my shopping list.

She glanced over the crumbled column of items. "I don't know ... maybe $350 or $400 American."

"Wow, really," I responded, "I had it in the range of $550 to $600."

"Would you mind coming with me?" I asked. I set my empty glass down, missing two-thirds of the coaster, and took her by the hand. Mama San was engrossed in paperwork.

I looked first to Stacey, "Will you go shopping with me tomorrow?"

She answered, "Yes, if it's—"

I looked at Mama San before Stacey finished her sentence, handed her a hundred and a fifty and said, "See you in four days, boss lady."

Over the next four days, I turned my R&R into SSS&S, shopping, sex, slings, and smoke. Smoke was a first for me.

Ten of us were into our third hour of partying on our third night when Kim raised her voice to get everyone's attention. "Anybody want to take party ... ahhh ... how you say ... up a notch?" We all said yes before we even knew what she had in mind. After all, who wouldn't want a great party not to become even greater?

Kim and Stacey grabbed all the towels from David's bathroom and stuffed them under the door to the room. Kim then spun around displaying a huge marijuana cigarette between her thumb and her index finger. I looked at David and asked if he had ever done this before.

"Never in Nam, but a few times in the States," he said.

"Hey, we've been drinking slings all night. Do they mix? What if we get caught?

What kind of drug laws do they have over here? I'm not sure ...," I said rapidly.

"Shut up and toke," David interrupted.

I looked to my left, directly at a lit joint two or three inches from my face. I looked through the small cloud of smoke and grasped the joint with my thumb and forefinger.

Sucking hard, I began to cough uncontrollably. I had flashbacks to gas training in basic and didn't take a second hit until it was down to lip-burning length. I became addicted that night, but not to marijuana. My new love—the potato chip. Four bags of chips and two joints later we wrapped up the party. Stacey and I, while nursing a white wine and a sling, finished off the evening staring at the multicolored paper lamps floating above our heads at the bar in the lobby.

*****

At the end of our five days, we were again gathered to head to the Singapore Airport. Rosco had spent most of his time recuperating, smoking, drinking mildly, and reading as voraciously as he always did. But he had a great attitude about being under the weather. "Being sick in a Singapore hotel was way freakin' better than being healthy in a Pleiku hooch," he said rather philosophically.

David was sitting on his duffel bag with a makeshift ice pack on his forehead. One continuous, nonstop, uninterrupted, maintained, sustained, prolonged party was taking its toll. He pushed up and off his bag in one off-balanced movement. He still had two or three ounces of warm brew in a Tiger Beer can that he held with his finger in the pull-tab hole in the top. He flipped the mangled aluminum to a trash receptacle that he missed by six or seven feet and entered the bus for the trip back to the airport.

Eddie, however, was the talk of the group. It seems he had gotten engaged some time in the previous five days. No one knew any of the details yet, but a pool of sorts was forming regarding the chances of the engagement coming to fruition.

I spent my time checking my booty. I had spent a total of $404 on my shopping list. My R&R was an immense success on all levels.

A few short hours later we landed at Cam Ranh Bay and found the correct person to show our paperwork to so we could catch our connecting flight to Pleiku.

"You guys are in luck; there is one more C-130 to Pleiku. It's taking off in a few minutes, so you'd better haul ass to hanger C to catch it," he said.

David, Eddie, and I simultaneously threw our bags over our shoulders and started a mad dash for hanger C3. Rosco sat down on the floor, leaned up against the wall, placed two fingers in his mouth, took a deep breath, and let loose with a shrill whistle that turned every head within fifty yards.

"Where the hell are you guys going?" he asked shaking his head.

"Ahhhh, we're catching the last plane to Pleiku?" Eddie stated in the form of a question.

"Because our R&R is over, and it's time to return to the war?" David added.

"Because I miss the smell of burning troughs of shit at the edge of Enari. I just can't wait a second longer for the melodious smell-feast to attack my fully detoxed nostrils," I stated.

"One last time—why?" Rosco asked with outstretched arms.

Eddie, now a bit exasperated, started to explain. "Because if we don't catch this flight they will—"

"What? Send us to Vietnam?" Rosco interrupted.

Dave broke in, "Yeah, and why not? I could use a day of rest and relaxation. Count me in."

"No argument from me," I added.

"Well, Eddie, the ball's in your court," Rosco said.

An hour later we were in our bathing suits catching softballs, rays, and ocean waves. The water was incredible. It was cool, clear, and clean. If you walked out on the soft, sandy bottom till it reached your armpits, you could look down and see your feet. I turned around and around in the water marveling at the purple mountains in the distance. The only thing that kept this scene from making it a picture-perfect postcard was the roll of concertina wire that ran the length of the beach and out of sight.

While basking in the sun, a group of guys set up a couple of towels a few feet to our left. They all appeared to be laughing as if they had just heard the funniest joke ever. Their accents gave away their origins. Rosco looked over at them and said, "Where are y'all from, mate?"

"We're all from Australia. Sounds like *y'all* are from the southern states in America," answered the only one standing, in a thick Mancunian accent. Rosco clarified, "Two south and two north; you don't sound like an Aussie," Rosco answered.

Well, they take all sorts, I'm from Manchester, UK, serving in the Australian Army since the early '60s," he replied with a wink in his eye as he stretched out his hand, which Rosco shook. He continued his introduction, "Sergeant Tom Entwistle, First Armored Regiment, Royal Australian Corps, Phuoc Tuy Province."

The next couple of minutes we traded names and locations. It turned out that there were two Davids and two Toms—another small reminder that it's a small world filled with hate and love. I broke the formalities with, "Sounded like someone just told the funniest joke ever."

"Naw, mate, just recalling a story from just before we went on leave," said a man named Stanley.

Tom jumped in with, "Our unit had a pet kid goat. The padre, pretty new to the bush, adjusting to its sights and sounds—he came over with us from home—he wanted to spend some time with us in the boonies. Some of our blokes put the kid outside of the padre's tent. Goats are noted for their lively and frisky behavior. This goat's favorite activity for self-amusement was to climb up one side of the tent and slide down the other … all night long. Needless to say the padre got no sleep."

He continued as he sat down and opened a can of Victoria Bitter beer: "Word came down that the 'mascots' in the unit had to go. A bloke by the name of Arnie had sort of adopted the goat. He knew of a Vietnamese teacher in a village close to Nui Dat and felt very good about having her take over caring for the goat.

"We brought the goat to the teacher, who was living with her family. The teacher sent her brother out to get us an orange soft drink, and when he came back, we all looked at each other like, 'I'm not drinking that shit.' But we didn't want to offend the grandmother's hospitality, so we accepted the drinks. We had all guessed that they had been sitting in the sun since the beginning of the war. Forget hospitality; wasn't worth dying for.

"Two days later David told Arnie that the teacher said to say beaucoup thank you again and that the goat was number one chomp chomp. Arnie was in instant shock, eyes wide, mouth agape, pulling at his hair."

David concluded the tale: "Everyone initially tried to stifle laughs. That didn't last long before all were slapping furniture, doubling over with laughter, and trying to catch our collective breaths."

We traded stories for the next half hour before going our separate ways. We all hoped that our new best mates made it back to their families intact.

We caught the first flight to Pleiku the following morning and reported to HQ with our tails between our legs and well-rehearsed excuses on our lips. The XO, obviously preoccupied with more important things, clearly said, "OK, whatever. Dismissed."

A SPC-4, whose name tag read Slawinowski (I think) stopped me on my way out. "Ah, are you aware that you are eligible for five days of leave?" he said as he closed the jacket to my file.

"I thought I lost those when my early-out had been granted," I responded.

"Unless there's a problem that your file doesn't show, you're free to take five more days," he said, proud of his observation. I knew right then that round two of shopping would continue in Hong Kong. I would need to practice my college letter-writing skills: "Dear Mom and Dad, please send money. Thanks. Love, your son, Tom."

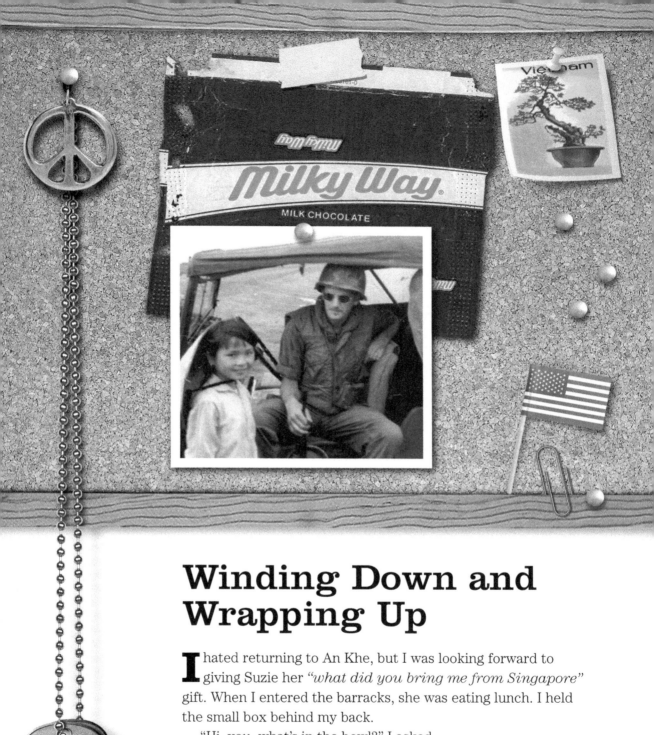

Winding Down and Wrapping Up

I hated returning to An Khe, but I was looking forward to giving Suzie her *"what did you bring me from Singapore"* gift. When I entered the barracks, she was eating lunch. I held the small box behind my back.

"Hi, you, what's in the bowl?" I asked.

"Hi, you too. Chicken feet soup. What you got behind you?" she asked as she jumped to her feet.

Chicken feet soup? I had flashbacks to AIT, shook my head, and kept my mouth shut.

"For you," I said, pulling the package from behind my back.

SNAFU

The box of assorted oriental gourmet foods sat fully in the palm of both my hands. It somehow seemed an inappropriate gift for someone who was, at the moment, eating chicken feet soup. She stood up, tucked her hair behind her ears, and tore into the package.

"Thank you, thank you, thank you beaucoup," she said as she gave me a tight hug.

I then showed her a stack of colorful picture postcards and described the city of Singapore. So close, yet so far away.

The next couple of weeks were pure hell, long days filled with stress-loaded details. With just three days before the start of my leave for Hong Kong, I was put in charge of a troubleshooting team to reorganize an arms room—top to bottom. The paperwork alone could take three days, but we pulled it off.

This assignment was my first and only responsibility as an E-5. I viewed the promotion as some form of a mind game to convince me to stay in the army. If that were the intent, it wouldn't work. It would be just one more wasted allotment of an available E-5 slot.

When I returned from Hong Kong on November 3rd, I was so short I could pee a puddle without any splash. I was sent to An Khe to finish out the week and then back to Pleiku to start my out-processing.

On Thursday, November 6, 1969, I was packed and ready to return to the real world. I looked everywhere for Suzie but couldn't find her. Chico's head and a hand appeared in the doorway. "Sorry, man, but I drew blanks everywhere. Couldn't find Mia either."

I placed a note on the same spot where she had left a Montagnard bracelet for me a week earlier, said farewell to Chico, and headed to HQ.

I threw my bag into a waiting truck, followed by my M16, and then myself. As the open deuce-and-a-half bounced through the camp, instead of looking at each landmark for the last time, I found myself scanning each walkway and side street for any hint of Suzie or Mia. The truck stopped and picked up two more passengers. The driver exited his very worn and rusted truck and called for a twenty-minute break.

I grabbed my camera, jumped to the ground, and focused on a row of hooches. I was about to click the shutter when a round, smiling face appeared, out of focus, in the viewfinder. It was Mia.

"What? Where is—"

"No time talk. Come," she interrupted, grabbing my hand and leading me into the building behind the truck.

Once inside, she and another girl, whom I had never seen before, covered the windows and scurried off. Before I had a chance to try my sentence again, Suzie appeared in the doorway.

Her beauty radiated. She wore a bright-yellow áo dài and white, silk pants, instead of the usual black pajama pants that she had worn every day since we met. I tried for a third time to start a sentence, but she hurriedly stepped forward into the room, closed the door behind her, ran to me, and held a finger to my lips.

She put her arms around me and buried her head in my chest. I pulled her tighter into my grasp and inhaled the sweet smell of her freshly washed hair. We relaxed our tight embrace.

I broke the silence. "I'm going to miss you very, very, very much."

"I miss you beaucoup already," she responded.

"I … I just wish that—" I started to say until she again put her finger to my mouth. I kissed her finger. She pulled it aside and replaced it with her lips. I pulled her tight and felt her heartbeat. She felt mine. We fell into a long, full kiss—our first—and our last.

We talked and held hands for about ten minutes. Then it was time to separate and live our lives 8,548 miles apart. My eyes never left her as we separated. She fought back a tear; I didn't.

The trip back to Camp Enari seemed to take just minutes. With Pleiku in sight, we slowed to avoid a small crater in the road. A dozen dirty children rushed the truck.

"Candy, cigarettes, you give, OK, number one GI," they shouted in unison. We tossed what we had in our pockets. I threw a Milky Way high into the air and watched it land in the midst of six or seven children. A tiny girl with dirty blond hair came up with the prize.

"Hey, I know that girl. Driver, slow up. I know that little girl," I said while trying to open my bag. "Hey driver, slow up." He didn't. Using all ten of my thumbs, I fumbled frantically with the cord. When the bag opened, I reached inside and pulled a small, brown teddy bear from the top of the fully packed interior.

"Do you know Little Shit?" I hollered.

"Yes!" she hollered back.

I threw the bear as hard as I could. It landed in the middle of the road, kicking up a small amount of dust. She ran to the bear, held it up in one hand, and waved with the candy bar in the other until we were out of sight.

I sat down hard in the center of the truck. I heard no sound.

Pleiku, Vietnam

Guard Duty

After the satchel charge, I saw nothing until my funeral. The scene was full of mixed emotions: anger, loss, pride, shock, and sadness. The day was cool, the air carrying a very soft breeze across the open field. The mountain leaves were a colorful collage of orange, red, and yellow. The manicured grass was a rich, lush green, and the sky was a bright blue. The clouds were full and white.

There was a curious contrast between the bright colors of nature and the dark clothing worn by the mourners scattered across the landscape. My friends and relatives grieved over my dead body. But what about Abe and the other guys on guard duty? What happened to them?

SNAFU

The casket, draped in a large, American flag with my peace medallion pinned to the corner of the last blue stripe, was a foreboding sight. While the coffin was slowly lowered into the ground, I limped over to the hole and gazed at the big, shiny box. I started to drip blood onto the casket, so I drew myself back. When I pulled to a straight-back position, my knee gave out, and I fell into the grave and crashed with a dull thud. I heard a collective gasp from everyone inside the green tent.

I struggled to turn over. My left arm was useless, and my left leg was numb, but with one final surge I rolled over and came face to face with Abe.

"Abe, what the hell are you doing here?"

"I'm here to wake your ass up. The captain said we're about to come under attack, and he could use your help in fighting the war." ...

Staring at him through the thin layer of mosquito netting, I tried to shake my left arm to restore circulation. I must have slept on it for hours. There was absolutely no feeling whatsoever from my shoulder to the tips of my fingers. Abe went back to his post.

"Fuck, the whole thing was a dream," I blathered to myself. *"God, oh God, it was only a dream."* I directed my next sentence to Abe. "Hey, Abe, what did you just tell me? Are we under attack? Hey man, seriously, are you shitting me, is this for real? Am I still dreaming? Shit!"

"I have no idea what you're babbling about, but your ass is in very deep shit if you don't get out of that rack. Is that real enough for you?" Abe hollered, each word growing louder as he spoke.

While slinging my arm to reactivate the flow of blood, I spun around on my poncho liner, pushed up and off with my right arm, and caught my right foot in the mosquito net. Approaching the ground fast and headfirst, I snapped to a stop, body-slamming into the back wall. A 16-penny nail found its mark. The netting broke loose from the ceiling, and I hit the ground hard.

I pulled off the netting with a flailing right arm and grabbed my boots and flak jacket. I stood on wobbly legs and felt instant panic. *What was real? What wasn't? What was waiting for me outside the bunker?* I looked at my right arm, which was bleeding from a 16-penny nail-sized hole. Disoriented and confused, I grabbed Thumper by her strap and headed outside.

It was still pitch dark but not as quiet as before. Abe, his M16 set on automatic, fired his first burst just before I made it out of the bunker, causing my ears to ring like giant church bells. The air, filled with activity, had me looking in all directions at the same time. The brain-numbing quickly diminished, but the tingling sensation in my arm and leg was clearing at a much slower pace.

The captain in the tower next to ours was yelling instructions, vehicles were speeding by, between the berm and our bunker, and the crackling of automatic M16 gunfire echoed. The sky came alive with the arrival of a C-47. Nicknamed "Puff the Magic Dragon," she was loaded with three multibarrel 7.62 mm Vulcan machine guns. Every fifth round fired from her miniguns was a tracer; at 6,000 rounds a minute, the sky rained red.

The confident, powerful voice from the command tower brought me a small sense of security. However, having a chunker instead of my ever-present M16 gave me a horrible sense of insecurity.

I joined in the sounds of war. I locked and loaded my M79. The insecurity was overwhelming. I envisioned the VC breaking through the wire and me waiting for them to get close enough, so I could hit them over the head with my blooper. My knees started to shake—not just a slight quiver or flutter, not a trembling or vibrating, but rather a full-blown case of the wobbles. The shaking became intense; I thought I wouldn't be able to continue to hold up my full weight. Panic, fear, inexperience, or more than likely, a combination of all three, caused my knees to give out. I leaned against the bunker and concentrated as much as I could on firing round after round in the "general direction" of the enemy. Open the barrel, push in the grenade, snap shut, hold at a forty-five-degree angle from the hip, fire, and repeat. My legs began to steady, but I couldn't tell if my ears were still ringing.

The sound of a truck coming to a halt directly behind me interrupted the routine. It was Specialist Billy Ray Kelleher. I greeted him with a glance and a nod as he exited his truck and then immediately returned my full attention to the pitch-black open field in front of me. I still couldn't see shit.

I felt Billy's presence directly behind me. "Hey, this is cool as shit, huh?" he said in an excited voice. I didn't respond. *Click, THUMP!*

"Niceshotletmetryoneok?" he asked, making his request with one long sound like Hutchison used to do.

"Are you out of your mind? We're not in a training exercise; it's the real thing. Don't you have somewhere you're supposed to be?" I said in a very irritated manner.

"Come on, man, I only want to fire it once," he said.

I looked out over the wire and saw no movement. Not wanting to argue and needing a moment to gather myself, I said, "Alright, just one. Do you know how to use a 79?"

"Yeah, no sweat," he responded, taking the weapon and a round from my belt.

I stepped back behind the bunker for a deep breath. I looked up at the peak of my air intake and saw Billy standing in the wide open holding the 79 like a 16.

"No, you dumb shit," I screamed. I lunged at him, but it was too late.

SNAFU

He pulled the trigger while the barrel rested against his shoulder. The grenade that looked like a giant snub-nosed bullet flew out straight and then quickly dove toward the earth. The round exploded as it struck the first row of concertina wire and set off a flare that lit up the area like Christmas in November. *Déjà vu.* Billy tossed me the launcher with a quick apology as he disappeared into the night.

Seconds hadn't passed before the captain was screaming at the top end of his vocal power. "Who the hell out there doesn't know how to operate his weapon?"

Stuttering and stammering that it wasn't me, I looked over my shoulder at a barren berm. I was the only one in sight. I felt alone. I was alone.

The flare died down, as did our firing. A few seconds later, a call of cease-fire from the command tower could be heard echoing up and down the line. The inning was over—no hits, no runs, one error. The word on the line was that there were, as yet, no reported casualties on either side, so I assumed we scared them off. Scaring, versus killing, was more than fine with me. I had no desire to see an expressionless VC with a mission.

I went back into the bunker and began to straighten my personal belongings. I spotted something shiny. I pulled back a pile of netting, reached down, and picked up my new sunglasses piece by piece.

I wandered back outside, dripping blood from my 16-penny nail wound, ignoring the cry of, "Hey, Sarge, we got one wounded," and left the war.

The End and a New Beginning

OK, so that wasn't the best way to end this tale because there was still one more day to face. Processing in Vietnam went smoothly, as did the return trip to the real world. Back in Fort Lewis, out-processing continued. We were issued brand-new sets of dress greens as we automatically became members of the inactive reserves for the next six years, the key word being "inactive." After the final salute to the officer in charge of setting us free, we exited the Quonset hut regular citizens of the US of A. Three guys in front of me deposited their new uniforms into a fifty-five-gallon oil drum that was given a second life as a trash can. That made me cringe a little because I would soon become a full-fledged tax paying member of society.

I arrived at the airport an hour before departure, so I took advantage of a free service that the captain at Fort Lewis mentioned in our final minutes as soldiers. Volunteers were busy sewing the proper insignia on our unadorned jackets. When it was my turn, I handed her my discharge papers and DD214, and I was informed that the final specialist E-5 patch was sewn on the uniform of the guy just ahead of me. The woman helping me looked up over the top of her glasses sitting near the end of her nose and said, "Honey, a new box of patches will be arriving shortly." Not wanting to chance missing my flight, I pointed to the box next to the empty one and said, "OK, I'm changing my MOS for the last time. Sew on E-5 sergeant stripes. What are they gonna do? Send me to Vietnam?"

I walked at time and a half to my flight so that I wouldn't have to acknowledge stares and dirty looks. I'd heard stories from a couple of my buddies about getting spit on and called names like baby killer and murderer. It was a strange, almost surreal trek, quickly glancing at businesspeople, families, college students, and other soldiers, none that appeared to be aware of my existence. As it turned out, I got a thumbs up, from a hippie no less, before I got my only dirty look. That one nasty stare came from another hippie wearing a three-piece suit. I wondered how he interpreted my return stare. His look was pretty innocuous considering that my imagination had me running through a gauntlet of hate and disgust the length of the concourse.

The final leg of my journey halfway around the world was out of Fort Lauderdale, Florida, many hundreds of miles from Endicott, New York. As luck would have it, my parents were on vacation in the Bahamas, and that's where I would officially start my new life. I was the last to board the plane and took the only empty seat. Just as I got settled in, the captain's voice came over the intercom with the usual greeting.

"Ahhhhhhhh, welcome aboard flight 38 to the island of Grand Bahama, home of Freeport and Lucaya. Before I give you times and temperatures, we would like to welcome on board a returning soldier from Vietnam."

"Oh, shit, here come the spitballs," I thought.

He continued, "If no one objects, I would like to invite this young man to first class."

I flushed from head to toe as the air filled with applause. *Really—applause? Damn,"* I thought, *"I don't remember getting the Medal of Honor."* But, hey, I wasn't going to argue. I headed to the front while receiving a couple of pats on the back. Now that was my kind of gauntlet.

I was pretty vague with my mom and dad regarding my arrival time so that I could surprise them. I arrived at their door at a condo in Harbor House Towers in Lucaya and tapped lightly. I heard my mom ask, "Who is it?"

"Some guy looking for clean sheets, a rum and Coke, and a dip in the ocean." A millisecond later I was in the grasp of a women who hugged and sobbed with equal commitment. I dropped my bags and said, "Hi, Mom. Hi, Dad. Oh, my God."

Endnotes

1   Military physical exam regulations state that "use of non-medical personnel for medical functions should be minimized to the greatest extent possible. Non-medical (opposite gender) personnel can be used as urine collection observers and chaperones, but not used where they directly contact or independently test applicants (i.e., draw blood, conduct an eye exam, conduct a hearing test)." Chaperones were almost exclusively female. This was changed to "same-sex medical-only observers" during the updating of the medical regulations in 2002 and 2009. Barack Obama signed off on the final changes. (page 29)

2   I used my cousin John, who received his "all nude all the time" physical in Syracuse in 1966 for a lot of the details in the writing of this chapter. Our physicals were separated by just a matter of months. (page 29–30)

3   In truth, I found out about the change in policy two weeks later from one of the guys still in the program. Nothing in the Army that involved would take place in just two days. I changed the timing in my story for dramatic effect. (page 86)

4   Rosco passed away in 2009 due to his exposure to Agent Orange. He was sixty-five years old. Rest in Peace, brother. (page 136)

5   The Central Highlands were labeled on military maps as "II Corps," the second Allied military region, which contained the provinces of Binh Dinh, Binh Thuan, Darlac, Khanh Hoa, Kontum, Lam Dong, Ninh Thuan, Phu Bon, Phu Yen, Pleiku, Quang Duc, and Tuyen Duc. Many of these provinces contained only a few thousand people. (page 191)

**Situation Normal
All Fucked Up**

**Fucked Up
Beyond All Repair**

Glossary

11B10 – The Vietnam-era military occupational code for an infantryman of the rank E-1 to E-3.

76Y20 – The Vietnam-era military occupational code for a unit supply specialist of the rank E-4.

Agent Orange – A powerful and toxic defoliant sprayed on vegetation, not to be confused with orange juice which only becomes toxic if vodka is added. Agents Orange, Blue, Pink, Green, White, and Purple were known as the Rainbow Agents, each causing varying degrees of harm to the living, including plants, animals, insects, and humans. Its purpose was to eliminate forest cover and crops for North Vietnamese and Vietcong troops. Agent Orange and most of the Rainbow Agents were phenoxy herbicides contaminated with dioxin, the third-most dangerous chemical known to man.

It killed plants on purpose and then people due to lack of proper research. Nineteen million gallons of these herbicides were sprayed over Vietnam from 1961 to 1971. The most number of gallons sprayed was in 1969, then came '68 and then '67. It was a mixture of equal parts of two herbicides, 2,4,5-trichlorophenoxyacetic acid and 2,4-dichlorophenoxyacetic acid. The two main companies that produced this defoliant were Monsanto and Dow Chemical. The use of Agent Orange in Vietnam was called Operation Ranch Hand or, as I renamed it, Operation Ranch Hand, Heart, Lung, Liver, Prostate, White Blood Cells, Spleen, Lymph Nodes ….

AIT (abbreviation) – Advanced individual training in a specialty that takes place for eight weeks after basic training.

AIT (abbreviation) – Advanced infantry training. What? They couldn't come up with three words that gives it the same meaning. How about "AKT," advance kill training?

AO (abbreviation) – Area of operation. Here, there, wherever.

áo dài – The traditional dress of young Vietnamese women. Nice enough, but it doesn't show any leg. In Vietnamese, the words literally mean "long clothing."

APO (abbreviation) – Army post office based in San Francisco through which all mail to Vietnam was funneled. APO was the second most popular word or abbreviation used while in country, right behind "short." (See definition of "short" in this glossary.)

areca – Betel nuts that were chewed by many Vietnamese and Montagnards; an opiate that stains the teeth. Apparently when you are that high you don't mind looking like Steve McQueen and Dustin Hoffman in *Papillon*.

army shade 107 – The official color of the United States Army, also known as olive-drab green or baby-shit green.

Article 15 – A nonjudicial punishment given to enlisted men for minor offenses, such as assault, passing bad checks, or not saluting a general because one's right hand was busy scratching one's butt. Hey, it could happen to anybody.

ARVN (abbreviation) – Army of the Republic of Vietnam. The good guys.

AWOL (abbreviation) – Absent without official leave. Claiming that you were sleepwalking when you were spotted 168 miles from base isn't accepted as a valid reason for being absent without official leave. I know this to be a fact.

back time – Slang for rear-area duty given to someone in the field. Also known as slack time, down time, or "recreational" time (uttered each time someone is told they are getting some back time).

bagged and tagged – Slang for the procedure of processing dead soldiers, sometimes mischievously carried out on *dead-drunk* soldiers.

beaucoup – French word for "many" (or "shitload" for those from the southern region of the United States), pronounced "boo coo." This word was used beaucoup millions of times during the Vietnam "Police Action."

bic – Derived from Vietnamese, meaning "comprehend" or (biet) "understand." Heard much more often were the words "no bic." *Example: "Where's my camera?" "Me no bic camera."*

big orange – The antimalaria pill taken once a week. A small white pill that was taken daily was called "daily-daily." Soldiers that didn't take the pills in the hopes that they would catch malaria and then be sent home were called "dumb shits."

bird – Slang for helicopter, also slang for a one-finger salute.

birdbath – A place, usually in the motor pool area, where vehicles were washed. During certain months the monsoons took care of this detail. Thank you, monsoons.

boom boom – Slang for sexual intercourse. All military personnel reverted back to the phrase "getting laid" upon returning to the world so as not to sound uncool.

boonies – Slang for the jungle, the field, the bush, the boondocks, and gruntville. Generally speaking, it's anywhere where the toilet is no further than wherever one happened to be standing at any given moment.

bug juice – Slang for Kool-Aid (sometimes refreshing, sometimes nasty). Also slang for insect repellant.

cherry – One of two slang terms used in reference to "new guys" in country. (Look in the letter F section for the other slang term.)

chicken hawk – Slang for someone who has not made up his or her mind whether to be a dove or a hawk. See also "dawk."

chopper – In Vietnam, it was the most popular slang term for a helicopter. In the

US, it is the most popular slang term for motorcycle.

cluster fuck – When grunts bunched up in the field, it was called a cluster fuck. Those that created the bunching were called "dumb fucks."

CO (abbreviation) – Commanding officer, the highest-ranking officer of a military unit.

combat pay – Those who actually participated in combat received $65 extra pay per month (separate from hazardous duty pay).

concertina wire – Coiled barbed wire used to protect perimeters of base camps and fire bases. It was highly recommended to stay at least three feet away from this wire when one was in the process of consuming alcohol.

conflict or police action – The US government never declared war, so it was referred to as the Vietnam Conflict or Vietnam Police Action. *Ha, ha, ha, ha, ha, ha, ha, ha, ha, ha, ha, ha, ha, ha, ha, ha, ha*—that's a good one. Over 3 million people died during this "conflict." I wonder how many would have died if we were actually fighting a "war."

crotch rot – Infections of the genital area, many brought on by the damp tropical climate (also known as "jungle rot" or "athletes dick").

DA (abbreviation) – The Department of the Army.

dap – An African-American handshake and greeting. Caution: dap is not to be attempted by white people unless the aforementioned white person has logged thirty hours of practice so as not to embarrass himself and his race.

dawk – Slang for a fence rider, someone who is neither a dove nor a hawk. It's a good thing the symbols weren't a _____ and a _____. (You fill in the blanks.)

delta dust – A variety of marijuana especially popular in the delta region of Vietnam. Believed to be more potent than Maui wowie, Acapulco gold, and cousin Ernie's hide-a-bud grown exclusively behind Uncle Earl's shed in Paducah, Kentucky.

deuce-and-a-half – A 2.5-ton military-transport truck or Mama Cass after a large whole pizza with the works for lunch.

devil's teeth – Slang for the three-pronged bards that the Vietcong (VC) spread on roads to cut tires. Sorry, no humor added here. There is nothing funny regarding those sons of bitches.

dinky dau – GI slang for "crazy," comes from the Vietnamese "dien cai dau" or crazy in the head.

DI (abbreviation) – Drill instructor, also known as the noncommissioned (noncom) officer in charge of making sure your life is hell on earth.

DOD (abbreviation) – Department of Defense. Duh O Duh.

dog-and-pony show – Slang phrase for giving guided tours of bases to important people, both civilian and military, such as Bob Hope, Robert MacNamara, and Jane

Fonda (oops, wrong guided tour).

DR (abbreviation) – Delinquency report given by military police for minor traffic regulations. "Your honor, I was innocent … every time."

E-4 and E-5 – Rank for a corporal or specialist E-4 (SPC-4) and the lowest-ranking noncommissioned officer, a sergeant or specialist E-5 (SPC-5) in the army.

elephant grass – A tall, razor-sharp plant located mostly in the Central Highlands of Vietnam. This plant generally did not cause a problem for any soldier over eight feet eight inches tall.

FIDO (abbreviation) – Fuck it. Drive on. (We don't have time to fix this situation.)

firebase – An artillery fire-support base fortified by the infantry. Generally located out in the middle of freakin' nowhere.

FNG (abbreviation) – Fucking new guy. One of two slang terms used for maligning new arrivals to Vietnam. Cherry, the other slang term for "new guys," was also popular, especially when talking with your mother, the chaplain, or FNGs over six feet four inches and 240 pounds.

Fourth Infantry – The division with its headquarters at Camp Enari outside of the city of Pleiku in the Central Highlands (moved to Camp Radcliff outside of An Khe in 1970) was nicknamed the Ivy Division, Poison Ivy, the Funny Fourth, Famous Fourth, and Funky Fourth.

FUBAR (abbreviation) – Fucked up beyond all recognition. Don't get me started. No, seriously, don't get me started.

GI (abbreviation) – Government issue.

Golf Course, The – Slang for Camp Radcliff in An Khe because of its size and low-cut grass on the helicopter landing area, a five iron away from my AO. Originally built in 1965 by the First Air Cavalry Division.

gook – A derogatory term used to refer to the Vietnamese people, both friendly and the enemy. The enemy was also referred to as a dink, slant, slope, little man, and the ever-popular Charles, Charlie, Chuck, and Chas. Since many of these names are derogatory, they were rarely used by US military personnel … and Santa Claus is real. VC, short for Vietcong (Vietnamese Communist guerrillas), was used through most of this book except in one direct quote.

grenade launcher M79 – A single-shot, break-open, breech-loaded weapon that fires 40 mm grenades. Also nicknamed the chunker, clunker, thumper, and blooper, as well as elephant gun, thump-gun, burp gun, and "hell in a fourteen-inch hole."

hard spot – Slang for a temporary overnight infantry position, except during the monsoons, at which time it was referred to as Mudville.

hooch – Slang for most any dwelling in Vietnam, both military and civilian.

HQ (abbreviation) – Headquarters, the nerve center of any military unit.

infantryman – The GI who lived and fought in the bush. The long list of nicknames included ground-pounder, grunt, straight-leg, boonie rat, and in my book, hero.

it don't mean nothin' – A heavily used phrase that meant just the opposite. The first person to use this phrase had just finished a hit of fresh delta dust.

KP (abbreviation) – Kitchen patrol. All the manual work in the kitchen where soldiers were assigned duties for up to twelve hours a day, peeling potatoes, and other necessary drudgery.

lifer – A soldier who makes a career of the military.

loser – A soldier who makes a career of the military—as a private.

LZ (abbreviation) – Landing zone; a forward area from where landed troops patrolled into the AO.

M151 – A quarter-ton Ford jeep used widely throughout Vietnam. My butt occupied the driver's seat of this vehicle for more days than I care to remember.

Monopoly money – Slang for military payment certificates. It was illegal to possess or use US greenbacks in-country, which denied money to the black market. A surprise inspection would have wiped out a forest for the paper needed for the soon-to-follow Article 15s.

Montagnard – Originally from a French term for "mountain people." They are tribal people found in the mountain regions of Vietnam. The Vietnamese considered them a lower class of people. Their culture was generally described as primitive. The good guys, personified.

MOS – Military occupation specialty, the actual job that a soldier was employed to do in the military. For example, 11B10 was an infantry soldier.

MP (abbreviation) – Military police.

MPC (abbreviation) – Military payment certificates.

Operation Ranch Hand – The military code name for the spraying of 19 million gallons of herbicides from 1962 through 1971, 11 million of which consisted of Agent Orange. (Don't forget to send a thank you note to Dow Chemical and Monsanto for their caring and concern and "cash" for the lives of millions that were exposed to dioxin, the fourth-most dangerous element know to man.)

Orange – See Agent Orange.

piaster – Vietnam currency worth US $0.01, thus the reason for oversized pockets on jungle fatigue pants.

R&R (abbreviation) – Rest and recuperation or rest and relaxation, generally a five-day vacation from the war taken in Australia, Bangkok, Hawaii, Hong Kong, Kuala Lumpur, Manila, Singapore, Taipei, Tokyo, or Chicago (in your dreams). Also called I&I for intercourse and intoxication or B&B for booze and broads.

REMF (abbreviation) – Rear echelon mother fucker; derogatory slang for army personnel who performed support duties from a base camp. A less derogatory term was Remington Raiders. REMF's generally referred to themselves as lucky shits.

rock and roll – Putting a weapon on full automatic fire. Also the music of Creedence Clearwater Revival, the Beatles, Jimi Hendrix, the Doors, Steppenwolf, Traffic, the Rascals, Bob Dillon, Otis Redding, Simon and Garfunkel, the Animals, Marvin Gaye, the Rolling Stones, and a new band called Led Zeppelin.

sapper – An enemy soldier armed with explosives who infiltrated base camps at night. Those little fuckers created a whole generation of light sleepers.

satchel charge – A canvas bag containing explosives used by the VC, especially the aforementioned sapper dude.

short – When a soldier's tour of duty was almost over, most often in the last month of service. Quite often used in a sentence starting, "I'm so short I could …."

SNAFU (abbreviation) – "Situation normal: all fucked up" if you're talking to the guys or "situation normal: all fouled up" if you're talking to your mom.

VC (abbreviation) – Vietcong, guerrilla fighters for the Vietnamese Communist movement. Or in today's world, "venture capital."

wheel jockey – Slang for truck drivers or any other wheeled vehicle driver. A strange nickname for drivers over six feet tall, i.e., me.

world, the – A specific reference to home (the United States) or generally anyplace but Vietnam.

We Weren't Alone

■ 400,000 soldiers from six other countries fought alongside the US on behalf of South Vietnam: South Korea (320,000), Australia (61,000), Philippines (10,000), and New Zealand (3,800). Thailand, Taiwan, Spain, and Canada also participated in the effort. Allies of North Vietnam included the Soviet Union, China, North Korea, and Cuba. We weren't alone.

■ 9,087,000 military personnel served on active duty during the official Vietnam era from August 5,1964, to May 7,1975.

■ 2,709,918 Americans served in Vietnam, including 7,484 women. The Department of Defense reports that 58,220 of those Americans died overseas.

■ 514,300 offshore personnel served in the SE Asia Theatre or South China Sea Waters (Blue Water Vets).

■ 9,492,958 Americans claimed on the 1995 census to have served in-country in Vietnam. In the 2010 census, the number jumped to 13,853,027. Man, that's a lot of people claiming to be "murderers and baby killers."

■ 240 men were awarded the Medal of Honor during the war.

■ By 2015, roughly 300,000 Vietnam veterans had died due to their Agent Orange exposure. More are currently dying from the sixteen diseases and conditions linked to AO exposure.

1969   **1980**   **2015**

About the Author

Now it's time to wrap things up with some self-serving info and a bunch of name-dropping, switching to third person, and boring you with what I've been doing since 1969. Stop here if you aren't into yada, yada, yada or wordy sentences.

Tom was honorably discharged (yes, that's right—he never got caught) from active service on 11/14/1969 and entered the Bachelor of Fine Arts program at East Carolina University (ECU) in Greenville, North Carolina.

In 1971, ECU tripled the tuition for out-of-state students (those bastards!). The taxpayers provided the paltry sum of $175 a month to cover tuition, books, art supplies, rent, food, gas, insurance, clothes, whips, chains, leather underwear, and … ahh … other necessary stuff. The money that Tom made as a figure-drawing model (shudder, shudder) hardly paid for breakfast. So Tom looked for a job that he could hold down for six months to become a resident of North Carolina and then attend ECU as a bona fide Pirate. He was informed that the owner of a defunct upstairs nightclub wanted to reopen. All they needed was a qualified manager. That would be Tom. He convinced the owner that knowing what beer tasted like and what rock 'n' roll sounded like was all that one needed to know to run a bar. The owner then convinced Tom that he should accept being paid a percentage of profits as compensation; after all, he knew what beer tasted like and what rock 'n' roll sounded like, so how could he lose?

The Attic opened its doors on September 7, 1971. On January 7, 1972, Tom was handed his W-2. The gross wages were just that, coming in at $728.40. Not discouraged—OK, he was totally bummed—Tom decided to give it one more semester. Eighteen years later—that's 1,389,268 customers (give or take a dozen), 36,510 T-shirts, 3,708 performances by live bands, 520 comedian performances, four major foosball tournaments, one nationally televised concert on NBC (OK, here's the first batch of name dropping) by the Pointer Sisters, one cover of *Performance Magazine* shared with the Nighthawks, and hundreds of diverse concerts from The Byrds to The Ramones, Greg Allman to Tim Weisberg, Wendy O. Williams to Nicolette Larson and Bill Hicks to Steve Harvey—in 1988, Tom and partner Stewart Campbell turned over the Attic's keys to manager Joe Tronto. Joe continued the diversity with the best in music and comedy from Dave Matthews to Maynard Ferguson, Phish to Hootie and The Blowfish, Train to The Black Crows and Jeff Foxworthy to Tommy Chong. In 1997, the Attic was chosen by *Playboy* magazine as one of the top 100 college bars in the country.

In July of 1988, Tom and his wife, Nancy (who said "I do" in 1974 and has been saying "what was I thinking" ever since), and their family, Tracy (10), Adam (8), Seniah (6) (the last a golden retriever, not an oddly named child), packed up the U-Haul (or whatever truck company that will pay to have their name mentioned here for the next printing of this book) and headed to Charlotte. Tom joined Creative Entertainment, the headquarters for the Comedy Zone chain of comedy clubs and settled into a work schedule of twenty-eight hours per day (those bastards). From 1988 to 1996, he and booking partner Jeff Chester booked more comedians than any other two people on earth. He became part owner of the Comedy Zone Comedy Club in Charlotte featuring such names as (OK, round two of name dropping) Jerry Seinfeld, Dennis Miller, Ritch Shydner, Dave Coulier, Chris Rock, Bill Maher, and Ellen DeGeneres. In the mid '90s he joined the Carrot Top management team and comanagement for Rodney Carrington and wrote comedy for many touring comedians and, for a short time, was on the fax team of writers for *The Tonight Show* with Jay Leno. In 1997, he decided the stress of booking comedians (those bastards) was more than he wanted to deal with, so Nancy and he formed an ad specialty company called Stand Up Stuff. Tom sold T-shirts and other marketing products to comedians while Nancy (the company president) serviced the corporate community. Tom remained in comedy by becoming the senior instructor of the Comedy Zone Comedy School from 2001 to 2010. In 2015, East Carolina University called and said they would be honored to archive the Attic. Tom said, "What? A major university wants to archive a rock 'n' roll nightclub. OK, what's the punchline?" The Attic was officially archived in May 2015.

The journey is currently at the stage known as "the present." Tom retired in January 2016 because of his exposure to Agent Orange while in Vietnam. The VA is doing an awesome job of taking care of Tom. He is currently looking for a number of individuals or one very wealthy person to offer him grant money to pursue a number of art projects. What he has in mind is … hey, where are you going? He just wants a few minutes of your time to explain. … No, really, he just—hey, don't close this book! This will only take a few short minutes … hey … hey … shit.

Other Titles by Tom Haines*

CHICKEN SHIT FOR THE SOUL
Stories from Your Life

SEX AND OATMEAL
Why the Republications Don't Want You to Know the Connection

SIX ONE WAY, A HALF DOZEN THE OTHER
America's Obsession with the Term "Whatever"

RUSH LIMBAUGH AND MICHAEL MOORE
Twin Sons of Different Mothers

3 KEYS TO BEING # 1
Money, Power, and I Can't Remember the Third One

SLEEPING WITH ONE EYE OPEN
Zzzz ... Zzzz ... Zzzz

*These are not actual books, just other "titles" by Tom Haines.

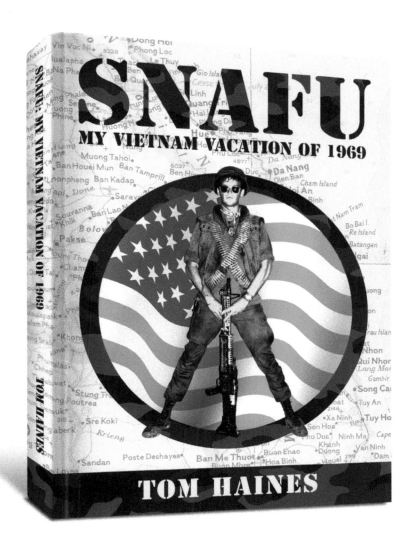

SPARK Publications made part of this dream project come true by publishing this book for Tom and his eternally dedicated friend, wife, and caregiver, Nancy. Thank you for reading and stepping into Tom's experiences.

I should have figured out that I was exposed to Agent Orange when I got this photo back from Camera World.

Tom "Skinner" Haines